PASSWORD 4

THIRD EDITION

A READING AND VOCABULARY TEXT

Linda Butler

To Peter Montgomery-Baecher, with love

Password 4: A Reading and Vocabulary Text
Third Edition

Copyright © 2017 by Pearson Education, Inc. or its affiliates.

Pearson Education, 221 River Street, Hoboken, NJ 07030

Staff credits: The people who made up the *Password* team, representing editorial, production, design, and manufacturing, are Pietro Alongi, Tracey Cataldo, Mindy DePalma, Dave Dickey, Warren Fischbach, Pam Fishman, Niki Lee, Amy McCormick, Robert Ruvo, Kristina Skof, Joseph Vella, and Rebecca Wicker.

Development Editor: Penny Laporte
Cover image: Venera Salman / Shutterstock
Text composition: ElectraGraphics, Inc.

Library of Congress Cataloging-in-Publication Data
A catalog record for the print edition is available from the Library of Congress.
ISBN-10: 0-13-439938-2   ISBN-13: 978-0-13-439938-6

Printed in the United States of America
ScoutAutomatedPrintCode

CONTENTS

Scope and Sequence iv
The Third Edition of the *Password* Series ix
Overview of *Password 4* xi
References, Acknowledgments, Credits, and About the Author xiii

Unit 1: Into the World of Business 1
   Chapter 1: Dreamers and Doers 2
   Chapter 2: Word-of-Mouth Advertising 14
   Chapter 3: A Language on the Move 25
   Chapter 4: When the Employees Own the Company 36
   Unit 1 Checkpoint 48

Unit 2: Health Matters 55
   Chapter 5: Living to 100 and Beyond 56
   Chapter 6: What Causes the Placebo Effect? 67
   Chapter 7: Tears 79
   Chapter 8: The Power of Touch 90
   Unit 2 Checkpoint 101

Units 1–2 Vocabulary Self-Test 1 107

Unit 3: Exploring Technology 109
   Chapter 9: A History of Telling Time 110
   Chapter 10: The Screen vs. the Printed Page 121
   Chapter 11: Appropriate Technologies 133
   Chapter 12: Technology in Science Fiction 144
   Unit 3 Checkpoint 155

Unit 4: The Environment 161
   Chapter 13: Small Ride, Big Trouble 162
   Chapter 14: Your Trees, My Trees, Our Trees 173
   Chapter 15: Would You Eat Bugs to Save the World? 184
   Chapter 16: A Small Creature with a Big Job 195
   Unit 4 Checkpoint 206

Units 3–4 Vocabulary Self-Test 2 211

Unit 5: Economics 215
   Chapter 17: Economics—What's It All About? 216
   Chapter 18: Supply and Demand 227
   Chapter 19: Behavioral Economics 238
   Chapter 20: The Economics of Happiness 250
   Unit 5 Checkpoint 261

Units 1–5 Vocabulary Self-Test 3 267

Vocabulary Self-Tests Answer Key 271

Index to Target Vocabulary 273

SCOPE AND SEQUENCE

Unit/Chapter	Developing Reading Skills	Learning Target Vocabulary	Building on the Vocabulary	Using Critical Thinking	Practicing Writing
Unit 1 INTO THE WORLD OF BUSINESS					
Chapter 1: *Dreamers and Doers* Page 2	• Guessing meaning from context • Understanding topics and main ideas • Understanding text features • Reading for details: Recognizing what the writer does and doesn't say **Tips** • Reading first for the gist	*ad, client, come up with, design drive, earn, fair, hire, make a living, mean, risk, service, set up, turn (something) into, willing* **Tips** • Meanings of *drive* • *Client* vs. *customer* • Understanding parts of speech • Uses of *willing* • Meanings of *text* • Learning by writing sentences	• Word Grammar: Nouns, Verbs, and Phrasal Verbs	• **Examining** text structure • **Analyzing** human character • **Drawing** logical conclusions • **Citing evidence** from the text to support your opinion **Tips** • Practicing critical thinking	• Writing a paragraph about a young entrepreneur • Writing a paragraph about a career in business **Tips** • Citing evidence
Chapter 2: *Word-of-Mouth Advertising* Page 14	• Understanding text features • Understanding topics and main ideas • Reading for details **Tips** • Scanning • Understanding the writer's purpose	*advertising, announce, appear, as long as, avoid, consumer, developing, get rid of, goods, in return, major, sign up, volunteer, while, within* **Tips** • Meaning of *goods* • Uses of *in return for* • Meanings of *while*	• Word Grammar: Adjectives	• **Determining** what the text does and doesn't say • **Inferring** reasons for opinions • **Identifying** author purpose • **Drawing** comparisons **Tips** • Making inferences	• Writing a paragraph about an ad you remember • Writing a paragraph about your reaction to ads **Tips** • Taking time to revise
Chapter 3: *A Language on the Move* Page 25	• Understanding topics of paragraphs • Reading for details: Recognizing what a writer does and doesn't say • Summarizing **Tips** • Making a mental map of a text • Recognizing details	*deal with, economic, employee, financial, gain, huge, influence, invest, market, nature, particular, political, quality, quite, spread* **Tips** • Uses of *influence* • Meanings of *deal with* • Meanings of *particular*	• Word Grammar: Suffixes	• **Identifying** reasons for quotations • **Analyzing** word choice • **Applying** information from the reading to other contexts • **Supporting** your opinion **Tips** • Analyzing quotations	• Writing a paragraph about advice for learners of English • Writing a paragraph about your first experience learning English **Tips** • Writing a summary • Prewriting activities
Chapter 4: *When the Employees Own the Company* Page 36	• Understanding topics and main ideas • Reading for details: Recognizing what a writer does and doesn't say • Using graphic organizers **Tips** • Marking up a text	*believe in, besides, committee, community, condition, in charge of, organize, profit, provide, quality, react, right, security, such, uncertain* **Tips** • Uses of *profit* • Uses of *react (to)* • Use of *conditions*	• Studying Collocations: *Condition* and its word partners	• **Identifying** author purpose • **Examining** text structure • **Applying** ideas from the text to other situations • **Citing evidence** from the text **Tips** • Citing evidence from the text	• Writing a paragraph about the most important working conditions • Writing a paragraph about an experience organizing something **Tips** • Reading your writing aloud
Unit 1 *Checkpoint* Page 48	• Look Back • Reviewing Vocabulary • Expanding Vocabulary: *Word Families* • A Puzzle: *A Crossword Puzzle* • Building Dictionary Skills: *Superscripts, Finding Words* and *Phrases within Entries*				

Unit/Chapter	Developing Reading Skills	Learning Target Vocabulary	Building on the Vocabulary	Using Critical Thinking	Practicing Writing
Unit 2 HEALTH MATTERS					
Chapter 5: *Living to 100 and Beyond* **Page 56**	• Understanding the main idea of the reading • Taking notes • Stating major points • Using details to support major points **Tips** • Avoiding translating as you read	*actually, as well, beyond, forever, generally, increase, lifestyle, likely, limit, make a difference, make it, possibly, process, similar, treat* **Tips** • Meanings of *difference* • *Actual* and *actually* • Uses of *make it* • Uses of *increase* • Meanings of *beyond*	• Word Grammar: Adverbs	• **Inferring** the writer's meaning • **Analyzing** word use • **Evaluating** support for claims • **Supporting** your opinion **Tips** • Looking for evidence to support inferences	• Writing a paragraph about living to be 100 • Writing a journal entry about celebrating your 100th birthday **Tips** • Practice using new vocabulary
Chapter 6: *What Causes the Placebo Effect?* **Page 67**	• Quoting and paraphrasing • Understanding reference words • Summarizing **Tips** • First reading vs. rereading • The function of *actual/actually*	*affect, block, break a habit, chemistry, explanation, further, have something to do with, prove, recent, response, role, simply, staff, treatment, trick* **Tips** • Meanings of *response* • Meaning of *play a role* • *Affect* vs. *effect* • Uses of *staff* • Meaning of *findings*	• Word Grammar: *Farther* vs. *Further*	• **Synthesizing** information • **Analyzing** word choice • **Applying** information from the text • **Assessing** implications	• Writing a paragraph about volunteering for a research study • Writing a paragraph about going to the doctor **Tips** • Making lists to organize ideas
Chapter 7: *Tears* **Page 79**	• Quoting and paraphrasing • Understanding major points • Summarizing **Tips** • The function of *in fact*	*blow, chemical, differ, emotional, flow, go ahead, liquid, material, mental, normal, notice, rate, surface, throughout, view* **Tips** • *Emotion* and *emotional* • Uses of *throughout* • Uses of *notice*	• Studying Collocations: Verbs Used with *View*	• **Analyzing** language used in the text • **Citing evidence** from the text • **Identifying** the writer's point of view • **Supporting** your opinion **Tips** • Being aware of the writer's point of view	• Writing a paragraph about a personal experience of crying • Writing an opinion paragraph about crying **Tips** • Using quotations to express the writer's ideas
Chapter 8: *The Power of Touch* **Page 90**	• Understanding text features: Uses of parentheses • Understanding topics and main ideas • Quoting and paraphrasing **Tips** • Reading about scientific studies	*benefit, condition, culture, development, drop, hug, key, improve, independent, physical, press, raise, reduce, set, stress* **Tips** • Uses of *benefit* • Meanings of *stress* • Uses of *improve* • *Drop* and *reduction*	• Word Grammar: The Suffix *-al*	• **Differentiating** between fact and opinion • **Recognizing** author purpose • **Inferring** information • **Reacting** to claims in a text • **Analyzing** language used in the text **Tips** • Facts vs. opinions	• Writing a paragraph about researching observations • Writing a paragraph about the sense most important to you **Tips** • Using the five senses in descriptive writing
Unit 2 *Checkpoint* **Page 101**	• Look Back • Reviewing Vocabulary • Expanding Vocabulary: *Transitive and Intransitive Verbs* • A Puzzle: *Word Search* • Building Dictionary Skills: *Understanding Codes in the Dictionary*				

Unit/Chapter	Developing Reading Skills	Learning Target Vocabulary	Building on the Vocabulary	Using Critical Thinking	Practicing Writing
Unit 3 EXPLORING TECHNOLOGY					
Chapter 9: *A History of Telling Time* **Page 110**	• Recognizing text organization • Understanding reference words **Tips** • The function of reference words	*accurate, advanced, attend, demand, equal, exact, fairly, high-tech, measure, modern, portable, set, shadow, technology, transportation* **Tips** • Gerunds • Meanings of *technology* and *technologies* • *Advanced* and *advance* • Meaning of *chronological order* • Understanding *solution*	• Word Grammar: Using *Port* to Form Words	• **Identifying** problems and solutions • **Explaining** the text • **Brainstorming** examples • **Examining** your own position **Tips** • Connecting problems with solutions	• Writing a paragraph about a popular saying about time • Writing a paragraph about being on time **Tips** • Providing reasons for your opinions
Chapter 10: *The Screen vs. the Printed* **Page 121**	• Recognizing text organization • Supporting details • Summarizing **Tips** • Noticing text organization	*at least, behavior, carry out, deserve, electronic, in particular, on the other hand, practice, replace, resource, respond, section, so far, take (something) seriously, whenever* **Tips** • Meaning of *deserve* • The prefix *e-* (for *electronic*) • Collocations with *resources* • Uses of *on the other hand*	• Word Grammar: *Behavior, Practice,* and *Habit*	• **Identifying** author purpose • **Drawing** comparisons • **Inferring** opinions • **Understanding** a metaphor **Tips** • Recognizing the purpose of a comparison	• Writing a paragraph about reading electronic texts • Writing a paragraph comparing reading purposes **Tips** • Using a T-chart to organize ideas
Chapter 11: *Appropriate Technologies* **Page 133**	• Identifying problems and solutions • Recognizing cause and effect • Supporting details **Tips** • Reviewing advice for readers	*appropriate, attach, be better off, engineering, grain, load, method, model, plenty, pollution, production, realize, rural, solve, the environment* **Tips** • The meaning of *environment* • The meaning of *engineering* • *Rural* vs. *urban*	• Word Grammar: The Suffix *-tion*	• **Analyzing** cause and effect • **Interpreting** a person's actions • **Distinguishing** fact from opinion • **Examining** a writer's word choices **Tips** • Making inferences about the people in a text	• Writing a paragraph about a technology you depend on • Writing a summary paragraph about a situation from the reading **Tips** • Ordering your reasons
Chapter 12: *Technology in Science Fiction* **Page 144**	• Scanning • Paraphrasing • Summarizing	*adventure, century, confused, description, exist, imagination, in spite of, make up, neither . . . nor, predict, scientific, set, society, style, take off* **Tips** • *Predict* and *prediction* • Using *in spite of* • *Confused* vs. *confusing* • *Imagine, imagination,* and *imaginary*	• Word Grammar: *In Spite of* and *Despite*	• **Identifying** examples that illustrate a concept • **Applying** ideas from the text to another context • **Examining** language in the text • **Interpreting** clues in the text **Tips** • Using clues to make inferences	• Writing a paragraph about science fiction • Writing a paragraph about your future life and technology **Tips** • Writing titles • Describing the setting
Unit 3 *Checkpoint* **Page 155**	• Look Back • Reviewing Vocabulary • Expanding Vocabulary: *Antonyms* • A Puzzle: *A Crossword* • Building Dictionary Skills: *Words with Multiple Meanings*				

Unit/Chapter	Developing Reading Skills	Learning Target Vocabulary	Building on the Vocabulary	Using Critical Thinking	Practicing Writing
Unit 4 THE ENVIRONMENT					
Chapter 13: *Small Ride, Big Trouble* **Page 162**	• Understanding the main idea of the reading • Recognizing the writer's point of view • Recognizing cause and effect • Recognizing problems and solutions **Tips** • Questioning the writer's point of view	*blame, border, competition, decrease, engine, estimate, fuel, harm, income, interest, loan, maintain, meanwhile, passenger, vehicle* **Tips** • Uses of *blame* • Uses of *decrease* • Uses of *estimate* • *Competition* and its word family	• Word Grammar: Words Related to Money	• **Interpreting** figurative language • **Brainstorming** alternative solutions • **Inferring** people's motivations • **Citing evidence** from the text **Tips** • Literal meanings and metaphors	• Writing a paragraph about pollution • Writing a paragraph about the environment **Tips** • Using transition words
Chapter 14: *Your Trees, My Trees, Our Trees* **Page 173**	• Understanding main ideas • Supporting details • Differentiating between fact and opinion **Tips** • Rereading the introduction and conclusion	*carbon dioxide, consume, diameter, get involved, grateful, ink, keep up with, look into, oxygen, population, renewable, rubber, shade, soil, valuable* **Tips** • Uses of *keep up (with)* • *Value* and *valuable* • Meanings of *consume*	• Studying Collocations: Using *Involve*	• **Identifying** author purpose • **Evaluating** reasons • **Examining** word choice • **Citing evidence** from the text **Tips** • Making an argument	• Writing a paragraph about an experience changing your behavior • Writing a paragraph about feeling grateful **Tips** • Writing a topic sentence
Chapter 15: *Would You Eat Bugs to Save the World?* **Page 184**	• Understanding main ideas, major points, and supporting details • Using graphic organizers: Venn diagram • Differentiating between fact and opinion **Tips** • Taking notes in a chart or diagram	*be open to, current, destroy, educate, environmental, expert, force, in favor of, in terms of, protein, require, set out, source, speak out, unless* **Tips** • Uses of *force* • Uses of *source (of)* • Uses of *speak out* • Meaning of *current events*	• Word Grammar: *Unless*	• **Interpreting** figurative language • **Evaluating** an argument • **Citing evidence** from the text • **Understanding** author purpose **Tips** • Following the writer's argument	• Writing a letter about David Gracer's efforts • Writing a paragraph about an experience speaking out **Tips** • Identifying sources
Chapter 16: *A Small Creature with a Big Job* **Page 195**	• Understanding main ideas, major points, and supporting details • Determining text organization • Recognizing cause and effect **Tips** • Paying attention to chronological order	*agriculture, at least, call on, crisis, crop, essential, hunt, immediately, lie, motor, occur, pesticide, productive, threat, yet* **Tips** • *Crisis* and *crises* • Meaning of *essentials* • *Threat* and *threaten* • *Productive* and its word family • Meanings of *hunt* • Meanings of *call on*	• Word Grammar: *Occur, Take Place,* and *Happen*	• **Analyzing** word choice • **Identifying** author purpose • **Synthesizing** information • **Perceiving** connections between texts **Tips** • Citing experts to strengthen a argument	• Writing a paragraph about environmental problems • Writing a paragraph about urban vs. rural life **Tips** • Using your dictionary to find synonyms
Unit 4 *Checkpoint* **Page 206**	• Look Back • Reviewing Vocabulary • Expanding Vocabulary: *Word Families* • A Puzzle: *Word Search* • Building Dictionary Skills: *Words with Multiple Meanings*				

Unit/Chapter	Developing Reading Skills	Learning Target Vocabulary	Building on the Vocabulary	Using Critical Thinking	Practicing Writing
Unit 5 ECONOMICS					
Chapter 17: *Economics – What's It All About* Page 216	• Understanding main ideas, major points, and supporting • Recognizing cause and effect • Understanding the writer's purpose **Tips** • Understanding *after all*	*after all, approach, debt, economics, exchange, individual, labor, loss, necessary, opportunity, property, rise, scarce, since, trade* **Tips** • Uses of *after all* • *Loss* and its word family • Meanings of *rise* • *Exchange* vs. *trade* • Uses of *trade*	• Word Grammar: *Economics* and Its Word Family	• **Applying** ideas from the reading • **Examining** word choice • **Analyzing** costs and benefits • **Comparing** ideas • **Citing evidence** from the text **Tips** • Using a T-chart to make comparisons	• Writing a paragraph about the costs and benefits of studying English • Writing a paragraph about decisions your government has made **Tips** • Organizing a paragraph about pros and cons
Chapter 18: *Supply and Demand* Page 227	• Understanding the main idea • Understanding text features: Subheadings • Understanding major points and supporting details **Tips** • Making and checking predictions about a text • Studying diagrams in a text	*as, assume, attractive, balance, bring in, bring up, cross, drive up, effective, other than, quantity, run out (of), significant, term, to sum up* **Tips** • Uses of *run out (of)* • Uses of *to sum up* • Meanings of *as* • Uses of *term*	• Word Grammar: Prefixes Meaning *Not*	• **Examining** word choice • **Analyzing** a diagram • **Interpreting** figurative language • **Applying** ideas from the reading	• Writing a paragraph about your behavior as a consumer • Writing a paragraph about luxuries and necessities **Tips** • Using quotation marks when you quote
Chapter 19: *Behavioral Economics* Page 238	• Reading for details: Recognizing what a writer does and doesn't say • Understanding the writer's purpose • Summarizing	*admit, borrower, even though, fake, frequently, get in the way, go through, hand out, help oneself, in relation to, nevertheless, ordinary, sensible, surround, thought* **Tips** • *Borrower* and *lender* • Uses of *go through* • Uses of *admit (to or that)*	• Word Grammar: *Even Though* and *Nevertheless*	• **Judging** behavior described in a text • **Imagining** a person's motivation • **Analyzing** word choice • **Synthesizing** information **Tips** • Synthesizing information	• Writing a paragraph about your own economic decision making • Writing a paragraph about a choice you made as a consumer **Tips** • Using transition words
Chapter 20: *The Economics of Happiness* Page 250	• Understanding the main idea • Understanding text organization: Chronological order • Understanding major points **Tips** • Determining the timing or order of events	*argue, as for, central, citizen, growth, percentage, poll, position, rate, reveal, satisfied, scale, tear apart, therefore, wealth* **Tips** • Meanings of *argue* • *Therefore* and *so* • Uses of *reveal*	• Studying Collocations: Prepositions	• **Interpreting** figurative language • **Distinguishing** among various beliefs • **Citing evidence** from the text • **Inferring** information from the text **Tips** • Inferring ideas from the structure of a text	• Writing a paragraph about the happiness of people in your country • Writing a paragraph comparing ourselves with others **Tips** • Developing your skills as a writer
Unit 5 *Checkpoint* Page 261	• Look Back • Reviewing Vocabulary • Expanding Vocabulary: *Word Families* • A Puzzle: *A Crossword* • Building Dictionary Skills: *Phrasal Verbs with Multiple Meanings*				

THE THIRD EDITION OF THE *PASSWORD* SERIES

Welcome to the third edition of *Password*, a series designed to help learners of English develop their English-language reading skills and expand their vocabularies. The series offers theme-based units which include:

- engaging nonfiction reading passages,
- a variety of activities to develop reading and critical thinking skills, and
- exercises to help students understand, remember, and use new words and phrases.

Each book in the *Password* series can be used independently of the others, but when used as a series, the books will help students reach the 2,000-word vocabulary level, at which point, research has shown, learners can begin to read unadapted texts.

The *Password* approach to reading skill development for English-language learners is based on the following ideas:

1. The best way for learners to develop their English reading skills is to read English-language materials at an appropriate level.

Attractive, high-interest materials will spark learners' motivation to read, but to sustain that motivation, "second language reading instruction must find ways to avoid continually frustrating the reader."[1] Learners of English need reading materials at an appropriate level of difficulty, materials that do not reduce them to struggling to decipher a puzzle. Materials at an inappropriate level will not allow learners to develop reading strategies but rather will discourage them from reading.

The level of difficulty of ELT materials is determined by many factors, such as the learner's familiarity with the topic, the learner's L1 reading skills, the length and structure of the words, sentences, and paragraphs, and the structure of the text as a whole. These are among the factors that influence the construction of all good ELT reading materials and the way they gradually increase in difficulty. However, an additional, critical factor in determining the difficulty of a text for English language learners is the familiarity of the vocabulary. Note that:

> There is now a large body of studies indicating that poor readers primarily differ from good readers in context-free word recognition, and not in deficiencies in ability to use context to form predictions.[2]

Learners of English must be able to recognize a great many words on sight so that they can absorb, understand, and react to the text much as they would to a text in their first language.

The *Password* series is distinguished by its meticulous control and recycling of vocabulary so that the readings consistently maintain an appropriate level of difficulty. When learners can recognize enough of the words in their reading materials, they can then develop and apply reading skills and strategies. The result is an authentic reading experience, the kind of experience learners need to become proficient readers of English.

2. An intensive reading program is essential to prepare English language learners for the demands of college and careers.

An intensive reading program means students engage in the careful reading of nonfiction texts with the goal of understanding them in detail, under the guidance of the teacher. A well-designed textbook can play a critical role in helping students not only meet that goal but also acquire reading skills and strategies they can apply to further reading. Course materials should provide practice with the types of thinking skills that students need, not only to comprehend explicitly stated information but to interpret texts, draw inferences, analyze the language, make comparisons, and cite evidence from the text to support their views. The materials should also facilitate collaboration with classmates throughout the process. When their classroom discussions are stimulating and rewarding, students are motivated to do the assigned readings, and thus get the reading practice they need.

3. An ELT reading textbook should teach the English vocabulary that will be most useful to learners.

Corpus-based research has shown that the 2,000 highest-frequency words in English (as identified in Michael West's classic *General Service List*) account for about 80 percent of the running words in academic texts.[3] The *New General Service List*, with 2,368 high-frequency "word families," goes even further, providing 90 percent coverage of the words in most general English texts.[4] Clearly, the highest-frequency words are highly valuable words for students of English to learn.

The *Password* target word lists are based on analyses of high-frequency word data from multiple sources, including the Longman Corpus Network. Also taught in the series are common collocations and other multiword units, such as phrasal verbs, while a few target words have been chosen for their value in discussing a particular topic. With the increasing interest in corpus-based research in recent years, a wealth of information is now available as to which words are the highest-frequency, be it in US and/or British academic contexts, in

---

[1] Thom Hudson, *Teaching Second Language Reading* (Oxford, UK: Oxford Universit y Press, 2007) 291.
[2] C. Juel, quoted in *Teaching and Researching Reading*, William Grabe and Fredericka Stoller (Harlow, England: Pearson Education, 2002) 73.
[3] I. S. P. Nation, Learning Vocabulary in Another Language (Cambridge, England: Cambridge University Press, 2001) 17.
[4] "A New General Service List (1.01)." (n.d.) Retrieved December 15, 2015, from http://www.newgeneralservicelist.org

written English of various types, in spoken English, and so on. Teachers may worry about how to choose from among the various lists, but at the level of the 2,000 highest-frequency words in general use—the level of the *Password* series—the lists are far more alike than they are different.

While becoming a good reader in English involves much more than knowing the meanings of words, there is no doubt that vocabulary knowledge is essential. To learn new words, students need to see and understand them repeatedly and in varied contexts. They must also become skilled at guessing the meaning of new words from context, but they can do this successfully only when they understand the context.

Research by Paul Nation and Liu Na suggests that "for successful guessing [of unknown words] . . . at least 95% of the words in the text must be familiar to the reader."[5] For that reason, the vocabulary in the readings has been carefully controlled so that unknown words should constitute no more than five percent of any reading passage. The words used in each reading are limited to those high-frequency words that the learner is assumed to know, or has studied in previous chapters, plus the new vocabulary being taught. New vocabulary is explained and practiced in exercises and activities, encountered again in later chapters, and reviewed in the Unit Checkpoints and Self-Tests. This emphasis on systematic vocabulary acquisition is a highlight of the series.

The chart below shows the number of words that each *Password* book assumes will be familiar to the learner, and the range of the high-frequency vocabulary targeted in the book.

The five books in the series vary somewhat in organization, to meet the diverse needs of beginning to high-intermediate students, as well as in the increasing complexity of the reading materials and exercises. All five books will help learners make steady progress in developing their reading, critical thinking, and vocabulary skills in English. Please see the Overview in each book for detailed information about its organization and contents, including the exciting new features the third edition has to offer.

Linda Butler, creator of the Password *series*

Additional References

Grabe, William. *Reading in a Second Language: Moving from theory to practice.* Cambridge: Cambridge University Press, 2009.

Liu, Dilin. "The Most Frequently Used Spoken American English Idioms: A Corpus Analysis and Its Implications," *TESOL Quarterly* 37 (Winter 2003): 4, 671-700.

Nation, I.S.P. *Teaching Vocabulary: Strategies and techniques.* Boston: Heinle, Cengage Learning, 2008.

Schmitt, Norbert, and Cheryl Boyd Zimmerman. "Derivative Word Forms: What Do Learners Know?" *TESOL Quarterly* 36 (Summer 2002): 145–171.

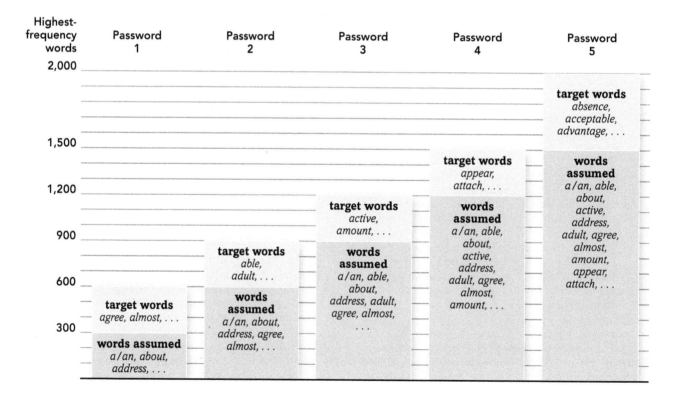

OVERVIEW OF *PASSWORD 4*, THIRD EDITION

Password 4 is intended for students who need to build a solid foundation for reading in English, whether for academic purposes or for their careers. Each chapter features an engaging nonfiction reading passage as the basis for a variety of activities to help students develop their reading, critical thinking, speaking, writing, and vocabulary skills.

The book assumes students start out with a vocabulary of about 1200 words in English, and it teaches over 300 more of the high-frequency words and phrases that students most need to know at this point in their study of English. In each chapter, fifteen words and phrases are highlighted in the reading passage and practiced in the exercises. Additional terms are taught in Tips in the margins and in the Critical Thinking sections. All are recycled in later chapters. Because of the systematic building of vocabulary, as well as the progression of the skills work, it is best to do the chapters in order.

The target vocabulary consists primarily of words found among the 1500 highest-frequency words in English. Occasionally, lower-frequency words and phrases are targeted for their usefulness in discussing a particular theme, as in the unit on the environment, where the words *resource*, *renewable*, and *agriculture* are taught.

Organization of the Book

Password 4 contains five units, each with four chapters and a *Checkpoint* chapter. Vocabulary *Self-Tests* are found after Units 2, 4, and 5. The answers to the Self-Tests and the Index to the Target Vocabulary are at the end of the book.

THE UNITS   Each unit is based on a theme, and each chapter in the unit is built around a nonfiction reading. The reading passages are about people, situations, concepts, and events.

★ **New in this edition:** Each unit opens with a *Think about This* question, designed to activate prior knowledge of the unit theme. It will get students thinking and talking about the topic from the start.

THE CHAPTERS   Each of the four chapters in a unit is organized as follows:

Getting Ready to Read—The chapter opens with a photo and pre-reading tasks. The tasks are for class discussion or pair or small-group work. *Getting Ready to Read* improves students' reading comprehension by activating schema. The tasks get students to connect with the topic before they read by raising questions, eliciting what they already know, asking for their opinions, and introducing key vocabulary.

★ **New in this edition:** The new, color photo will spark interest in the topic. The *Learning Outcome* tells students the content objective of the chapter: what they will be reading, talking, and learning about by working through the chapter.

Reading—This section begins with a *Read to Find Out* question, which gives students a reading goal. The reading passage for the chapter follows. The passages progress from about 600 to about 800 words over the course of the book. Students should do the reading the first time without stopping to look up or ask about new words. Careful control of the vocabulary in each passage means that students will not get derailed by too many new words and can have the authentic reading experience they need to build their reading skills.

Audio recordings of the readings are available in the **Essential Online Resources,** for which this book contains an access code inside the front cover. Students can play the audio recording of the passage while they reread it, as listening while reading can aid comprehension, retention, and pronunciation.

Each reading passage is followed by *Quick Comprehension Check* which is a brief true/false exercise to help students monitor their general understanding of the text. At this point, students focus only on comprehension of the major points in the reading. Vocabulary study and an in-depth examination of the text will follow.

★ **New in this edition:** All of the readings have been updated for this edition, and three chapters are entirely new: Chapter 8: The Power of Touch, Chapter 10: The Screen vs. the Printed Page, and Chapter 18: Supply and Demand. Also new are the *Read to Find Out* questions and part B of the *Quick Comprehension Check*: students must locate and cite evidence from the reading to support their answers and to make corrections to the false statements. The ability to cite evidence from a text is an essential skill for academic reading.

Exploring Vocabulary—This section teaches the target vocabulary from the reading. In *Thinking about the Target Vocabulary*, students complete a chart with the target words and phrases from the reading, organized according to parts of speech. After they circle those terms that are new to them, students return to the reading to see what they can learn about the words from the context in which they are used. Students can do the vocabulary independently or in pairs, but they may benefit from working on this first as a whole class, with the teacher's guidance.

Understanding the Target Vocabulary follows, with two exercises to help students understand the meanings of the target words and phrases as they are used in the reading. The exercises also serve as a recap of key ideas from the text. They can be done in class, by students working individually or in pairs, or for homework. In *Building on the Vocabulary*, students learn more about the parts of speech, collocations, or particular target words or phrases. In the final section, *Using the Target Vocabulary in New Contexts*, students broaden their understanding of the meanings and uses of the words.

★ New in this edition: *Vocabulary Tips* in the margins teach vocabulary strategies, introduce new terms, and provide extra information about the meanings and uses of particular target words and phrases.

Developing Your Reading Skills—Re-reading is a vital part of the reading process, and the tasks in this section motivate students to delve back into the reading passage and thereby deepen their understanding of the text. Among the tasks are exercises on identifying topics and main ideas (of both paragraphs and entire texts), scanning, recognizing cause and effect relationships, distinguishing fact from opinion, quoting and paraphrasing, and summarizing the reading. See the Scope and Sequence on page iv for a full list of the reading skills practiced. Developing these skills is essential preparation for academic reading in English.

★ New in this edition: Essential skills for academic reading have been added throughout the chapters. New tasks help students understand text features and use graphic organizers. *Reading Tips* in the margins teach reading strategies, offer advice on good reading habits, and raise awareness of text structure.

Critical Thinking—This new section for the third edition adds rigor to the discussion of the reading passages by requiring students to analyze and evaluate the text before they offer their own opinions and reactions to it. Students are guided to examine the text, make inferences, draw comparisons, determine author purpose, cite evidence--in short, to apply a range of vital thinking skills and demonstrate a thorough understanding of the text. This section may also include community-building questions, inspired by the readings, that get students to brainstorm, use their imaginations, and share their own experiences and ideas.

★ New in this edition: Questions for discussion promote the critical thinking skills expected and required for success in college and careers in the 21st century. *Critical Thinking Tips* in the margins help students to develop those skills and become more aware of them.

Writing—Part A, *Use the Target Vocabulary*, gives students tasks for using the target vocabulary in sentences, which students then share with a partner. In Part B, *Practice writing*, students write a paragraph on either of two topics related to the reading. These writing tasks can be used for brief in-class writing, as prompts for journal entries or online discussions, or for longer, more formal assignments that may require multiple drafts. Writing in response to reading is a way for students not only to develop writing and vocabulary skills but to deepen understanding of what they have read and make connections to the unit theme. Students are encouraged to share their paragraphs, a practice which helps them develop awareness of writing for an audience and gives their partner an additional theme-based reading experience.

★ New in this edition: *Writing Tips* in the margins provide strategies to help students become more successful writers.

UNIT CHECKPOINT   Each unit ends with a Checkpoint chapter, designed to help students review and expand on the content of the unit. The Checkpoint begins with a *Look Back* section, in which students are asked to recall and reflect on what they learned (*Think about This*), and think about their own response to each of the reading passages (*Remember the Readings*). *Reviewing Vocabulary* gives students another point of interaction with the target vocabulary from the unit; *Expanding Vocabulary* teaches students about word families and word parts; and *A Puzzle* puts target vocabulary into a crossword or word search puzzle. The final section, *Building Dictionary Skills*, provides practice based on excerpts from Longman dictionaries of American English. Knowing how to use a dictionary effectively is an essential skill for the independent language learner.

★ New in this edition: A *Learning Outcome* introduces each Checkpoint chapter. The *Look Back* section provides a valuable follow-up to the students' reading experiences in each unit.

THE VOCABULARY SELF-TESTS   Three multiple-choice vocabulary tests appear in the book, the first covering Units 1 and 2, the second covering Units 3 and 4 , and the third, all five units. The answers are given at the back of the book, as these tests are intended for students' own use so that they can review the target vocabulary and assess their progress.

★ New in this edition: The Self-Tests have been updated to include the new target vocabulary.

NEW Essential Online Resources

A new set of resources is available online for *Password 4*. It contains:

- An audio recording of each reading
- Bonus activities for extra practice in timed reading and study skills
- The Teacher's Manual, containing:
  - An introduction
  - The answer key for all exercises in the book, updated for this edition
  - Five unit tests with answers, updated for this edition (each test containing a theme-based reading passage, four reading skills tasks based on the passage, and 10-12 test items on the unit vocabulary)
- *Quick Oral Reviews*, sets of prompts to use in class for rapid drills of the target vocabulary for each chapter. These drills can be an important part of the spaced repetition of vocabulary—repeated exposures to newly learned words and phrases at increasing intervals—that helps students remember the vocabulary. The Introduction in the Teacher's Manual contains tips on how to use the prompts.

To the Student

Welcome to *Password 4!* This book will help you become a better reader of English and expand your English vocabulary. I hope you will enjoy using it.

REFERENCES, ACKNOWLEDGMENTS, CREDITS, AND ABOUT THE AUTHOR

References

Akst, D. "Q&A: Betsey Stevenson and Justin Wolfers: It turns out money really does buy happiness. Uh-oh." Boston Sunday Globe, November 23, 2008.

Anderson, C. "The Correlation between Wealth and Happiness – Is There One?" Retrieved September 23, 2016, from https://www.linkedin.com/pulse/correlation-between-wealth-happiness-one-camilla-anderson.

Ariely, D. *Predictably Irrational*, New York: Harper, 2008.

Asimov, I. "The Fun They Had." *The Best of Isaac Asimov.* New York: Doubleday & Company, 1974.

Barasch, D. "Letter from the Editor: Why I Ain't Blue." *OnEarth Magazine*, Vol. 28, No. 2, Summer 2006, p. 3.

Brehm, D. "MIT Grad Student Designs Low-Cost Solution for High-Tech African Problem." *MIT News.* Retrieved October 26, 2016, from http://news.mit.edu/1999/incubator.

Field, L. "Young entrepreneur turns hobby into career." *Opelika-Auburn News*, September 29, 2007.

Field, T. *Touch*, second edition. Cambridge, MA: The MIT Press, 2014.

Glausiusz, J. "Want to Help the Environment? Eat Insects." Retrieved September 9, 2016, from http://discovermagazine.com/2008/may/07-want-to-help-the-environment-eat-insects.

Jabr, F. "The Reading Brain in the Digital Age." Scientific American, retrieved August 2, 2016, from http://www.scientificamerican.com/article/reading-paper-screens/

Kaptchuk, T.J., et al. "Components of placebo effect: randomized controlled trial in patients with irritable bowel syndrome." (2008) Retrieved October 22, 2016, from https://www.ncbi.nlm.nih.gov/pubmed/18390493.

Konnikova, M. "The Power of Touch." *The New Yorker*, March 4, 2015 [electronic version].

Krulwich, R. "Going Out on a Limb with a Tree-Person Ratio." National Public Radio. Retrieved September 6, 2016, from http://www.npr.org/templates/story/story.php?storyId=96758439&sc=emaf.

Leonhardt, D. "Maybe Money Does Buy Happiness After All." *New York Times*, April 16, 2008 [electronic version].

Levy, S. "The Vanishing." *OnEarth Magazine*, Vol. 28, No. 2, Summer 2006, pp. 14–22.

Lutz, T. *Crying: The Natural and Cultural History of Tears.* New York: W. W. Norton & Company, 1999.

Nadkarni, N. M. *Between Earth and Sky: Our intimate connections to trees.* Berkeley, CA: University of California Press, 2008.

Ola, P., and D'Aulaire, E. "Baking Up a Business." *Smithsonian* (November 2000): 114–115.

Roser, M. "Happiness and Life Satisfaction." *Published online at OurWorldInData.org.* Retrieved October 26, 2016, from: https://ourworldindata.org/happiness-and-life-satisfaction.

Tozzi, J. "Should You Hire Your Parents?" *Business Week.* Retrieved October 26, 2016, from http://www.bloomberg.com/news/articles/2008-09-08/should-you-hire-your-parents-businessweek-business-news-stock-market-and-financial-advice.

Silverman, G. "Book Summary: *Secrets of Word of Mouth Marketing.*" Retrieved January 12, 2009, from http://www.bizsum.com/articles/art_the-secrets-of-word-of-mouth-marketing.php.

Stevenson, B., and Wolfers, J. "Economic Growth and Subjective Well-Being: Reassessing the Easterlin Paradox." Retrieved October 26, 2016, from http://users.nber.org/~jwolfers/papers/EasterlinParadox.pdf.

"Teen Millionaires . . . How Did They Do It?" *The Morning Show.* Retrieved October 26, 2016, from https://www.youtube.com/watch?v=MZXHlLQGquQ.

"The World's Richest and Poorest Countries." *Global Finance.* Retrieved October 26, 2016, from https://www.gfmag.com/global-data/economic-data/worlds-richest-and-poorest-countries.

Watson, J.B., and Watson, R.A. *Psychological Care of Infant and Child.* New York: W.W. Norton & Company, 1928.

Acknowledgments

I would like to thank the following reviewers, whose contributions have been much appreciated during the development of *Password 4*: Allan Hislop, Northern Essex Community College, Massachusetts; Lewis Spates, Northern Essex Community College, Massachusetts; Simon Weedon, NOVA ICI Oita School, Japan; Joe Walther, Sookmyung Women's University, Korea; Kevin Knight, Kanda University of International Studies, Japan; Guy Elders, Turkey; Wendy Allison, Seminole Community College, Florida; Kimberly Bayer-Olthoff, Hunter College, New York; Ruth Ann Weinstein, J. E. Burke High School, Massachusetts; Vincent LoSchiavo, P.S. 163, New York; Kelly Roberts-Weibel, Edmunds Community College, Washington; Lisa Cook, Laney College, California; Thomas Leverett, Southern Illinois University, Illinois; Angela Parrino, Hunter College, New York; Adele Camus, George Mason University, Virginia.

I am grateful to Miles Montgomery-Butler and Sam Daniel for their feedback on selected readings and to Miles for his advice on the readings on economics in particular.

I would also like to thank developmental editor Penny Laporte for her outstanding work on the entire *Password* series.

Finally, it has been a pleasure working with Pearson English, and for all their efforts on behalf of this book and the entire *Password* series, I would like to thank everyone on the Pearson English team.

Photography Credits

Page 1: Shutterstock; 2: Photographee.eu/Shutterstock; 14: Iakov Filimonov/Shutterstock; 25: Shapiso/Shutterstock; 36: Toby Talbot/AP Images; 48: Shutterstock; 55: Kzenon/123RF; 056: Lisa F. Young/Shutterstock; 67: XiXinXing/Shutterstock; 79: Mel Yates/DigitalVision/Getty Images; 90: XiXinXing/Shutterstock; 092: Asife/Shutterstock; 101: Kzenon/123RF; 109: NASA; 110: Chursina Viktorii/Shutterstock; 121: Wavebreakmedia/Shutterstock; 133: ©Tomas Bertelsen/Rolex Awards; 135: John Warburton Lee Photography/Alamy Stock; 144: CSA Images/Mod Art Collection/Getty Images; 155: NASA; 161: Lone Wolf Photos/Shutterstock; 162: Russell Young/Danita Delimont, Agent/Alamy Stock Photo; 173: Henn Photography/Cultura/Getty Images; 184: kwanchai.c/Shutterstock; 195 (bottom left): Goran cakmazovic/Shutterstock; 195 (bottom, right): Brandt Bolding/Shutterstock; 195T: Alexey Laputin/Shutterstock; 206: Lone Wolf Photos/Shutterstock; 215: Isak55/Shutterstock; 216: DragonImages/Shutterstock; 227: Breakingthewalls/Shutterstock; 238: Stocked House Studio/Shutterstock; 261: Isak55/Shutterstock.

Illustration Credits

Electragraphics, Inc.

About the Author

Linda Butler began her English language teaching career in Italy in 1979. She earned a master's in TESOL at Boston University and has since taught in several college ESL programs in the United States. She writes and edits online and print materials for learning, teaching, and testing English, and she is the author of many ESL/EFL textbooks, including Books 1 through 4 of the *Password* series and *Longman Academic Writing Series 1: Sentences to Paragraphs*.

INTO THE WORLD OF BUSINESS

THINK ABOUT THIS

If you were to choose a career in business, what would you most want to do?

Rank your choices from 1 (the most) to 4 (the least).

- Start my own business
- Work in a family-owned business
- Work for a small locally-owned company
- Work for a large international company
- Your idea:

CHAPTER 1

Dreamers and Doers

Young entrepreneurs

LEARNING OUTCOME

> Learn about some young entrepreneurs

GETTING READY TO READ

Talk about these questions in a small group.

1. Do you know the word *entrepreneur*? Read the definition. Can you name any famous entrepreneurs?

> **en·tre·pre·neur** / ŏn′trə-prə-nûr′, -noŏr′ / *n* a person who starts a new company, often someone who takes a chance on a new idea

* *CEO* = Chief Executive Officer, the person at the head of a company

2. Is starting your own business something that you would like to do? Can you picture yourself as a CEO?* Explain why or why not.

READING

Read to Find Out: What do young entrepreneurs have in common with older ones?

Look at the words and definitions next to the reading. Then read without stopping. If you see a new word, try to understand the sentence without it. You will learn the word later.

Dreamers and Doers

1   The world has always had entrepreneurs—people who **come up with** an idea and **turn it into** a business. Today, however, these people seem to be everywhere! They also seem to be getting younger and younger. Some very well-known businesses, such as Facebook and Microsoft, were started by college students, and other businesses have been started by students who were even younger.

2   At age nine, Ashley Qualls learned how to **set up** a website. At fourteen, she created a website where girls could get free help to set up websites for themselves. Before long, her site was getting more than 100,000 page views[1] a day. Then Ashley got a call from a business that wanted to put **ads** on her site and would pay her to do that. She agreed, and from those ads, she **earned** enough while still in high school to buy her family a house. Cameron Johnson was also nine when he started his first business: he began with printing party invitations, for his parents' friends. By the time he graduated from high school, he had started three more businesses and made his first million.[2]

3   What **drives** young entrepreneurs like these? Ashley Qualls would say that she was just having fun. She might call herself "an accidental CEO," someone who ends up at the head of a company without really planning on it. Pierre Omidyar might say the same thing. He created the world-famous eBay[3] but he says he did not **mean** to start a business. He was just trying to look good for his girlfriend. Cameron Johnson, on the other hand, knew *exactly* what he wanted. He grew up reading books about famous businessmen, and he dreamed of making millions.

4   Other young entrepreneurs, like Constanza Ontaneda, dream of making the world a better place. At age eighteen, while visiting Peru, she met some people who were highly skilled at making clothes but could not **make a living** at it. Instead, they supported themselves washing dishes or cleaning rooms. Constanza came up with a plan: She would **hire** them at a **fair** wage[4] to make clothes that she would **design**, and she would sell the clothes in the United States. After she opened her store, the Peruvians started earning more in a few weeks—at work they enjoyed—than they used to make in a year.

[1] *page views* = how many times people look at a website

[2] *made his first million* = earned his first $1,000,000

[3] *eBay* = a website for buying and selling things online

[4] *wage* = an amount of money a worker earns, usually paid by the hour

5   Young people who start their own businesses may face problems that older people do not. Matt Spain is one example. He started a computer **service** company at age fifteen. That was old enough for him to be good at fixing computers but not old enough for him to drive, so his **clients** had to pick him up at his house and take him to their offices.

6   Young CEOs may also face a question that older ones do not: Should they hire their parents? Ashley Qualls hired her mother, and Daniel Negari did, too. He started working in real estate[5] at age eighteen, and at twenty-two, he had fourteen people working for him. He got his mother to leave her high-paying job to work for him by showing her that with his company, she would earn even more. He was happy to hire someone he knew so well and trusted completely.

[5] *real estate =* the business of selling houses, other buildings, or land

7   Young or old, most entrepreneurs are alike in some ways. For example, they're **willing** to take **risks**, and they believe they'll succeed. If you would like to know more about starting your own business, you can pick up a book about it. Cameron Johnson wrote his first at age fifteen.

Quick Comprehension Check

A. Read these statements **about the reading**. Circle T (true) or F (false). On the line, write the number of the paragraph with the answer.

1. Entrepreneurs are people who start their own businesses.   (T)   F   _1_

2. Starting your own business usually means taking chances.   (T)   (F)   _7_

3. Some famous businesses have been started by college students.   (T)   F   _4_

4. Young entrepreneurs get good experience but little money.   T   (F)   _2_

5. The young people in the reading all had the goal of getting rich.   T   (F) _2, 3, 4_

6. Young CEOs and older ones share all the same problems.   T   (F)   _5, 6_

B. Work with your class. Share your answers from part A. Go back to the reading to find the reason why a statement is true or false. Correct the false statements.

EXPLORING VOCABULARY

Thinking About the Target Vocabulary

The Target Vocabulary

The words and phrases in **bold** in "Dreamers and Doers" are the **target vocabulary** for this chapter. They are listed in the chart below in the same order as in the reading.

In the chart, you can see five columns:

- In the column on the left are the paragraph numbers. The symbol "¶" means *paragraph*.
- The next three columns are for nouns, verbs, and adjectives—three important **parts of speech**. The last column is for all other kinds of words and phrases.

The chart shows:

- the singular form of any plural noun from the reading.
- the base form, or simple form, of each verb. Verbs include phrasal verbs, such as *come up with*. (See page 8 for more information.)

A. Look at the chart with the target vocabulary from "Dreamers and Doers." One noun, one verb, and one adjective are missing. Scan the reading to find them, and add them to the correct places in the chart. Use the singular form of the noun. Use the base form of the verb.

¶	Nouns	Verbs	Adjectives	Other
1	entrepretor ~~toebtetacbook~~ Business	come up with	yonger well-known *use 11*	always ihavedr , also srcnas also
		turn (something) into		
2	Website High school Girls	set up was having was getting	yang yang	fun-adverb was
3	Ashley early	drive ends up mean		On the other hand - Prep Phrase
4				make a living
		hire		
		fair		
		design		

¶	Nouns	Verbs	Adjectives	Other
5	service	*start itake*	*older, good*	
	client	*Pick fixing*		
7				
	risk			

B. Which words or phrases are new to you? Circle them in the chart. Then find them in the reading. Look at the context. Can you guess the meaning?

Guessing Meaning from Context

We use words in a **context**. The context of a word means the words and sentences before and after the word. The context can help you guess the meaning of a word or phrase. For example, look at the context of *make a living*:

[Constanza] met some people who were highly skilled at making clothes but could not **make a living** at it. Instead, they supported themselves washing dishes or cleaning rooms.

People work to support themselves, so the context of *make a living* tells you that the phrase refers to work. The people could not make a living at one thing, so they did other work. *Make a living* means to make enough money from your work to support yourself.

Understanding the Target Vocabulary

A. These sentences are **about the reading**. Complete them with the words and phrases in the box.

✓came up with	drives	fair	service	turned it into
designs	earned	mean	set up	willing

1. If someone was the first person to think of an idea or a plan, for a business or anything else, you can say that he or she ___came up with___ the idea.

2. If someone takes an idea and does the work to change it into something else—a business, for example—you can say the person took the idea and ___turned it into___ a business.

3. Ashley Qualls learned how to build a website. She learned the steps to create one, and then she ___set up___ a website of her own.

4. Ashley made a lot of money from her website while still in high school.

   She _earned_ enough money to buy a house.

5. Young entrepreneurs have to do a lot of work to make a business succeed. Something strongly influences them to work so hard. What _drives_ them to do it?

Vocabulary Tip:
Drive can also be a noncount noun meaning "energy and desire to succeed:" *He has a lot of drive.*

6. Pierre Omidyar was *not* planning on becoming an entrepreneur. Starting a business wasn't his goal. He didn't _mean_ to do it. It happened almost by accident.

7. Some workers do not get paid as much as they should. Constanza wanted to pay her workers the right amount. When she hired them, she paid them a _fair_ wage.

8. Constanza comes up with new ideas for clothes and draws pictures of them. She _designs_ clothes.

9. Matt Spain started a business fixing computers for people. He did not sell a product, as many businesses do. He offered people a _service_ —a kind of help.

   fair - willing service

10. Some people don't want to take chances. The idea makes them unhappy. But entrepreneurs are usually ready and _willings_ to take risks.

B. Read each definition and look at the paragraph number. Look back at the reading on pages 3–4 to find the **boldfaced** word or phrase to match the definition. Write the word or phrase in the chart.

Definition	Paragraph	Target Word or Phrase
1. pictures, words, short movies, etc., used to get people to buy a product, use a service, etc. (short for *advertisements*)	2	ads
2. earn enough money to live	4	make a living
3. give a job to	4	hire
4. people who pay for services or advice from a professional, a company, etc.	5	clients
5. chances that bad things may happen	7	risks

Vocabulary Tip:
Use *client* to mean someone who pays for a service and *customer* to mean someone who buys products from a store, a restaurant, a company, etc.

EXPANDING VOCABULARY

Building on the Vocabulary

> **Grammar: Nouns, Verbs, and Phrasal Verbs**
>
> The **parts of speech** are the different kinds of words, such as nouns and verbs.
>
> **Nouns**: These are words for people (*boy, clients, Ashley*), things (*book, ads, Honda*), places (*home, airport, Los Angeles*), and ideas (*risks, education, time*).
>
> **Verbs**: Every sentence must have a verb. Verbs are words for actions (*dance, go, run, wash*) or for states or experiences (*be, have, feel, understand*). Remember that a verb can be more than one word (*is working, has been*). **Phrasal verbs** combine a verb with a particle, as in *set up* and *turn into*. The meaning of a phrasal verb can be very different from the meaning of the verb alone.

Vocabulary Tip: Understanding the parts of speech will help you understand how to use words in sentences.

A. Circle the nouns in these sentences.

1. Who came up with the idea for the movie?
2. Most entrepreneurs take risks.
3. The company hired Paula right after her interview.
4. The magazine had many pages full of ads.
5. The client was very happy with the service.

B. Underline the verbs in these sentences. Note that some verbs are more than one word.

1. Who came up with the idea for the movie?
2. Business is slow these days, so no one is hiring.
3. Ashley learned how to set up a website.
4. Pam didn't know how difficult the job was going to be.
5. I'm sure the boys didn't mean to break the window.

Using the Target Vocabulary in New Contexts

A. Complete the sentences with the target words and phrases in the box. There are two extra words.

clients	drive	make a living	services
design	fair	mean	willing

1. Jack takes beautiful photos, but he can't _make a living_ at it.
2. An architect is a person whose job is to _design_ houses and other buildings.

3. A doctor has patients, a store owner has customers, and a lawyer has
   _____clients_____.

4. The company offers nighttime cleaning _____services_____ for office
   buildings.

5. Jan was angry that Peter wasn't doing his _____fair_____ share of the
   work.

6. I'm sorry about what I said. I didn't _____mean_____ to upset you.

B. These sentences also use the target words and phrases **in new contexts**.
What is the meaning of each **boldfaced** word or phrase? Circle a, b, or c.

1. *Minimum wage* means the lowest hourly rate that someone can **earn** by
   law. *Earn* means

   a. pay as a tax.   **b.** get by working.   c. save in the bank.

2. Higher oil prices are **driving** price increases for everything else. In this
   sentence, *driving* means

   a. allowing.   b. holding back.   **c.** causing.

3. I have no idea yet what to get him as a gift, but I'll **come up with**
   something. *Come up with* means

   a. arrive with.   **b.** think of.   c. bring.

4. Chris has taken a bedroom and **turned it into** a home office. *Turn
   something into* means

   a. call it.   **b.** change it into.   c. imagine it as.

5. Nick and his friends are **setting up** a new after-school club. *Set
   something up* means

   a. start it.   b. ask for it.   c. join it.

6. I like the car, but I'm not **willing** to pay that price for it. *Be willing to
   do something* means

   a. know how to do it.   **b.** be ready to do it.   c. be too afraid to
   do it.

> **Vocabulary Tip:**
> *Be + willing*
> means "agree (to
> do something)."
> *Willing* + noun
> means someone
> is happy to do
> something: *a
> group of willing
> volunteers.*

DEVELOPING YOUR READING SKILLS

Understanding Topics and Main Ideas

Identifying Topics and Main Ideas

Every reading is about someone or something. That person or thing is the **topic** of the reading. The title of a reading may tell you what the topic is. The topic can usually be expressed in a word or a phrase. Each paragraph in a reading has its topic, too.

The **main idea** of a reading, or of a paragraph, is the most important information about the topic. Use a complete sentence to state the main idea of either a paragraph or an entire text.

Reread "Dreamers and Doers." Then answer the questions.

Reading Tip: The first time you read a text, read for **the gist**, or main ideas. Then reread for a better understanding and for details.

1. What is the reading about? Check (✔) the topic.
   - ☐ a. Dreams about the future
   - ☑ b. Young people who start up businesses
   - ☑ c. Ways you can make a lot of money

2. What does the reading say about the topic? Check (✔) the main idea.
   - ☑ a. It is important for a young person to have a dream about the future.
   - ☑ b. Some very young people have become successful entrepreneurs.
   - ☐ c. It is easier to start your own business when you are very young.

3. What is the main idea of paragraph 3?
   - ☑ a. Young entrepreneurs have various reasons for what they do.
   - ☐ b. Most young entrepreneurs start their businesses by accident.
   - ☐ c. The dream of becoming a CEO drives the average entrepreneur.

4. What is the main idea of paragraph 6? Write a sentence.

   the main idea is a guston about that olders
   shouldin hired their parents.
   hhing a family member can be binefsilcial to intrepreheurs.

Understanding Text Features

Vocabulary Tip: *Text* can mean a book or another piece of writing. *Password 4* is a text (or textbook). "Dreamers and Doers" is also a text (or reading passage).

Introduction to Text Features in *Password 4*

A feature is an element or part of something, often one that is important. **Text features** are elements added to a text to help readers understand it.

Punctuation is a text feature that helps show the writer's meaning. For example, an exclamation point (!) can show strong feeling or surprise. Dashes—like these—are used to add information and show that the information is something extra: it could be deleted without changing the meaning of the sentence.

Two other text features in *Password 4* are **boldface** and *italics*. The words in **bold** in a reading are the target vocabulary for the chapter. Italics are used:

- when the word itself is the topic of discussion: "*Drive* can also be a noncount noun . . ." (page 7).
- for extra emphasis: "Pierre Omidyar was *not* planning on becoming an entrepreneur" (page 7).

Read the sentences from "Dreamers and Doers." Match them with the type of text feature shown and the reason for its use.

__c__ 1. *page views* = how many times people look at a website

__a__ 2. Today, however, these people seem to be everywhere!

__b__ 3. At age nine, Ashley Qualls learned how to **set up** a website.

__c__ 4. Cameron Johnson, on the other hand, knew *exactly* what he wanted.

__d__ 5. After she opened her store, the Peruvians started earning more in a few weeks—at work they enjoyed—than they used to make in a year.

a. an exclamation point to show the writer's surprise

b. dashes used to add extra information

c. boldfaced text to identify a target word or phrase

d. italics to show the writer is talking about a word or phrase

e. italics for extra emphasis

Reading for Details

Are these statements about the reading true or false? If the reading doesn't give the information, check (✓) *It doesn't say.*

	True	False	It doesn't say.
1. Facebook and Microsoft are examples of businesses begun by college students.	✓	☐	☐
2. Ashley Qualls set up her website to make money.	☐	☒	☐
3. Cameron Johnson made a lot of money as a young entrepreneur.	☐	☐	☒
4. Pierre Omidyar set up his business and then sold it.	☐	☒	☐
5. The people who work for Constanza Ontaneda get a fair paycheck.	☒	☐	☐
6. Ontaneda hired her mother to work for her.	☐	☒	☐
7. Daniel Negari has a computer service company.	☐	☐	☒
8. Cameron Johnson has written more than one book.	☒	☐	☐

Does *Critical Thinking* Mean?

Critical thinking is used to describe ways of thinking that help you be a better reader, not only in school but at work and in every area of your adult life. As a critical thinker, you begin reading a text with an open mind. You read closely to understand what the writer is saying. You work to figure out what the writer believes but does not say directly. You ask questions about the writer's thinking: *How is the writer supporting the claims they make? Is there enough support? Does it make sense? Do I agree with the writer's opinions?* When you speak about the text, you point to information in the text to support what you say.

Critical thinking means using certain thinking skills. You will practice these skills as you work through this book.

Discussion

Talk about these questions in a small group.

> **Critical Thinking Tip:**
> With this book, you will be able to practice critical thinking as you read the reading passages, do the exercises, and work with classmates on the Discussion questions.

1. Complete the chart with facts about each of the six young entrepreneurs in the reading. If the reading does not tell you someone's motivation (their reason for starting their business), put a question mark in the box.

Name	Business	Motivation
1. Ashley Qualls		
2. Cameron Johnson		
3. Pierre Omidyar		
4. Constanza Ontaneda		
5. Matt Spain		
6. Daniel Negari		

Of these six young entrepreneurs, whose story is most interesting? Explain why. Use information from the reading to support your opinion.

2. Which sentence in paragraph 5 gives the main idea of the paragraph? What is the purpose of the other sentences in the paragraph? Which of these other paragraphs is organized in the same way?

   a. paragraph 2

   b. paragraph 6

   c. paragraph 7

3. According to the writer, entrepreneurs of any age are alike in some ways: What two examples are given in the text? How would these two personal characteristics help someone succeed as an entrepreneur?

4. The writer also points out ways that young entrepreneurs are different from older people who start their own businesses. What two examples are given in the text? What other differences would you expect? Would each of these differences be an *advantage* for a young entrepreneur (something that might help them be more successful) or a *disadvantage* (something that might cause them problems)?

5. What does the title "Dreamers and Doers" mean? Why do you think the writer chose this as the title for the reading? Is it a good title? Use information from the reading to support your opinion.

WRITING

A. Use the Target Vocabulary: Choose five of the target words or phrases from the chart on pages 5–6. On a piece of paper, use each word or phrase in a sentence and underline it. Find a partner and read each other's sentences.

Vocabulary Tip: Don't choose the easiest words and phrases to practice. Writing sentences is a chance to learn more about the words you don't understand well.

Examples:

1. My friend's father helped me get a job by <u>setting up</u> an interview for me at his company.
2. I'm <u>willing</u> to work very hard to learn English.

B. Practice Writing: Choose one of these topics and write a paragraph about it. Then find a partner and read each other's paragraphs.

1. Choose a young entrepreneur from "Dreamers and Doers" whom you find interesting. Tell what you know about this person and what you think about his or her story.

2. When you answered the question on page 1 about a career in business, what was your first choice? Explain why that would be your first choice.

Writing Tip: When you use information from a text to support your opinion, you are citing evidence from the text. This is an important college and career skill.

CHAPTER 2

Word-of-Mouth Advertising

"Try it. You'll like it."

LEARNING OUTCOME

> Learn what word-of-mouth advertising can do

GETTING READY TO READ

Talk about these questions in a small group.

1. Where do you see ads? On a piece of paper, make a list of all the places you can think of.

2. How do you feel about the ads you see and hear? Check (✔) one or more answers. Explain your answers.

   ☐ Ads are a good way to learn about products.

   ☐ Ads are often interesting and fun.

   ☐ I don't usually pay much attention to ads.

   ☐ I don't like ads.

READING

Read to Find Out: What is special about word-of-mouth advertising?

Look at the picture, words, and definitions next to the reading. Then read without stopping. If you see a new word, try to understand the sentence without it. You will learn the word later.

Word-of-Mouth Advertising

1   Whether you want to or not, you probably see and hear ads every day. Ads are all around us and have been for a very long time. They have even been found painted on walls in the ruins[1] of Pompeii and ancient[2] Egypt. **Advertising** has come a long way[3] since then, but it's still all about getting people's attention.

2   Back when few people could read, ads usually took the form of pictures. A sign for a shoemaker might have a picture of a boot, and a sign for a baker might show a loaf of bread. Street callers were a common form of advertising, too. They were hired to **announce** in a loud voice what was for sale, where to find it, and how good it was, as in "Get your fresh fish, right here, right now! The best in town!"

3   In **developing** countries, some businesses still use street callers, and this form of advertising probably doesn't cost them very much. In other parts of the world, advertising has become much more sophisticated,[4] and it costs a great deal. If you add up all the money spent on advertising around the world, it comes to the equivalent of[5] hundreds of billions[6] of U.S. dollars a year.

4   Business owners will consider it money well spent **as long as** enough **consumers** pay attention and buy the product or use the service. But much of the time, consumers do *not* pay attention. When an ad comes on the TV or radio, they change the station. They turn the pages of magazines without really seeing the ads. If an ad **appears** on their computer screen, they **get rid of** it or just look away.

5   Dave Balter worked in advertising, and he knew that most people don't like ads. They **avoid** watching them, reading them, or listening to them. He also knew that people do pay attention when they hear about **goods** and services from people they know. So he said to himself, "If no one pays attention to advertising, but they *do* pay attention to the opinions of their friends and family, let's focus our attention there. Let's figure out a better way."

[1] *ruins*

[2] *ancient* = happening or existing very far back in history

[3] *has come a long way* = has changed a lot (for the better)

[4] *sophisticated* = having a complex and advanced design

[5] *the equivalent of* = an amount that is the same as

[6] *a billion* = 1,000,000,000

6   What Balter came up with was a website where consumers could **sign up** to receive free products. **In return**, they promised that if they liked the products, they would tell their friends. In most cases, the **volunteers** also got coupons[7] to give to their friends. All Balter asked was that they report back on two questions: What did you think of the product, and who did you talk to about it? Balter then reported back to his clients, the companies who had hired him.

7 *a coupon*

7   After four years, Balter had 65,000 volunteers trying products and telling people about the ones they liked. Then a reporter heard about Balter's idea and wrote a story on it for a **major** magazine. Free advertising! **Within** a year after that story appeared, Balter had 130,000 volunteers. Today, the company he started has over one million people spreading the word about a wide variety of products. They are doing word-of-mouth advertising, perhaps the best kind of advertising there is.

8   There may be a risk to advertising by word of mouth, however, according to George Silverman, author of *The Secrets of Word-of-Mouth Marketing*. What's the danger? Studies have shown that a customer who likes a product or service will tell an average of three people about it. But when a customer doesn't like one, on average they'll tell eleven. This means that **while** good word of mouth can help, bad word of mouth can really hurt.

Quick Comprehension Check

A. Read these statements **about the reading**. Circle T (true) or F (false). On the line, write the number of the paragraph with the answer.

1. Advertising was invented in the 1800s   T   (F)   1

2. Some forms of advertising are low-cost.   (T)   F   3

3. Hundreds of billions of dollars are spent on ads each year.   (T)   F   3

4. Dave Balter believes most people enjoy ads.   T   (F)   5

5. People usually listen to their friends' opinions of products.   (T)   F   5

6. Dave Balter paid people to try new products.   T   (F)   7

B. Work with your class. Share your answers from part A. Go back to the reading to find the reason why a statement is true or false. Correct the false statements.

EXPLORING VOCABULARY

Thinking about the Target Vocabulary

A. Look at the chart with the target vocabulary from "Word-of-Mouth Advertising." Four verbs are missing. Scan the reading to find them, and add them to the correct places in the chart. Use the base form of each verb.

¶	Nouns	Verbs	Adjectives	Other
1	advertising			
2				
3			developing	
4				as long as
	consumer			
				get rid of
5				
	goods			
6				in return
	volunteer			
7			major	
				within
8				while

Vocabulary Tip:
The noun *goods*, meaning "products for sale," is used in the plural only.

B. Which words or phrases are new to you? Circle them in the chart. Then find them in the reading. Look at the context. Can you guess the meaning?

Understanding the Target Vocabulary

A. These sentences are **about the reading**. Complete them with the words and phrases in the box.

advertising	as long as	in return	while
appears	avoid	sign up	within

1. The business of creating and using ads is called _____.

2. Business owners are willing to spend money on advertising if the ads get them customers. They don't mind spending the money _____ the ads work.

3. Sometimes you suddenly see an ad on your computer. The ad _____ on your screen.

4. Many people try not to watch, read, or listen to ads. They _____ ads.

5. Dave Balter set up a website where a person could put his or her name on a list to get free products. A person could _____ to get the products.

6. People promised Dave Balter that they would to do something as a kind of payment for the products they received. They got the products for free, but they promised to do something _____.

> **Vocabulary Tip:** Use *in return + for +* an object: *In return for the use of my car, he gave me concert tickets.* Use *in return* alone only when the meaning is clear.

7. Things changed for Balter's company in the 12 months after a story about it appeared in a magazine. _____ a year, he had twice as many volunteers as before.

8. Although word-of-mouth advertising *can* have good results, it doesn't always. _____ good word of mouth is helpful, bad word of mouth can really hurt.

> **Vocabulary Tip:** *While* can refer to time (*He checked his phone for messages while he waited*), but in sentence 8 and paragraph 8 of the reading, it means "although."

B. These sentences are also **about the reading**. What is the meaning of each **boldfaced** word or phrase? Circle a, b, or c.

1. The job of a street caller was to **announce** what was for sale. *Announce* means

    a. make a decision.   b. give out new information.   c. set something up.

2. In **developing** countries, most businesses cannot afford expensive advertising. A developing nation is

    a. trying to produce more.   b. full of successful businesses.   c. not willing to do business.

3. Advertisers want **consumers** to pay attention to ads. Consumers are people who

    a. work for a living.   b. buy products and services.   c. own personal computers.

4. If an ad appears on your computer screen, you may want to **get rid of** it. *Get rid of something* means to take action so that you

    a. don't have it anymore.   b. can pay for it later.   c. put it in a safe place.

5. We usually pay attention to our friends' opinions of **goods** and services. *Goods* means

    a. products.   b. nice people.   c. interesting places.

6. Dave Balter got **volunteers** to do word-of-mouth advertising for his clients. Volunteers are people who

    a. like to take risks.   b. work without pay.   c. earn a lot of money.

7. A story in a **major** magazine brought Balter a lot of attention. In this sentence, *major* means

    a. small.   b. fair.   c. important.

EXPANDING VOCABULARY

Building on the Vocabulary

Word Grammar: Adjectives

In addition to nouns and verbs, **adjectives** are one of the major parts of speech. Adjectives, such as *happy, hot, rich,* and *new,* describe people, places, things, and ideas. Adjectives come before nouns (*an old man, an interesting book*) or after linking verbs such as *be, seem,* and *look* (*I'm ready. It seems expensive. You look tired.*)

Most adjectives have a **comparative** form (*a lighter color, a more difficult test*) and a **superlative** form (*the fastest runner in the world, the worst storm of the year*).

Circle the adjectives in these sentences.

1. It used to be a common form of advertising.

2. Vietnam, Chile, and Somalia are all considered developing countries.

3. We agreed that it was fair.

4. I'm willing to try if you are.

5. Ashley Qualls might call herself "an accidental CEO."

6. Dave Balter said, "Let's figure out a better way."

7. The plan seems risky.

8. Major stories appear on page one of the newspaper.

Using the Target Vocabulary in New Contexts

A. Complete the sentences with the target words and phrases in the box. There is one extra word or phrase.

announced	consumers	got rid of	volunteers
as long as	goods	in return	while

1. The company president had some good news. He _____ the hiring of 1,000 new workers.

2. When we bought our new TV, we _____ our old one because it didn't work very well.

3. I'm not sure I want to accept this job offer. _____ the job would be interesting, the pay would be low.

4. The police say they found stolen _____ in the apartment.

5. At the public library, _____ help children with their homework.

6. U.S. _____ spend a lot of money Christmas shopping in December.

7. George smiled at Carmen, and she smiled at him _____.

B. Read the sentences with the target vocabulary used **in new contexts**. Write each **boldfaced** target word or phrase next to its definition. Put an X next to the extra definition.

  a. You'll get your test results **within** 24 hours.

  b. Nancy's cat sometimes goes away for days but then **appears** at her door.

  c. I try to **avoid** having to stand in lines.

  d. Are you going to **sign up** to take the class?

  e. Lisa's father said she could go out **as long as** she did her homework first.

Target Word or Phrase		Definition
1.	=	if
2.	=	enjoy, have fun doing
3.	=	starts to be seen or suddenly be seen
4.	=	put your name on a list because you want to join
5.	=	stay away from someone or something
6.	=	before (a certain amount of time) has passed

DEVELOPING YOUR READING SKILLS

Understanding Text Features

Using Text Features to Preview

When you **preview** a text, you try to learn as much as possible about it before you start reading. This can help you understand it better as you read. Looking at certain text features—the title, photographs, illustrations, and captions—is one way to preview. The title will often help you understand what the text will be about. Photos will help you picture what the writer is saying. In this book, illustrations in the margins of reading passages help explain new words. Captions help you understand what you are seeing in a photo or illustration.

Answer the questions about text features in Chapter 2.

1. Look at page 15. What is the title of the reading? _____

2. What words do the illustrations on pages 15 and 16 define?

   _____ and _____

3. What does the caption of the photo on page 14 say? _____

4. What does the photo on page 14 show? _____

5. How do the photo and caption on page 14 help readers understand what the reading passage will be about? _____

_____

Understanding Topics and Main Ideas

A. What is the main idea of "Word-of-Mouth Advertising"? Check (✔) your answer.

☐ 1. In the long history of advertising, word-of-mouth advertising is the newest idea.

☐ 2. Ads are everywhere, and most people don't like them, so they avoid them when they can.

☐ 3. Advertising is about getting consumers' attention, and the best way to do that may be by word of mouth.

B. Where in the reading can you find these topics? Write the paragraph number.

__3__ a. advertising costs

_____ b. a risk of word-of-mouth advertising

_____ c. two early forms of advertising

_____ d. what consumers often do about ads

_____ e. the early history and main purpose of advertising

_____ f. Balter's plan

_____ g. the success of Balter's plan

_____ h. Balter's ideas about consumers and ads

C. What is the main idea of each of these paragraphs? Complete the sentences. Use your own words.

1. Paragraph 6: Dave Balter found volunteers _____

_____.

2. Paragraph 8: Word-of-mouth advertising can be great for business, but

_____.

Reading for Details

Read the sentences about "Word-of-Mouth Advertising." Scan the reading for the information to complete them.

1. Advertising is "all about _____."

2. Before most people could read, business owners often used

_____ and _____ to advertise.

> **Reading Tip:** When you **scan** a reading, you look through the text very quickly to find a specific piece of information.

3. Worldwide, advertising costs _____ a year.

4. Dave Balter knew that consumers pay attention to what _____ say about _____.

5. Balter's idea was to get _____ to do word-of-mouth advertising.

6. Studies show that, on average, a customer will tell _____ people about a product or service that they like and tell _____ people about one that they don't like.

CRITICAL THINKING

Using Critical Thinking Skills

You are using critical thinking skills when you figure out the main idea of a text and when you study the relationships between the writer's major points and the details that support them. You are also using critical thinking skills when you look at the writer's choice of words and consider what they mean in context. Critical thinking skills help you when you need to cite evidence from a text (when you choose information from the text to point to when you explain it or give an opinion about it).

Discussion

Talk about these questions in a small group.

1. The reading begins with some information about the history of advertising. Why did people used to use pictures to advertise their products? How has advertising changed since ancient times? What has remained the same?

2. Dave Balter "knew that most people don't like ads" (paragraph 5). Does the reading say why not? Why do you think most people don't like ads? According to Balter, when *do* people pay attention to information about products and services? Do you agree? Why or why not?

3. According to the reading, the volunteers who signed up with Balter's company were doing word-of-mouth advertising, "perhaps the best kind there is" (paragraph 7). Whose opinion is it that word of mouth is best? What reasons for this opinion can you infer from the reading?

Critical Thinking Tip: When a writer does not say something openly, you may need to **infer**, or guess, what the writer is thinking. **Make inferences** based on other information in the text and your own understanding of the world.

4. For what purpose does the writer mention George Silverman? Reread the description of Balter's plan and what the volunteers promised to do. Do you think there's a danger that Balter's volunteers will hurt his clients rather than help them? Explain why or why not.

5. Why can word-of-mouth advertising be good for a business compared to other types of advertising? When would other kinds of advertising be better? Consider the type of product or service being advertised, the people who might want to buy it, the question of time, and so on.

Reading Tip: The writer's **purpose** is the reason why he or she writes something. Is it to share useful information? Is it to try to change the reader's mind about something?

WRITING

A. Use the Target Vocabulary: Choose five of the target words or phrases from the chart on page 17. On a piece of paper, use each word or phrase in a sentence and underline it. Find a partner and read each other's sentences.

B. Practice Writing: Choose one of these topics and write a paragraph about it. Then find a partner and read each other's paragraphs.

1. Describe an ad that you remember seeing. What was the ad for? What made the ad easy to remember? Did you buy the product or use the service because of the ad?

2. Think about your answer to question 2 on page 14: *How do you feel about the ads you see and hear?* Write a statement telling your general feeling about ads, and use it as the first sentence in a paragraph. Then explain why you feel that way.

> **Writing Tip:** Time is a writer's friend. After you write a paragraph, take a break. Look at it again later, or better still, the next day. That will help you see how you can make it better.

A Language on the Move

English for business

GETTING READY TO READ

Answer the questions. Then talk about your answers with your class.

1. Which number best describes the situation in your country?

   In your country: Very ⟵⟶ Not at all
   a. are English classes common in the schools?   1   2   3   4   5
   b. is English important for many jobs?   1   2   3   4   5
   c. is English important in the business world?   1   2   3   4   5

2. When, where, and why do people from your country use English to do business?

READING

Look at the words and definitions next to the reading. Then read without stopping. If you see a new word, try to understand the sentence without it. You will learn the word later.

A Language on the Move

1 Filiz Yilmaz works for a company in Istanbul and usually speaks Turkish at work. When she travels to England on business, she **deals with** people there in English. But when she goes to Germany or Brazil, she doesn't use German or Portuguese; again she uses English. "I use English in Japan and Thailand, too," she says. "It's the language of international business."

2 How did English get to be so widely used? It's not the oldest living language or the most beautiful to the ear. It has sounds that are hard to pronounce and words that are hard to spell. So why has this **particular** language **spread** so far?

3 Some people would answer by pointing to the **influence** of movies and music. However, films made in English often appear dubbed into[1] other languages, and many people enjoy songs in English without understanding the words. So the question remains.

[1] *dubbed into* = with the actors' words changed to and said in (another language)

4 Part of the answer can be found in the **nature** of the language. English has certain **qualities** that make it especially useful. For one thing, its grammar is **quite** simple, making it easier to learn. For example, learners of English don't have to worry about whether a noun is masculine, feminine, or neuter,[2] while learners of many other languages do. In German, for example, *der Mond* (the word for the moon) is masculine but *die Sonne* (the sun) is feminine. Anyone would expect the words for girl and woman (*das Mädchen* and *das Weib*) to be feminine, but they are neuter!

[2] *masculine, feminine, or neuter* = male, female, or neither

5 English also has a **huge** vocabulary. Early English developed from Germanic languages, which gave it its most common words, such as *the, is, of, go, you, man,* and *woman.* English has always taken words from other European languages, too, including Latin (*attract, design,* and *invent*) and Greek (*alphabet, mathematics,* and *theater*). After 1066, when invaders[3] from France came to power in England, English **gained** many French words, such as *officer, crime,* and *service.* Since that time, English has welcomed words from many other languages—Spanish, Arabic, Turkish, Urdu, Chinese, and Japanese, to name just a few.

[3] *invaders* = people who enter a country by force, as with an army

6   To understand the spread of English, we also have to look at **political** and **economic** history. During the 1600s and 1700s, people from England traveled all over the world, taking their language to North America, Africa, India, and Australia. New nations were born, and their governments used English. Then in the 1800s, England led the Industrial Revolution,[4] and London became the world's great **financial** center. That made English the language of money. In the 1900s, it also became the language of science and air travel.

[4] the Industrial Revolution = the start of producing many goods in factories with machines

7   Then came the Internet. As Filiz Yilmaz remembers it, "People at my company realized that the Internet could be quite useful to us. But at first, everything online was in English. It gave us another reason to know this language." Soon businesspeople in many countries were going online and using English more and more.

8   Today, there are business schools teaching all their courses in English, even in countries where English is a foreign language. These schools want their students to be ready to do business in international **markets**. Companies around the world are **investing** in English classes for their **employees**. They believe English will be the language of the future.

9   Today, there are about 400 million native speakers of English.[5] While many more people speak Mandarin Chinese—about 900 million—few of them are outside China. People who speak English, on the other hand, live and work all over the world. There are more than 1.5 billion people who speak it as a second, third, or fourth language. Yilmaz says, "With so many people using English, I can't imagine any other language taking its place. I think English for business is here to stay."

[5] native speakers of English = people whose first language is English

Quick Comprehension Check

A. Read these statements **about the reading**. Circle T (true) or F (false). On the line, write the number of the paragraph with the answer.

1. Companies around the world expect English to continue as the international language of business. (T) F   T 1,8

2. Hollywood movies are the biggest reason why English is so popular. T (F)   F 3

3. Many English words come from other languages. (T) F   5

4. England was a world power in the 1800s. (T) F   6

5. The same numbers of people speak Mandarin and English. T (F)   9

6. More people speak English as their second, third, or fourth language than speak it as their first. (T) F   ___

B. Work with your class. Share your answers from part A. Go back to the reading to find the reason why a statement is true or false. Correct the false statements.

EXPLORING VOCABULARY

Thinking about the Target Vocabulary

A. Look at the chart with the target vocabulary from "A Language on the Move." Three nouns and five adjectives are missing. Scan the reading to find them, and add them to the correct places in the chart. Use the singular form of any plural noun.

¶	Nouns	Verbs	Adjectives	Other
1		deal with		
2		Has	Beautiful	
		spread	Particular	
3		Made		
4	nature			
				quite
5				
		gain		
6				
	market			
8		invest		

B. Which words or phrases are new to you? Circle them in the chart. Then find them in the reading. Look at the context. Can you guess the meaning?

Understanding the Target Vocabulary

A. These sentences are **about the reading**. Complete them with the words in the box.

financial	invests	political	quite
influence	markets	qualities	spread

1. Music and movies can have a strong effect on us, and some people believe that music and movies in English have had a major _influence_ in making English so widely used.

Vocabulary Tip: *Influence* can be a count noun (*He was a huge influence*), a noncount noun (*I have little influence*), or a verb (*How will it influence the voters?*).

2. The number of English speakers has grown, and English is being spoken in more countries. The language has _spread_ around the world.

3. When you describe a language, you talk about the things that make the language different from other languages. The reading describes certain _qualities_ that English has that have made it useful around the world.

4. The grammatical rules of English are not very hard. Compared to the grammars of many other languages, the grammar of English is _quite_ simple.

5. To understand why English has spread over so much of the world, we have to study _political_ history. This is about power, governments, and relationships between countries.

6. When England led the Industrial Revolution in the 1800s, many new banks were started. They managed large amounts of money (that entrepreneurs needed and that other people wanted to invest). London became a great _financial_ center.

7. After finishing business school, some people go on to work in international _markets_ —that is, in areas that deal with buying and selling between or among countries.

quite - completamente
quiet - callar

8. When a company _injvests_ in English-language training for its workers, it feels this will be a good financial decision. It expects the training to bring good financial returns (that is, to make them more money later).

B. These sentences are also **about the reading**. What is the meaning of each **boldfaced** word or phrase? Circle a, b, or c.

1. Filiz Yilmaz **deals with** people in several countries. In this sentence, *deals with* means
   a. has trouble with.   b. does business with.   c. comes up with.

2. The reading gives some history about one **particular** language, English. In this sentence, *particular* means
   (a.) specific.   b. developing.   c. fair.

3. One reason for the spread of English is the **nature** of the language. In this context, *nature* means
   a. the spelling rules.   b. sound and music.   (c.) particular qualities.

4. Another important quality of English is its **huge** vocabulary. *Huge* means
   a. very, very big.   b. surprising.   (c.) friendly.

5. English has **gained** many words from other languages. In this sentence, *gain something* means
   a. lose it.   b. win it.   (c.) get it.

6. **Economic** history from the 1800s to the present helps explain the spread of English. *Economic* means relating to
   (a.) money, goods, and services.   b. art, music, and books.   c. movies and TV.

7. Many companies have invested in English classes for their **employees**. Their employees are the people who
   a. buy their products.   (b.) work for them.   c. volunteer for them.

> **Vocabulary Tip:**
> *Deal with* has several meanings in addition to "do business with," including "be about (a particular topic)" and "take action on (a problem)." See your dictionary for example sentences.

EXPANDING VOCABULARY

Building on the Vocabulary

> **Word Grammar: Suffixes**
>
> A **suffix** is a letter or letters added to the end of a word to make a new word. Look at the words and suffixes in the word family for *employ* ("give a job to"):
>
> *employ**er*** = a person who gives a job to someone
>
> *employ**ee*** = a person who works for another person, for a company, etc.
>
> *employ**ment*** = work; the fact or condition of having a job

A. Complete the paragraph with words from the word family for *employ*. Add *-s* as needed.

The hospital is the biggest _employee_ in our community. It has
                                        (1)

over 800 _employees_ . It _employs_ not only doctors and
            (2)   (3)

nurses but also managers, office workers, cooks, and so on. If you are

looking for a job, perhaps you can find _employment_ there.
                                            (4)

B. The **boldfaced** words have the suffixes *-er* and *-ee*. Can you guess their meanings? Write the words next to their definitions.

a. On the first day at my new job, I met the other **trainees**.

b. Martin is a racehorse **trainer**.

Word		Definition
1. _traineness_	=	a person who teaches skills, especially for a job or sport
2. _trainer_	=	people who are receiving training

Using the Target Vocabulary in New Contexts

A. Complete the sentences with the target words and phrases in the box. There is one extra word.

dealt with	employees	huge	invest	political
economic	financial	influence	nature	qualities

1. News about the company always spreads quickly among its

   Employees .

2. I've ___deal with___ that company for years, but I won't do it again. Their customer service has become terrible.

3. They plan to ___invest___ in oil, and they hope to get rich.

4. A good ad can have a big ___influence___ on consumers' buying decisions.

5. Everyone wants love. It is human ___nature___ to want to love and feel loved.

6. The phrase ___political___ *science* refers to the study of government.

7. The country's ___economic___ future is looking better: Businesses are hiring again.

8. Entrepreneurs often take risks. Some risks are small, but some are ___huge___.

9. Many students in the United States couldn't afford to go to college without ___financial___ aid.

B. Read these sentences. Write each **boldfaced** target word next to its definition. Put an X next to the extra definition.

a. Are you looking for a **particular** color shirt? 5

b. Her company has been **quite** successful. 3

c. When one member of a family gets a cold, it will often **spread** to the rest. 1

d. Ann has all the **qualities** the boss likes: She's smart, 2 hardworking, and a good team member.

e. The company has customers in Asia, but the main **market** for their software is the United States. 6

Target Word		Definition
1.	=	move and affect more people or a larger area
2.	=	parts of someone's nature or character
3.	=	more than a little but not extremely
4.	=	stop something bad from happening
5.	=	certain (not just any one)
6.	=	a particular area where a company sells its goods

Vocabulary Tip:
When *particular* describes a person, it can mean either "certain" or "not easily satisfied:" *He's very particular about his food.* The adverb *particularly* means "especially:" *The restaurant is particularly busy on weekends.*

DEVELOPING YOUR READING SKILLS

Understanding Topics of Paragraphs

Where in the reading can you find these topics? Write the paragraph number.

_____ a. facts about political and economic history

_____ b. numbers of English-speakers

_____ c. the effect of the Internet

_____ d. Filiz Yilmaz's use of English

_____ e. the influence of movies and songs in English

_____ f. how English got its huge vocabulary

_____ g. English for international markets

_____ h. English grammar

_____ i. reasons you might *not* expect English to be widely used

> **Reading Tip:**
> Identifying the topic of each paragraph in a text will help you make a map in your mind of how the text is organized.

Reading for Details

Are these statements about the reading true or false? If the reading doesn't give the information, check (✔) *It doesn't say.*

	True	False	It doesn't say.
1. Filiz Yilmaz uses English in Japan and Brazil.	☐	☐	☐
2. Popular music is the major reason for the spread of English.	☐	☐	☐
3. English has more difficult grammar rules than most languages.	☐	☐	☐
4. English has the largest vocabulary of any language.	☐	☐	☐
5. The Industrial Revolution started in England.	☐	☐	☐
6. English became the language of science in the 1700s.	☐	☐	☐
7. The Internet started in California (USA).	☐	☐	☐
8. Some companies pay for their employees to learn English.	☐	☐	☐

> **Reading Tip:**
> The details in a reading are the facts, examples, or other pieces of information that help explain, or support, the main ideas.

Summarizing

Summaries

A **summary** is a short report of what a longer text says. It has only the main information from the longer text. When you summarize a reading, you have to think about which ideas matter most and figure out how to put them into writing. Summarizing a text helps you understand and remember it and prepare to discuss it. Being able to summarize is an important college and career skill.

A. Complete the summary of "A Language on the Move." Use your own words. (That is, do not copy sentences from the reading.) Answer these questions in your summary:

What are the major reasons given in the reading for the spread of English?

What examples support the idea that English is the language of international business?

> **Writing Tip:** When you write a summary, be sure to include the title of the text in your first sentence.

> "A Language on the Move" explains how English became the language of international business.

B. Compare your summary with a partner's. Did you include the same major reasons for the spread of English?

CRITICAL THINKING

Using Critical Thinking Skills

You need to use critical thinking skills to understand the writer's purpose and the main idea of a text. You also use these skills to figure out how the parts of a text relate to each other and to identify the most important information to include in a summary.

Discussion

Talk about these questions in a small group.

1. Why does the writer quote Filiz Yilmaz? What is Ms. Yilmaz's opinion of English as an international language? Do you agree? Support your opinion with information from the reading and from your own experience.

2. In the opinion of the writer, have movies and songs in English had a major influence on English becoming an international language? What reasons does the writer give to support that opinion? Do you agree or disagree with the writer? Explain.

3. In paragraph 5, the writer says the English language has a huge number of words. Does the writer present this as a positive or negative quality? Use information from the reading to support your answer. In the last sentence of paragraph 5, why do you think the writer uses the verb *welcome*? What does it mean in this sentence?

4. English uses many words from other languages, and other languages use words taken from English. For example, two businesspeople in Shanghai might use *boss* and *CEO* even when they're speaking Chinese to each other. Can you give any examples of:

   - English words that are now used in your first language?
   - words from your first language that are used in English?

5. According to the reading, who is investing in English classes and why? Why are *you* investing in learning English? How will knowing English affect your future? How much English do you need to know?

> **Critical Thinking Tip:** When a writer quotes someone, ask yourself why the writer wants to use that person's words. What do they add to the reading passage?

WRITING

A. Use the Target Vocabulary: Choose five of the target words or phrases from the chart on page 28. On a piece of paper, use each word or phrase in a sentence and underline it. Find a partner and read each other's sentences.

B. Practice Writing: Choose one of these topics and write a paragraph about it. Then find a partner and read each other's paragraphs.

> **Writing Tip:** Before you write, do a prewriting activity. Take notes about your ideas, or discuss your ideas with a classmate.

1. People invest a lot of time and money in learning English, and nobody wants to waste either one. What three (or more) pieces of advice would you give a new learner on how to invest his or her time and money well? If you wish, you can begin:

   If you want to learn English without wasting time or money, here is my advice.

2. When, where, and why did you start to learn English? How did you feel about that experience?

CHAPTER 4

When the Employees Own the Company

LEARNING OUTCOME

❯ Learn about worker-owned businesses

Baker and worker-owner Christoph Stucker with freshly-baked bread at King Arthur Flour

GETTING READY TO READ

Talk about these questions in a small group.

1. Have you ever been the boss at work? Would you like a job where you were the boss? Explain your answer.

2. Who works harder, the owner of a business or the people who work for the business?

3. How would you complete this statement? Explain your answer.

    When you own a business,

    a. you don't have to work so hard.

    b. you have to work harder.

Read to Find Out: How do employees become worker-owners?

Look at the picture, words, and definitions next to the reading. Then read without stopping. If you see a new word, try to understand the sentence without it. You will learn the word later.

When the Employees Own the Company

1 King Arthur Flour is the oldest flour company in the United States. Its flour is of very high **quality**. Just ask the people who use it. All across North America, people who care about making fine bread buy King Arthur flour, and the company even has customers in Switzerland, Japan, China, and Saudi Arabia. King Arthur Flour began in 1790 as the Sands, Taylor, and Wood Company, and members of the Sands family have stayed with the company all these years. Frank Sands was the fifth member of the Sands family to lead the company. He started working there in 1963, when his father was **in charge of** the business, and eventually,[1] Frank's wife, Brinna, joined him there. When Frank and Brinna decided to retire,[2] none of their children wanted to take control of the family business, which meant that the future of King Arthur Flour was **uncertain**. Then one evening, Brinna asked Frank, "Who **besides** our kids is most like family?" The answer was clear: The people who worked at the company. Frank and Brinna trusted them to continue the family tradition, so they began to let the employees take charge of the business. Today, the 160 employees of King Arthur own and run the company.

2 Worker-owned businesses don't all start the same way. In some cases, workers at a successful company find a way to buy the business. In other cases, a company fails, but the employees **react** by working as a team to start it up again. Often, a group of people decide to set up a new business together. What makes them want to do this? Some want to be part of the decision-making at their workplace. Others want a chance to share in a company's **profits**.

3 There are various types of worker-owned businesses. Some of them make a product, like flour, and others **provide** a service, such as health care or cleaning offices. There are also various ways to **organize** these businesses. However, most worker-owned businesses share certain important ideas. One idea is that all the workers—not just the people in charge—should have the chance to be owners. A second is that all financial information about the company should be shared openly with the workers. A third is that the workers should have the **right** to vote

[1] *eventually* = after a long period of time

[2] *retire* = stop working at the end of a career or at a certain age

on business decisions. Then they have real control. The worker-owners at King Arthur **believe in** these ideas. They are proud to call King Arthur "an employee-owned, open-book, team-managed company."

4   Here are the stories of how two more **such** companies began:

- Eight employees at a photocopy shop[3] in Massachusetts (USA) were unhappy with their jobs. "Working **conditions** were terrible and the pay was low," says one of the eight. "Plus,[4] we had no job **security**— the manager could get rid of any one of us at any time for any reason. We ran the shop for the owners, and we started to ask, 'Why can't we do it for ourselves?'" So they went into business together and started Collective Copies. Thirty-three years later, they have two shops. One afternoon a month, they close their doors to meet and make business decisions.

- In Coamo, Puerto Rico, there weren't many jobs for young people. Miriam Rodriguez, who lived in Coamo, wanted to do something about it. She organized a **committee** to work on the problem, and the result of their efforts was a furniture business, Las Flores Metalarte. The business now has more than 150 worker-owners producing tables, chairs, kitchen cabinets,[5] and so on. The success of the company has led to other new businesses in the town, including a sandwich shop and a childcare center.

5   Worker-owned businesses are not unique to[6] the United States, and their effects are not limited to the worker-owners themselves. According to a study in Italy, worker-owned businesses are good for their **communities**. They lead to a higher quality of life. The researchers who did the study looked at things like health care, education, and social activities in many Italian towns. They also considered problems in the towns, such as crime. They found that towns with more worker-owned businesses were better places to live in almost every way.

[3] *a photocopy shop* = a business that uses machines to make copies of print materials

[4] *plus* = and also

[5] *kitchen cabinets*

[6] *unique to* = happening only in, or relating only to

Quick Comprehension Check

A. Read these statements **about the reading**. Circle T (true) or F (false). On the line, write the number of the paragraph with the answer.

1. There are worker-owned businesses only in the United States.   T   F   ____

2. All worker-owned companies start out as family businesses.   T   F   ____

3. King Arthur Flour was a family business for many years.   T   F   ____

4. The workers at King Arthur bought the company after it failed.   T   F   ____

5. Worker-owned businesses can be quite different
   from one another.   T   F ____

6. Workers gain more control when they become
   worker-owners.   T   F ____

B. Work with your class. Share your answers from part A. Go back to the reading to find the reason why a statement is true or false. Correct the false statements.

EXPLORING VOCABULARY

Thinking about the Target Vocabulary

A. Look at the chart with the target vocabulary from "When the Employees Own the Company." Five nouns and four verbs are missing. Scan the reading to find them, and add them to the correct places in the chart. Use the singular form of any plural noun. Use the base form of each verb.

¶	Nouns	Verbs	Adjectives	Other
1				
				in charge of
			uncertain	
				besides
2				
3				
4			such	
	condition			
	committee			
5				

B. Which words and phrases are new to you? Circle them in the chart. Then find them in the reading. Look at the context. Can you guess the meaning?

Understanding the Target Vocabulary

A. These sentences are **about the reading**. What is the meaning of each **boldfaced** word or phrase? Circle a, b, or c.

1. The people who use King Arthur flour for baking bread say that this flour is of very high **quality**. *Quality* means

   a. how expensive something is.
   b. how good something is.
   c. how difficult something is.

2. Frank Sands was the last of his family to be **in charge of** King Arthur Flour. *In charge of something* means

   a. in need of it.
   b. happy about it.
   c. responsible for it.

3. Who would run King Arthur after Frank and Brinna? The company's future was **uncertain**. *Uncertain* means

   a. not willing.
   b. not clear or decided.
   c. not surprising.

4. Brinna asked who **besides** their children was most important to them. *Besides* means

   a. because of.
   b. in addition to.
   c. in order to.

5. Some workers want to be owners so they can share in the company's **profits**. A profit is

   a. money earned from doing business.
   b. a decision to be made.
   c. a risk in trying something new.

> **Vocabulary Tip:**
> *Profit* can be a noun or a verb (usually followed by *from*): *Certain companies profited from the change in the law.*

6. There are many worker-owned businesses in the world. The reading describes three **such** companies. In this sentence, *such* means

   a. of the kind described.
   b. on a regular basis.
   c. in addition.

7. It's good for a **community** to have employee-owned businesses. A community is

   a. a way to spend money carefully.
   b. a political party that wants strong government.
   c. a group of people living in the same area.

B. These sentences are also **about the reading**. Complete them with the words and phrases in the box.

believe in	conditions	provide	right
committee	organize	react	security

1. In most cases, after a company fails, the employees feel sad and go find other jobs. But in some cases, after a company fails, the employees feel and do things differently. They _____ differently.

   Vocabulary Tip: Use *react + to +* an event or situation: *How did they react to the news?*

2. Some employee-owned businesses produce goods (such as flour) and others _____ services (such as giving health care).

3. Employee-owned businesses are not all set up in the same way. There are various ways to _____ and run a business of this kind.

4. In a worker-owned business, the rules of the company say workers can do certain things. For example, workers usually have the _____ to vote.

5. The people who set up employee-owned businesses usually feel that certain things are right and good, such as sharing information and decision-making. These people _____ certain ideas.

6. The workers at the photocopy shop in Massachusetts didn't have a safe and healthy place to work. The working _____ in the shop were bad.

   Vocabulary Tip: *Conditions* is always plural when it refers to a situation: *Weather conditions are making it unsafe to fly.*

7. At the photocopy shop, none of the workers felt safe in their jobs. They could lose their jobs at any time for any reason. They had no job _____.

8. Miriam Rodriguez organized a group of people to work on a particular problem. This _____ came up with the idea for Las Flores Metalarte.

EXPANDING VOCABULARY

Building on the Vocabulary

> ### Collocations: *Condition* and Its Word Partners
>
> **Collocations** are words that often go together. For example, to speak about security as a worker, use the collocation *job security*, not *work + security*.
>
> The noun *condition* has several meanings. With each meaning, there are certain nouns, verbs, and adjectives that form collocations with *condition*.
>
> 1. condition = the state of something: *The roads were in excellent/good/poor condition.*
> 2. condition = a sickness: *The patient's condition is getting better/is stable/is getting worse.*
> 3. conditions = situation: *weather conditions, working conditions, living conditions, political conditions, market conditions*

Choose the words that can form a collocation with *condition* or *conditions*.

1. I bought a used car in (very high / excellent) condition.

2. I'm afraid my heart condition is (getting worse / going down).

3. The employees were unhappy with the (job / working) conditions at the photocopy shop.

4. She's studying (government / political) conditions in developing countries.

5. During the Industrial Revolution, (life / living) conditions were terrible for many factory workers.

Using the Target Vocabulary in New Contexts

A. These sentences use the target words **in new contexts**. Complete them with the words in the box.

besides	profits	quality	security
organizing	provide	react	such

1. It is a new business and not yet making any _____.

2. _____ taking four courses, Greta is working fifteen hours a week.

3. No one understands why these people are getting sick, but we hope new research will _____ some answers.

4. If you thought someone wasn't being fair to you, how would you _____ in that situation?

5. *Cheap* can mean either "not expensive" or "of poor _____."

6. A regular schedule can give a child a sense of _____.

7. Alan has to write a twenty-page paper. He has never written

   _____ a long paper before.

8. Beatriz is _____ the class party. She knows who is bringing

   what food, who is taking care of the music, and all the other details.

B. These sentences also use the target words and phrases **in new contexts**. Complete them with the words and phrases in the box. There are two extra words.

believe in	community	in charge	rights
committees	conditions	quality	uncertain

1. Ben volunteered to serve on two _____.

2. I _believe in_ giving everyone a chance to give his or her opinion.

3. The fight for women's _conditions_ resulted in women getting the

   vote.

4. The parents went out and left a baby-sitter _in charge_.

5. After Ted and Sue had children, they moved to a _community_ with

   good public schools.

6. With such _____ economic conditions, it's hard to make

   business decisions.

DEVELOPING YOUR READING SKILLS

Understanding Topics and Main Ideas

A. Reread "When the Employees Own the Company." What's the main idea of the reading? Check (✓) your answer.

☐ 1. King Arthur Flour is a company with a long history, hard-working employees, and happy customers.

☐ 2. Employee-owned businesses are good for both the worker-owners and their communities.

☐ 3. An unusual way to set up a business is by having the employees own and manage it themselves.

> **Reading Tip:** The time to mark up a text and take notes is when you reread it. Underline or highlight important parts of the text, and write the topics of paragraphs in the margin.

B. Write the topic of each paragraph.

Paragraph 1: _____

Paragraph 2: _____

Paragraph 3: _____

Paragraph 4: _____

Paragraph 5: _____

C. What is the main idea of paragraph 5? Write a complete sentence. Do not copy a sentence from the paragraph.

_____

_____

Reading for Details

Are these statements about the reading true or false? If the reading doesn't give the information, check (✓) *It doesn't say.*

	True	False	It doesn't say.
1. King Arthur has an international market for its flour.	☐	☐	☐
2. Frank and Brinna Sands' children did not want to take charge of King Arthur Flour.	☐	☐	☐
3. King Arthur Flour now has sixteen worker-owners.	☐	☐	☐
4. Some employee-owned businesses produce goods, and others provide services.	☐	☐	☐
5. Worker-owned businesses do not make as much money as traditional businesses.	☐	☐	☐
6. Collective Copies was set up by people who wanted better working conditions.	☐	☐	☐
7. Coamo, Puerto Rico, now has several businesses that are employee-owned.	☐	☐	☐
8. Researchers have studied Italian towns that have worker-owned businesses.	☐	☐	☐

USING GRAPHIC ORGANIZERS

Graphic Organizers

A **graphic organizer** is a kind of diagram or chart used to show relationships between facts or ideas from a reading passage. When someone puts information from a text into a graphic organizer, it makes it easy to see how the facts or ideas relate to each other. For example, you can list the order of events in a graphic organizer (see the chart on page 119 for an example), or you can use a graphic organizer to compare and contrast people, as in the page 12 chart on the young entrepreneurs.

You will work with several types of graphic organizers in this book. Knowing how to use them to organize and show information is an important skill for college and careers.

Complete the chart with facts from the reading about the three worker-owned companies described in the reading.

Name of business	Type of business	Number of worker-owners	How it became a worker-owned business
1. King Arthur Flour			
2. Collective Copies			
3. Las Flores Metalarte			

CRITICAL THINKING

Critical Thinking Skills

When you read, you must work to understand not only what the writer is saying but *why* the writer is saying it. What is the writer's purpose? What is the writer's point of view? You use critical thinking skills to figure out the answers and get a good understanding of the text. Then you use critical thinking skills to evaluate, or judge, the text: How strong are the writer's claims? Has the writer shown good thinking and presented enough support for his or her ideas? Do you agree? Being a critical thinker also means being aware of your own point of view, your own interests and feelings, and the ways they affect your reading of the text.

Discussion

Talk about these questions in a small group.

1. How do you think the writer feels about worker-owned businesses? What do you think the writer's purpose was in writing "When the Employees Own the Company"? Cite evidence from the text to support your ideas.

Critical Thinking Tip: Remember that citing evidence from a text means using information found in the text to show that your ideas are correct.

2. Look back at the first paragraph of "When the Employees Own the Company." How does the writer begin?

   a. with basic facts about what a worker-owned company is

   b. with the writer's opinion of worker-owned companies

   c. with the history of one worker-owned company

   Why do you think the writer chose to begin the reading this way? What is the effect of introducing the topic of worker-owned companies in this way?

3. The reading says that *most* worker-owned companies "share certain important ideas" (paragraph 3), and it gives three of those ideas. What are they? Enter them in the chart. Do you think the three companies described in the reading believe in each of these ideas? Find information from the text to support your opinion. Make a check (✔) in the chart when your answer is yes, and put a question mark if you can't find (or infer) any evidence.

	Idea 1:	Idea 2:	Idea 3:
King Arthur Flour			
Collective Copies			
Las Flores Metalarte			

4. The employees at a worker-owned business each own a part of their company. Do you think that being an owner influences how they do their jobs? Explain.

5. In paragraph 4, the reading reports on eight employees who were unhappy with their jobs. Do you think those eight employees are happier now? Cite evidence from the text to explain your answer. Does the reading include any information about problems with worker-owned businesses? What problems can you think of that worker-owners might experience?

6. The reading says that researchers in Italy found that "worker-owned businesses are good for their communities" (paragraph 5). In what ways do those communities become better places to live? What other evidence can you find in the reading of a worker-owned business being good for the community? How did it influence the community?

WRITING

A. Use the Target Vocabulary: Choose five of the target words or phrases from the chart on page 39. On a piece of paper, use each word or phrase in a sentence and underline it. Find a partner and read each other's sentences.

Writing Tip: Before you show your paragraph to a partner, read it out loud to yourself. That can help you make sure your paragraph is clear and correct.

B. Practice Writing: Choose one of these topics and write a paragraph about it. Then find a partner and read each other's paragraphs.

1. The phrase *working conditions* refers to all the things about your job that affect how you feel about it. They can include everything from the air quality in your workplace to your sense of job security. What working conditions do you think are most important? What does "great working conditions" mean to you? Why? If you wish, you can begin:

   The most important working conditions at a job are . . .

2. Are you good or bad at organizing things? Write about an experience you had organizing something. It could be something you organized by yourself (your closet, for example) or something you organized with a group (such as a party or a group project for school).

Checkpoint

LEARNING OUTCOME

❯ Review and expand on the content of Unit 1

LOOK BACK

A. Think About This

Look back at your answers to the *Think About This* question on page 1:

If you were to choose a career in business, what would you most want to do?

Do you want to change your answers? Do you want to add anything new?

B. Remember the Readings

What do you want to remember most from the readings in Unit 1? For each chapter, write one sentence about the reading.

Chapter 1: Dreamers and Doers

_____

Chapter 2: Word-of-Mouth Advertising

_____

Chapter 3: A Language on the Move

_____

Chapter 4: When the Employees Own the Company

_____

REVIEWING VOCABULARY

A. Circle the correct words in each group.

1. Circle the nouns: *client, customer, employee, invest, political, volunteer*

2. Circle the verbs: *appear, earn, fair, hire, nature, react*

3. Circle the adjectives: *developing, financial, particular, quite, uncertain, while*

B. Complete the sentences with words and phrases from the box. There are two extra words or phrases.

believe in	come up with	mean	qualities	set up	turn into
besides	deal with	provide	right	sign up	within

1. My friends are bringing the food for the party, and I'll _____ the drinks.

2. They don't _____ hitting their children for any reason.

3. At what age do people get the _____ to vote in your country?

4. Clara works fifteen hours a week _____ going to school full-time.

5. The business should begin making a profit _____ a year.

6. My grandmother has many _____ that I respect.

7. They have to _____ a plan to save the company.

8. I'm sorry, I didn't _____ to step on your foot.

9. How did their discussion _____ a fight?

10. The president _____ a committee to deal with the problem.

EXPANDING VOCABULARY

Word Families

Each form of a word belongs to the same **word family**. For example, the nouns *service* and *server*, the verb *serve*, and the adjective *serviceable* all belong to the same word family.

Two members of a word family may look the same. The words *design, drive, gain, risk,* and *spread* can be nouns or verbs.

A. What part of speech is the **boldfaced** word? Circle *noun* or *verb*.

1. They'll try to keep the new **designs** secret.   *noun*   *verb*

2. Someone so successful must have a lot of **drive**.   *noun*   *verb*

3. They were pleased with the baby's weight **gain**.   *noun*   *verb*

4. The UN peacekeepers **risk** their lives every day.   *noun*   *verb*

5. They are working to stop the **spread** of AIDS.   *noun*   *verb*

B. The **boldfaced** words in these sentences belong to two word families, *profit* and *influence*. Are they nouns, verbs, or adjectives? Write the words in the correct place.

1. It's a very **profitable** business.

   He collects comic books for fun, not for **profit**.

   Will they **profit** much from the sale?

   Noun: _____

   Verb: _____

   Adjective: _____

2. A CEO has a lot of **influence** over a company.

   She's an **influential** business leader.

   Is there any way to **influence** the committee?

   Noun: _____

   Verb: _____

   Adjective: _____

A PUZZLE

Complete the sentences with words you studied in Chapters 1–4. Write the words in the puzzle.

Across

1. The cost of health care is a
   _____ problem.

5. Don't worry, you'll get your
   _____ share of the profits.

6. She buys cheap clothes. She can't afford
   anything of high _____.

8. There are five people on the hiring
   _____.

9. The teacher _____ that there
   would be a test on Friday.

10. Is he _____ to help?

Down

1. The housing _____ is strong,
   and home prices are going up.

2. The teachers _____ a trip
   with the students.

3. He has lived in the same
   _____ all his life.

4. _____ Jack enjoys dealing
   with customers, his brother hates it.

7. Job _____ means fewer
   worries about the future.

8. Working _____ were very
   bad, so many employees quit.

BUILDING DICTIONARY SKILLS

Finding Words in the Dictionary

Superscripts

Do you see profit¹ and profit² in the dictionary entries below?

> **prof·it¹** /ˈprɑfɪt/ *n* **1** [C,U] Money that you can gain by selling things or doing business: *NovaCorp* **made a** *pretax* **profit** *of $39 million.* | *They sold the company* **at a huge profit**. **2** [U] an advantage that you gain from doing something: *reading for profit and pleasure*
>
> **prof·it²** *v* **1** [I,T] to get something useful or helpful: *Everyone* **profits from** *an education.* **2** [I] to get money from doing something: *The states have* **profited from** *cigarette taxes.*

The small, raised numbers are called **superscripts**. They tell you that there is more than one entry for *profit*. When a word can function as more than one part of speech, that information may all be in one entry or the word may have separate entries for each part of speech.

Look for superscripts when you look up a word in the dictionary. When there is more than one entry for a word, scan all its meanings and uses.

A. Answer the questions about the dictionary entries for profit¹ and profit².

1. What parts of speech can *profit* be? A _____ or a

   _____

2. What preposition follows the verb? profit _____ something

3. Which verb is used with the noun *profit*? *Get, make,* or *take?*

   _____ a profit

Finding Words and Phrases within Entries

Sometimes words and phrases do not have their own entries in the dictionary. They may appear as part of, or following, the entry for another word in the same family.

- An adverb ending in *-ly* may appear at the end of the entry for an adjective in the same family.

  For example, at the end of the entry for po•lit•i•cal, you may see this: " —politically *adv.*"

- When you look for a multi-word phrase in the dictionary, look for it under the first important word in the phrase.

  For example, look for *in other words* in the entry for oth•er. However, when the first important word is a very common verb, then you may find the phrase somewhere else: look for *go wrong* in the entry for wrong, and look for *put your foot down* under foot.

- Look for phrasal verbs at the end of the entry for the verb.

  For example, look for *come up with* at the end of the entry for come. The list of phrasal verbs that start with *come* will be in alphabetical order, so you will find *come up with* after *come between, come out,* and *come under.*

B. Look at the dictionary entries and answer the questions.

> **charge**[1] /chärj/ *n* **1 MONEY** [C,U] the amount of money you have to pay for something: *an admission* **charge** *of $5* | *There's a $70* **charge for** *every extra piece of luggage.* | *We deliver* **free of charge** (= at no cost) **2 CONTROL** [U] the position of having control over or responsibility for something or someone: *Who is* **in charge of** *the department?* | *Diane took* **charge of** *the business when her father died.* **3 CRIME** [C] a statement that says that someone has done something . . .

1. Find the phrase *in charge of* in the entry for *charge*. Circle it. Does it refer to money, control, or crime?

> **a·void** /ə-void'/ *v* [T] **1** to prevent something bad from happening: *Exercise will help you avoid heart disease.* | *He had to swerve to avoid being hit by the other car.* Don't say "avoid to do something" **2** to deliberately stay away from someone or something: *Paul's been avoiding me all day.* **3** to deliberately not do something: *To avoid paying tax, he moved to Canada.* —**avoidable** *adj* —**avoidance** *n* [U]

2. a. Does the adjective *avoidable* have its own entry in this dictionary? YES   NO

   b. What noun is related to *avoid*? _____

3. In each phrase, circle the **boldfaced** word that you would look up in your dictionary to find the phrase. Then find the phrase in your dictionary.

   a. If you help him out, I'm sure he'll do something for you **in return**.

   b. I cleaned out my closet and **got rid of** clothes I no longer wore.

   c. Yes, you can take the DVDs—**as long as** you promise to return them tomorrow!

   d. Can she really **make a living** as an artist?

   e. The actor's first Hollywood movie **turned him into** a star.

HEALTH MATTERS

THINK ABOUT THIS

How much do you know about health?

Read these health-related questions. Check (✓) the ones you think you can answer.

- What is the average life expectancy for men and women in your country?

- What is the placebo effect?

- How many types of tears do people produce?

- How are tears good for you?

- Why is it important for babies to be held?

CHAPTER 5

Living to 100 and Beyond

People today are living longer than ever.

LEARNING OUTCOME

❯ Learn about ways to add to your life expectancy

GETTING READY TO READ

Read the definition of *life expectancy*. Then talk about the questions with your class.

Life expectancy means the number of years a person will probably live. The average life expectancy for a country is how long people in that country usually live. For example, for people in the United States, the average life expectancy is about 78 years. For Canadians, it is about 82.

1. What do you think the average life expectancy is for people in your country? If you can, look up the information online.

2. Do you think the average life expectancy in your country is the same for both men and women? Tell why or why not.

3. In what countries do you think people have the longest life expectancy? And the shortest? Why?

READING

Read to Find Out: What can you do to increase your life expectancy?

Look at the pictures, words, and definitions next to the reading. Then read without stopping. If you see a new word, try to understand the sentence without it. You will learn the word later.

Living to 100 and Beyond

1 Would you like to live to 100? Many people would. Some have dreamed of living even longer—perhaps **forever**. We know this has long been a popular idea because for hundreds of years, many cultures have had legends[1] about ways to avoid growing old.

2 In Europe in the 1400s, people heard one such legend about a wonderful spring[2] somewhere in eastern Asia. Drinking the water from this spring was supposed to make a person young again. It's **likely** that this story reached the Spanish explorer[3] Juan Ponce de Léon, and it may have been on his mind when he traveled to the Americas in the 1490s. After arriving in Puerto Rico, Ponce de Léon heard about an island with a **similar** spring, and he decided to go look for it. He invested in three ships, and in 1513, he went searching for the island. However, he ended up in Florida, never finding the island or the spring, which people now call the "Fountain[4] of Youth." When Ponce de Léon died eight years later, he was 61, which may not seem very old, but living to 61 was **actually** a very long life for a man of his times and his **lifestyle**.

3 It used to be **generally** agreed that the human body could not **possibly** last more than 120 years. No scientist today believes 120 to be the **limit** because people have already lived **beyond** that age. A woman in France, Jeanne Louise Calment, **made it** to 122 years and 164 days. Today, people in many parts of the world are living longer lives than their ancestors[5] did, partly because of better public health services and safer drinking water. Greater understanding of how to **treat** heart problems has **made a big difference** in life expectancy **as well**. Scientists are learning more all the time about how we can live longer, healthier lives, and maybe someday they'll even learn how to stop the aging **process** completely.

4 While you're waiting for that day to come, there are things you can do to **increase** your life expectancy. Do you think you can follow these three rules?

[1] *a legend* = an old, well-known story, often about brave people or magical events

[2] *a spring* = a place where water comes up naturally from the ground

[3] *an explorer* = someone who travels to learn about unknown places

[4] *a fountain*

[5] *their ancestors* = members of their families who lived long before

5   *Rule Number 1: Treat your body well.*

Your everyday lifestyle influences how long you will live. For example, smoking can take years off your life, and even if it doesn't make you sick, it will affect your skin and make you look older. So, don't smoke, get enough sleep, lead an active life, and be sure to eat right. In other words, eat foods that are good for you, and don't eat too much.

6   *Rule Number 2: Don't take risks.*

Forget about motorcycles,[6] and wear your seat belt when you travel by car. Also, try to choose a nice, safe way to make a living. If you can avoid it, don't do a dangerous job, like going to sea and working on a fishing boat.

7   *Rule Number 3: Choose your parents carefully.*

Perhaps you're asking, "How can anybody follow this one?" Well, that's a good question. However, about 70 percent of your life expectancy depends on your genes,[7] and you get your genes from your parents. Genes control not only your hair and eye color, but much, much more. If people in your family usually live long lives, then chances are good that you will, too.

8   It also helps to be born in Australia or Japan, and it helps to be born female. The average Australian or Japanese man can expect to see age 80, while his sister can expect to reach 85. Japan is home to more than 61,000 people who have made it to 100, and more than 87 percent of them are women.

[6] *a motorcycle*

[7] *your genes* = the parts of cells in your body that control qualities you get from your parents

Quick Comprehension Check

A. Read these statements **about the reading**. Circle T (true) or F (false). On the line, write the number of the paragraph with the answer.

1. Scientists all agree: Nobody can live past 120.   T   F   _____

2. The reading gives three rules for living longer.   T   F   _____

3. The way you live can add years to your life.   T   F   _____

4. People in certain countries often live especially
    long lives.   T   F   _____

5. There's no relationship between how long your
    family members live and your life expectancy.   T   F   _____

6. Many cultures have stories from the past about
    ways to stay young.   T   F   _____

B. Work with your class. Share your answers from part A. Go back to the reading to find the reason why a statement is true or false. Correct the false statements.

EXPLORING VOCABULARY

Thinking about the Target Vocabulary

A. Look at the chart with the target vocabulary from "Living to 100 and Beyond." Three nouns, two verbs, and two adjectives are missing. Scan the reading to find them, and add them to the correct places in the chart. Use the base form of each verb.

¶	Nouns	Verbs	Adjectives	Other
1	People idea	have, has know	old longer	forever
2				
		act, was	long, old,	actually
3		to be,		generally
				possibly
	People	Have,		beyond
	A woman, public health service			make it
	problems scientist		longer, healthier	
		Has, as well		make a difference
				as well
4				

B. Which words and phrases are new to you? Circle them in the chart. Then find them in the reading. Look at the context. Can you guess the meaning?

Understanding the Target Vocabulary

A. These sentences are **about the reading**. Complete them with the words and phrases in the box.

forever	lifestyle	limit	made it	process
increases	likely	made a difference	possibility	treat

1. Some people dream of a life without end. They want to live
   forever.

2. Juan Ponce de Léon probably heard the stories about a spring in Asia
   with special powers. It's _likely_ that he heard them.

3. As an explorer and a soldier, Juan Ponce de Léon had a way of life that
   put him at risk. A _lifestyle_ like his does not add years to a
   person's life.

4. Scientists used to think that people couldn't _possibility_ live
   more than 120 years. They thought there was no way it could happen.

5. Now, no one thinks of 120 years as the longest anyone can live. No one
   sees 120 as the _limit_ anymore.

6. A French woman managed to reach the age of 122. She
   made it to 122.

7. Today, doctors know more about heart problems. They can give heart
   patients new kinds of medical help. They can _treat_ heart
   problems better now.

8. Better understanding of heart problems has _made a different_
   in many people's life expectancy. It has caused a change (adding
   years to people's lives).

   > **Vocabulary Tip:**
   > A difference can be any way that two or more people or things are not alike. In the context of a problem, the phrase *make a difference* means "make things better."

9. We change as we grow older. We go through the aging
   process—that is, we experience a series of changes,
   actions, or events relating to our minds and bodies.

10. If something adds to your chances of living a longer life, then it
    increases your life expectancy.

B. Read each definition and look at the paragraph number. Look back at the reading on pages 57–58 to find the **boldfaced** word or phrase to match the definition. Write it in the chart.

Definition	Paragraph	Target Word or Phrase
1. really, truly (but perhaps surprisingly)	2	
2. almost the same, alike in some way	2	
3. usually, in most cases	3	
4. past or later than (a certain time or date)	3	
5. too, also	3	

> **Vocabulary Tip:**
> The adverb *actually* is related to the adjective *actual*, used to stress what is real or true: *The actual cost of the service was higher than I expected. It actually cost twice as much.*

EXPANDING VOCABULARY

Building on the Vocabulary

Grammar: Adverbs

Adverbs have many uses. An adverb can modify (or describe):

a verb	They **worked** quickly.
an adjective	The two plans are quite **similar**.
another adverb	She sings very **well**.
an entire sentence	**Luckily, we made it there on time.**

Possibly is an adverb which usually means "perhaps, maybe": *He's going to buy a car soon, possibly this week.*

When *possibly* follows *cannot, can't,* or *couldn't,* it means "(not) in any way:" *I can't possibly get there today.*

A. Circle the adverb(s) in each sentence.

1. The news spread fast.
2. You may not want to believe it, but it's actually true.
3. I thought you dealt with the problem quite well.
4. Generally, they hire part-timers.

B. What is the meaning of *possibly* in these sentences? Circle your answers.

1. I'm sorry, but I couldn't possibly go out tonight.   perhaps   in any way
2. This is possibly your best work ever.   perhaps   in any way
3. You can't possibly mean what you're saying!   perhaps   in any way
4. Is it going to rain? Possibly.   perhaps   in any way

as well – also
too

Using the Target Vocabulary in New Contexts

A. Complete the sentences with the target words and phrases in the box. There are two extra words.

actually	likely	make it	similar
increase	limit	process	treat

Vocabulary Tip:
Use _make it_ when someone manages to arrive in time for something or succeeds in getting to a difficult goal.

1. The speed ____limit____ on this street is 35 miles per hour.

2. The train won't leave for an hour. Don't worry, we'll ____make it____ in time.

3. The two companies offer ____similar____ services, so it's hard to choose.

4. I didn't need a doctor. I was able to ____treat____ the cut myself.

5. Getting a college education is a long ____process____.

6. In the past year, the company was able to ____increase____ profits by 20 percent.

Vocabulary Tip:
Increase can be a noun or a verb. The verb can be **transitive** (used with a direct object: _They increased the price_) or **intransitive** (with no direct object: _The price has increased_).

B. Complete the sentences with the target words and phrases in the box. There are two extra words.

as well	forever	lifestyle	makes a difference
beyond	generally	likely	process

1. After their baby is born, they won't be going out with their friends so much. Having a baby usually changes a couple's ____lifestyle____.

2. It's ____likely____ to rain later, so take an umbrella.

3. With so much about the future uncertain, I can't make plans ____beyond____ next week.

4. The job offers good pay and good working conditions ____as well____. Both are important.

5. The movie had a happy ending. The two main characters promised to love each other ____forever____.

6. The fresh paint really ____makes a____ difference in the look of the room. It looks great now!

Vocabulary Tip:
Beyond can mean "past or later than (a time or date)," or "farther than (a place)," as in _beyond the river_, or "past (a limit)," as in _beyond my ability_.

DEVELOPING YOUR READING SKILLS

The Main Idea

Reread "Living to 100 and Beyond." Then complete this sentence to give the main idea of the reading. Write one or more words on each line.

If you want to _like to be a 100 years_, then you should
(1) old

treat your body well and _don't take risks_, but a lot
(2)   (3)

depends on your _____ genes _____, and these you cannot control.
(4)

Taking Notes

Marking Up a Text

The first time you read a text, read for the gist. Don't focus on the details. When you reread, read more slowly and take notes—about both the main ideas *and* the most important details.

One way of taking notes is to mark up the text.

- Mark topics of paragraphs and main ideas in one way, such as underlining or highlighting words and sentences. You might add a star or another symbol in the margin.
- Mark important details in another way, such as highlighting with a different color or using a different kind of underlining.
- Marking up a text helps guide your thinking about the text and helps you remember what matters most about it.

Write in the margin, not in the spaces between the lines. Writing between the lines makes it more difficult to reread the text.

Answer the questions about what to mark up in "Living to 100 and Beyond."

1. Which part of paragraph 1 would you highlight as the main idea?
   - ☐ a. "Would you like to live to 100? Many people would."
   - ☒ b. "Some have dreamed of living even longer—perhaps forever."

2. Which note about the topic would you write in the margin next to paragraph 2?
   - ☐ a. Europe, 1400s
   - ☐ b. the story of the Fountain of Youth

Reading Tip: It's fine to use your first language when you take notes, but avoid translating as you read. It will slow you down.

3. Which part of paragraph 3 would you highlight as the main idea?
  - ☑ a. "Today, people in many parts of the world are living longer lives. . . ."
  - ☐ b. ". . . maybe someday they'll even learn how to stop the aging process completely." ↑ conclusion

4. Which part of paragraph 3 would you underline as an important detail?
  - ☐ a. ". . . the human body could not possibly last more than 120 years" — opinion
  - ☑ b. "No scientist today believes 120 to be the limit. . . ." — fact

5. Which note would you write in the margin next to paragraph 8?
  - ☑ a. Australia and Japan = healthy places to live — main point
  - ☐ b. women live longer than men - no focus in this

Understanding and Using Supporting Details

A. Supply a detail from the reading to support each of the major points below. Use your own words and write complete sentences.

1. People have told many stories about ways to avoid growing old.

   For example, people used to talk about drinking water from a

   certain spring.

2. Some people have already lived to be more than 120 years old.

   _____

   _____

3. There are several reasons why people in many countries live longer lives now.

   _____

   _____

4. Some things beyond our control have an effect on our life expectancy.

   _____

   _____

B. Write a general statement that relates to each supporting example.

1. _Take care of yourself. / Live a healthy lifestyle._

   For example, eat well, exercise, and don't smoke.

2. _____

   For example, avoid riding motorcycles.

3. _____

   For example, don't take a job working on a fishing boat if you can avoid it.

4. _____

For example, your hair and eye color depend on them, as well as about 70 percent of your life expectancy.

5. _____

For example, people in Japan are more likely to make it to 100.

CRITICAL THINKING

Discussion

Talk about these questions in a small group.

1. The writer begins "Living to 100 and Beyond" with a question for the reader. What is that question? What answer does the writer expect from the reader? How do you know? What answer would _you_ give to writer's question? Why?

2. _Be supposed to_ has more than one meaning. What does it mean in each of these sentences? Match the uses of _be supposed to_ and their meanings.

   ____ a. People are supposed to pay their taxes.

   ____ b. The party was supposed to be a surprise.

   ____ c. That restaurant is supposed to have the best food in town.

   1. used to say that something is believed by many people, although it might not be true or you might not agree

   2. used to say what is expected or planned, especially after it didn't happen

   3. used to say what someone should or should not do, especially because of rules or laws

> **Critical Thinking Tip:** Remember, sometimes you need to infer, or guess, what a writer is thinking. Look for evidence in the text that suggests what the writer is saying between the lines.

   What does _be supposed to_ mean in the sentence "Drinking the water from this spring was supposed to make a person young again" (paragraph 2)? How does the context for this sentence—especially the sentences that come before it—help you understand its meaning?

3. In paragraph 3, the writer refers to public health services and drinking water. Why? What does "public health services" mean? What is the writer implying about living conditions in the past? The writer also refers to heart problems. What has changed? How do these changes influence life expectancy for people in general?

4. In paragraph 7, what does the writer mean by saying "That's a good question"? Look again at Rules 1, 2, and 3 in the reading. Do you think the writer gives enough support to make you believe in each of these pieces of advice? Think about the things these rules say to do. What piece of advice do you think is easy to follow? What's hard? What's impossible? Give the reasons for your answers.

5. The three rules in the reading say nothing about a person's relationships with other people. Are relationships important in living a long life? Explain your opinion.

6. What do you think is the secret to living a long life?

WRITING

A. Use the Target Vocabulary: Choose five of the target words or phrases from the chart on page 59. On a piece of paper, use each word or phrase in a sentence and underline it. Find a partner and read each other's sentences.

B. Practice Writing: Choose one of these topics and write a paragraph about it. Then find a partner and read each other's paragraphs.

1. Would you like to make it to 100 or beyond? Explain why or why not. If you like, you can begin:

   There are several reasons why I would (not) like to live to be 100.

2. Imagine that today you celebrated your 100th birthday. Write in your journal about how you spent your day.

> **Writing Tip:**
> When you write a paragraph, try to use words and phrases you've learned recently.

There are several reasons why I do want to live to 100 years old. First, I want to live to 100 years because I can spend more time with my family. I would also like to live more years to enjoy nature.

CHAPTER 6

What Causes the Placebo Effect?

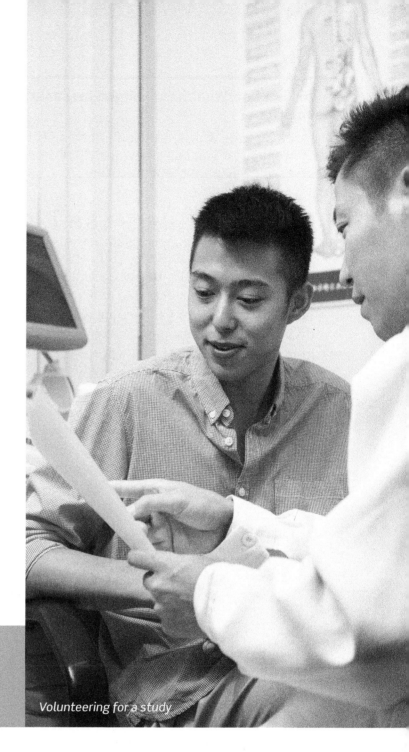

Volunteering for a study

LEARNING OUTCOME

> Learn what researchers have found out about the placebo effect

GETTING READY TO READ

Talk about these questions in a small group.

1. When you are sick, what do you usually do? Do you take medicine? Do you see a doctor?

2. When you go to the doctor because you feel sick, do you expect to get a prescription?[1] Explain why or why not.

3. Does a sick person's state of mind (how he or she thinks and feels) influence how quickly the person gets well? Explain your answer.

[1] a prescription = a doctor's written order for a specific medicine

Read to Find Out: What has changed in researchers' understanding of the placebo effect?

Look at the picture, words, and definitions next to the reading. Then read without stopping. If you see a new word, try to understand the sentence without it. You will learn the word later.

What Causes the Placebo Effect?

1   Harry S. wanted to quit smoking. So, when he saw an ad for a study on ways to **break the habit**, he called and offered to be part of it. The research was being done at a local university, where Harry and the other volunteers—all people who wanted to quit smoking—were divided into three groups. The volunteers in Group A received nicotine gum. (That's chewing gum[1] with nicotine, the drug in tobacco[2] that gives smokers the good feeling they get from smoking.) When these smokers felt the need for a cigarette, they could chew a piece of this gum instead, and it would give them the nicotine their bodies were used to. The volunteers in Group B, including Harry, got some gum, too. Theirs was just plain chewing gum, but they didn't know it had no nicotine. The people in Group C got nothing. A group like this in a study is called the control group.

2   After a four-hour period with no cigarettes, Harry and the other volunteers had to write answers to a series of questions. Their answers showed how badly they wanted a cigarette. Not surprisingly, the smokers in Group C—the control group, which got no gum—showed the strongest cravings.[3] The smokers in the other two groups didn't feel such a strong need to smoke.

3   What surprised the researchers was that the results for Groups A and B were exactly the same. That meant that the plain chewing gum worked just as well as the gum with the nicotine. Why? The researchers thought it was most likely the placebo effect.

4   A placebo is something that seems like a medical **treatment** (such as a pill or a medical procedure[4]) but that doesn't actually have any *direct* effect on the body. Sometimes a patient has a good **response** to a placebo, and when that happens, it's called the placebo effect. The placebo effect was long believed to result **simply** from a patient expecting to feel better. In 1757, Benjamin Franklin, the American scientist and inventor, described it as "the Spirits given by the Hope of Success." People thought placebos **tricked** patients into thinking they were better when they really weren't, and doctors who didn't believe in tricking patients saw no **role** for placebos as a form of treatment.

[1] *a pack of chewing gum*

[2] *tobacco* = the plant whose leaves are used to make cigarettes and cigars

[3] *a craving* = a very strong wish for something (such as a certain food)

[4] *a medical procedure* = a way of doing something to fix a health problem

5   However, **recent** research has **proven** that placebos can have *indirect* effects on the body. They can cause changes in brain **chemistry**, the same kinds of changes produced by drugs. For example, when patients in pain believe that they're getting treatment that will help control their pain, their brains produce natural painkillers. Those painkillers then help **block** the pain. This means that the placebo effect isn't a mistaken idea in the patient's mind. It's an actual event in the patient's brain. As a result of this new understanding of how placebos **affect** us, they may come to have a useful role in treating pain and other problems by making use of the brain's own neurotransmitters.[5]

6   We still can't be sure why the smokers in Harry's group felt fewer cravings than expected. Maybe just the idea of getting treatment— nicotine in this case—produced changes in their brain chemistry. But maybe the people working with the volunteers **had something to do with** it, too. A study at Harvard University showed that when people on the medical **staff** were especially kind and helpful, patients had a better response to a placebo (Kaptchuk, 2008). There could be other **explanations**, too. Maybe the sugar in the chewing gum helped the smokers in Group B feel better. One thing we *do* know about the placebo effect is that **further** research is needed.

[5] *a neuro-transmitter = a chemical in the body that carries a signal from one nerve cell to another*

Quick Comprehension Check

A. Read these statements **about the reading**. Circle T (true) or F (false). On the line, write the number of the paragraph with the answer.

1. Harry's doctor told him to join the study on quitting smoking.   T   (F)   4

2. Chewing gum helped the smokers feel okay without smoking.   (T)   F   1,2,3

3. A placebo has strong drugs in it.   T   (F)   4

4. A placebo can help a patient who is experiencing pain.   (T)   F   5

5. The brain can produce its own painkillers.   (T)   F   5

6. Doctors have often given their patients placebos.   (T)   F   ___

B. Work with your class. Share your answers from part A. Go back to the reading to find the reason why a statement is true or false. Correct the false statements.

EXPLORING VOCABULARY

Thinking about the Target Vocabulary

A. Look at the chart with the target vocabulary from "What Causes the Placebo Effect?" Five nouns and three verbs are missing. Scan the reading to find them, and add them to the correct places in the chart. Use the singular form of any plural noun. Use the base form of each verb.

¶	Nouns	Verbs	Adjectives	Other
1	He, volunteers, study, groups	wanted, gut, saw, called, put	plain	break the habit
	treatment			
4	placebo, inventor, scientist	seems, feel	long	
	pill, medical procedure	described, mark		simply
	nolc, disease	believe, saw		
	Benjamin Frank			
5	chemistry	block	recent	
	patients	prove		
	result	making, getting		
	problems	mark		
6				have something to do with
	effect		further	

B. Which words and phrases are new to you? Circle them in the chart. Then find them in the reading. Look at the context. Can you guess the meaning?

Understanding the Target Vocabulary

A. These sentences are **about the reading**. Complete them with the words and phrases in the box.

blocks	had something to do with	treatment
break the habit	response	trick
chemistry	role	

1. For Harry, smoking was a thing he did repeatedly. He wanted to stop doing it. He wanted to _break the habit_ of smoking.

2. When doctors take action to help a patient with a sickness or injury, they are giving the patient medical _treatment_.

3. Sometimes a person in a study receives a placebo and it makes no difference. In other cases, the person feels better. That reaction, or _response_, is called the placebo effect: feeling better based on something that is not an actual medical treatment.

4. People used to think that if a doctor gave a patient a placebo, the doctor was trying to fool the patient—that is, make the patient believe something that wasn't true. They thought a placebo was just a way to _trick_ a patient.

5. Doctors who "saw no _role_ for placebos as a form of treatment" did not want to use them. These doctors thought placebos should not be a part of their work helping patients.

6. We have chemicals in our brains that carry messages, like a pain message from a part of the body that gets hurt. The phrase "brain _chemistry_" refers to those chemicals and the way they work together. A placebo, like an actual drug, can cause changes in the way they work.

7. When a painkiller stops pain from traveling through the body to the brain, you can say it _blocks_ the pain.

> **Vocabulary Tip:**
> A response is the way you react to what someone has said or done. A response can also be a reply (spoken or written): *I got no response to my question.*

> **Vocabulary Tip:**
> When someone or something plays a role in an activity or a situation, they are part of it and may have an influence on it: *A CEO plays a major role in a company.*

8. It's possible that the way people spoke and acted with the patients in the Harvard University study had some effect on, or *had something to do* the results of the study.

B. These sentences are also **about the reading**. What is the meaning of each **boldfaced** word or phrase? Circle a, b, or c.

1. People used to think the placebo effect was **simply** a matter of a patient's mind at work. *Simply* means

   a. willingly.   b. only.   c. beyond.

2. There have been **recent** studies that have provided new information about placebos. *Recent* means happening

   a. a little while ago.   b. without pay.   c. accidentally.

3. Research has **proven** that a placebo can have an indirect effect on the body by changing brain chemistry. When you prove something, you

   a. increase it.   b. get rid of it.   c. show that it is true.

4. New research is increasing our understanding of how placebos **affect** us. *Affect* means

   a. influence or produce a change in.   b. avoid dealing with.   c. be in charge of.

5. One study showed that the way **staff** act when treating patients can influence the placebo effect. *Staff* means people who

   a. work for an organization.   b. are sick or hurt.   c. buy goods or services.

6. The reading offers several **explanations** why the placebo gum might have helped the smokers in Group B. An explanation provides

   a. a design for something.   b. a limit on something.   c. a reason why something happened.

7. Scientists would say that **further** research is needed. *Further* means

   a. international.   b. more.   c. uncertain.

> **Vocabulary Tip:**
> *Affect* is usually a verb. The verb always has a direct object. *Effect* is usually a noun. It can be a count or noncount noun.

EXPANDING VOCABULARY

Building on the Vocabulary

> **Word Grammar: *Farther* vs. *Further***
>
> ***Farther*** and ***further*** are both comparative forms of *far*. In conversation, many people use either one; in writing, follow these rules.
>
> - Use *farther* when you mean a longer distance: *They ran farther than we did.*
> - Use *further* when you refer to time, amounts, or processes: *We need to study the problem further.*
>
> These words can be adjectives (*the farther star, further research*) or adverbs (*it spread farther, we didn't discuss it any further*).

Complete each sentence with *farther* or *further*.

1. My classroom is _____farther_____ down the hall.

2. I need _____further_____ practice.

3. They never developed the plan any _____further_____.

4. Clear Lake is nicer than Heart Lake, but it's _____farther_____ away.

5. You can swim _____farther_____ than I can.

6. He will study math _____further_____ when he goes to college.

[handwritten margin notes: Farther – distance comparing / Further – time, amounts, processes]

Using the Target Vocabulary in New Contexts

A. Complete the sentences with the target words and phrases in the box. There are two extra words.

affected	break the habit	explanation	recent	treatment
blocked	chemistry	prove	simply	tricked

1. She is still in pain from a _____recent_____ accident. It happened just last weekend.

2. I'm tired of his calling me every time he has a problem. I wish he would _____break the habit_____

3. It wasn't fair. He _____tricked_____ me into doing his share of the work.

4. Cooks don't need to be scientists, but they can learn a lot if they study the _Chemistry_ of food.

5. We all hope the new manager will be able to do the job, but we have to wait and see. She has to _prove_ that she can.

6. I wondered why he arrived so late, but he offered no _explanation_.

7. Doctors are working on a new _treatment_ for patients with burns.

8. I would love to come to the party, but it's _simply_ not possible. I'll be away on a business trip.

B. Complete the sentences with the target words and phrases in the box. There are two extra words.

affects	has something to do with	responses	staff
block	recent	role	tricks

1. The organization has only a small paid _staff_ but many volunteers.

2. Your lifestyle or your genes: Which one plays a bigger _role_ in your life expectancy?

3. His most recent book _has something_ Mexican history, I think.

4. When trees come down during a storm, they sometimes _block_ roads.

5. When they advertised the job opening, they got hundreds of _responses_.

6. My doctor talked to me about how my lifestyle _affects_ my life expectancy.

> **Vocabulary Tip:**
> *Staff* usually refers to a group of employees. One person in the group is a member of the staff or a staff member.

DEVELOPING YOUR READING SKILLS

Quoting and Paraphrasing

Quoting or Paraphrasing Someone's Words

When you **quote** someone, you repeat the exact words the person said or wrote. Use quotation marks (" ") to mark the beginning and the end of the quotation.

We now know that "placebos can have indirect *effects on the body in the form of changes in brain chemistry, the same kinds of changes produced by drugs."*

When you **paraphrase**, you say the same thing as someone else but in a different way. There are two main ways to paraphrase:

- Change words and phrases to other words and phrases with similar meanings.

  Researchers have found that placebos can affect brain chemistry, just like drugs.

- Change the order of the parts of a sentence or the way the information is organized in a sentence.

  The same kinds of changes that drugs can produce in brain chemistry can be produced by placebos, too.

The following sentences are paraphrases of sentences in the reading. Find the sentence in the reading with the same meaning and copy it here. Use quotation marks (" ") because you are quoting someone else's exact words.

1. The researchers were surprised to see Groups A and B show the same results.

   <u>"What surprised the researchers was that the results for</u>

   <u>Groups A and B were exactly the same."</u>

2. Harry S. was a smoker who wanted to break the habit.

   _____

   _____

3. The volunteers in all three groups answered some questions after spending four hours without smoking.

   _____

   _____

4. This tells us that the placebo effect isn't just something a person imagines.

   _____

   _____

5. Clearly, scientists need to study the placebo effect some more.

   _____

   _____

Understanding Reference Words

Reference Words

A **reference word** takes the place of a noun, noun phrase, or a longer part of a text. The most common kinds of reference words are pronouns (such as *he, she, it*, and *they*) and demonstratives (such as *this, that, these,* and *those*).

Reference words usually refer back to someone or something already named (the **antecedent** of the reference word). The definite article *the* is also a reference word when it refers the reader back to something that came before.

From page 68:

antecedent

So, when he saw an ad for **a study** on ways to break the habit, he called and

reference words

offered to be part of **it**. **The** research was being done . . . .

Reading Tip: The first time you read a text, read for the gist. When you reread, make sure you know exactly who or what each reference word refers to.

What do the **boldfaced** reference words mean in these sentences? Look back at the reading.

1. Paragraph 1: . . . he called and offered to be part of **it**. _____

    _____

2. Paragraph 3: **That** meant that the plain chewing gum worked . . . _____

    _____

3. Paragraph 5: **Those** painkillers then help block the pain. _____

    _____

4. Paragraph 5: As a result of **this** new understanding . . . _____

    _____

5. Paragraph 6: But maybe the people working with the volunteers had

    something to do with **it**, too. _____

    _____

Summarizing

Complete this summary paragraph to give the main ideas of "What Causes the Placebo Effect?"

According to the reading "What Causes the Placebo Effect?," a placebo is

_____
(1)

The term the *placebo effect* refers to someone feeling better after

_____
(2)

Recent studies have shown that _____.
(3)

People who have studied the placebo effect probably all agree that

_____
(4)

CRITICAL THINKING

Discussion

Talk about these questions in a small group.

1. How was the nicotine gum study set up? Why do you think researchers set up studies this way? Did the researchers in this case get the results they expected? How do you know? What were their findings? Based on those findings, what do you think researchers should study in the future?

2. In paragraph 4, you read, "The placebo effect was long believed to result simply from a patient expecting to feel better." Which word or phrase is closest in meaning to *simply* as it's used in this context?

    a. easily   b. clearly   c. just

    How do you know? Do people still believe that the placebo effect results simply from what the patient is expecting? What two sentences in paragraph 5 contrast the old and new ideas about placebos?

3. Why does the writer talk about tricking people? After reading about new research on placebos, do you think doctors still see placebos as just a way to trick their patients? Do you see placebos this way? Explain.

4. What type of medical conditions or problems can a placebo be helpful for, according to the reading? What other types of conditions might placebos also be good for? What conditions do you think would *not* be influenced by a placebo?

5. The writer suggests that in the future, doctors might treat pain by giving the patient a placebo that would cause the brain to produce natural painkillers. How do you think this would be different from giving the patient a prescription for a painkilling drug?

> **Vocabulary Tip:**
> *Findings* is usually plural. It means "information discovered as a result of research (or similar work)."

> **Reading Tip:**
> Notice the sentence "It's an actual event . . ." (paragraph 5). *Actual* and *actually* are sometimes used to stress that new information contrasts with what came before or with what the reader might expect.

WRITING

A. Use the Target Vocabulary: Choose five of the target words or phrases from the chart on page 70. On a piece of paper, use each word or phrase in a sentence and underline it. Find a partner and read each other's sentences.

B. Practice Writing: Choose one of these topics and write a paragraph about it. Then find a partner and read each other's paragraphs.

1. Imagine that you are invited to be part of a study on a new drug that is supposed to make you smarter. Some of the volunteers will get the drug and some will get a placebo. Would you agree to volunteer? Why or why not? If you wish, you can begin:

   Researchers working on a new drug have invited me to be part of a study. The drug is designed to make people smarter. As a volunteer, I might get the drug, or I might get a placebo. I have decided . . . .

2. When do you go to see a doctor? How do you feel about going to doctors? What do you expect from a visit to the doctor?

> **Writing Tip:**
> Before writing about a decision you're making, make a list of reasons for and against it. This will help you organize your ideas.

Tears

Chopping onions may make you cry.

GETTING READY TO READ

Talk about these questions in a small group.

1. When was the last time you cried? What made you cry?

2. Do you agree with a, b, or c? Choose one and explain your choice.

   a. Crying is a healthy thing to do.

   b. Crying is bad for you.

   c. Crying is neither good for you nor bad for you.

3. When is it okay, and not okay, to cry? Give some examples. Are the rules about crying the same for everyone?

READING

Look at the words and definitions next to the reading and the illustrations that follow it. Then read without stopping. If you see a new word, try to understand the sentence without it. You will learn the word later.

Tears

1 Tears are good for our eyes. In fact, without them, our eyes would be so dry they wouldn't be able to move. Some people say tears help us in other ways, too. Maybe you know someone who likes to watch sad movies in order to "have a good cry." While it hasn't been proven, tears may be good not only for our eyes but for our **emotional** health as well.

2 We generally **notice** tears only when we cry, but we have them in our eyes all the time, and we need to. Without this **liquid** covering them, our eyes would be at risk of infection.[1] We also need tears in order to see. The cornea[2] of the eye does not have a perfectly smooth **surface**, and tears fill in the holes in the cornea, making it smooth so that we can see clearly. Without tears, the world would look very strange to us. These are the two basic jobs that tears do for us: They help us see the world while at the same time protecting our eyes from it.

3 There are three types of tears, called *basal*, *reflex*, and *emotional* (or *psychic*) tears, and these three types **differ** not only in purpose but also in composition.[3]

4 • Basal tears are the ones that we produce all the time. On average, our eyes produce these tears at the **rate** of five to ten ounces[4] a day. When we blink,[5] we spread basal tears across the surface of our eyes. If we do not blink often enough, like some people who spend long hours in front of a computer, our eyes get dry.

5 • Have you ever cut up an onion and felt tears come to your eyes? Tears of that type are called reflex tears. They're the ones that fill our eyes when a cold wind **blows**. These tears also protect our eyes, washing away dust and other **materials** that get into them.

6 • Emotional, or psychic, tears **flow** when we feel certain emotions. When we cry tears of sadness, disappointment,[6] or happiness, we are crying emotional tears. Emotional tears are the tears we think of most when we use the word *cry*.

7 Tom Lutz, the author of *Crying: The Natural and Cultural History of Tears*, writes, "**Throughout** history, and in every culture, . . . everyone, everywhere cries at some time." Even men and women who say they never cry can usually remember crying as children. Most of us

[1] *infection* = sickness in a part of the body

[2] *the cornea* = a covering for the eye; see the picture on page 81

[3] *composition* = the way something is made up of different things, parts, etc.

[4] *an ounce* = a small amount of liquid (less than 0.03 liters)

[5] *blink* = quickly close and reopen your eyes

[6] *disappointment* = unhappiness because something you hoped for didn't happen

probably think it's **normal** for men or women to cry at certain times. For example, it's no surprise when someone cries during a sad movie, and we often expect people to cry when a family member dies. At times such as these, we may even tell them, "**Go ahead** and cry." However, we don't always take this **view** of tears, and sometimes adults who cry—or even children who do—lose the respect of others. What would you think, for example, of an adult who cried over losing a card game? Most people are aware of the social rules about when, where, and why it is and isn't acceptable[7] to cry. These rules generally differ for children and adults, and often for men and women. They depend on things such as family, culture, and religion, and they change over time.

[7] *acceptable =*
generally
considered
good enough
or correct

8   Some people think it's not just acceptable to cry but actually healthy to let the tears flow. Over 2,500 years ago, doctors in Greece thought that tears came from the brain and that everyone needed to let them out. Today, many people still believe in getting tears out. They say that through crying, we get rid of emotions we have stored up, which is good for our **mental** health. Some people report that they feel better after crying. This could be because of the **chemicals** in emotional tears; one of which is a type of endorphin, a painkiller that the body produces naturally. Emotional tears increase the amount of endorphin that gets to the brain because tears flow from the eye into the nose and pass to the brain that way. This painkiller may make a person less aware of sad or angry feelings, and that could explain why someone feels better after "a good cry."

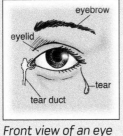

Front view of an eye

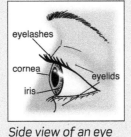

Side view of an eye

Quick Comprehension Check

A. Read these statements **about the reading**. Circle T (true) or F (false). On the line, write the number of the paragraph with the answer.

1. Tears are important for keeping our eyes healthy.	T	F	_____
2. Tears are important for our ability to see.	T	F	_____
3. There are two different kinds of tears.	T	F	_____
4. We have emotional tears in our eyes all the time.	T	F	_____
5. There are social rules about when it is okay to cry.	T	F	_____
6. Some people think it can be good for you to cry.	T	F	_____

B. Work with your class. Share your answers from part A. Go back to the reading to find the reason why a statement is true or false. Correct the false statements.

EXPLORING VOCABULARY

Thinking about the Target Vocabulary

A. Look at the chart with the target vocabulary from "Tears." Four verbs and three adjectives are missing. Scan the reading to find them, and add them to the correct places in the chart. Use the base form of each verb.

¶	Nouns	Verbs	Adjectives	Other
1				
2				
	liquid			
	surface			
3				
4	rate			
5				
	material			
6				
7				throughout
				go ahead
	view			
8				
	chemical			

B. Which words and phrases are new to you? Circle them in the chart. Then find them in the reading. Look at the context. Can you guess the meaning?

Understanding the Target Vocabulary

A. These sentences are **about the reading**. What is the meaning of each **boldfaced** word or phrase? Circle a, b, or c.

1. Tears may be good for your **emotional** health. *Your emotional health* means the condition of your

   a. body.   b. eyes.   c. mind and feelings.

2. We don't usually **notice** our tears, except when we cry. If you notice tears, that means you

   a. see or feel that they're there.   b. block them from coming.   c. increase the. supply

3. Your eye does not have a smooth **surface**. Like your skin, your eye has tiny holes and wrinkles. The surface of something is

   a. its top, outer layer.   b. the inside of it.   c. the color of it.

4. We may think it is **normal** for people to cry at certain times. *Normal* means

   a. surprising.   b. usual and. expected   c. strange and funny.

5. You might tell someone, "**Go ahead** and cry." Saying that someone can or should go ahead and do something tells the person

   a. that it's okay to do it.   b. to follow you.   c. to hurry up.

Vocabulary Tip:
The adjective *emotional* is related to the noun *emotion*, meaning a strong feeling: *Love is a powerful emotion.*

B. These sentences are also **about the reading**. Complete them with the words and phrases in the box.

blows	differ	liquid	mental	throughout
chemicals	flow	materials	rate	views

1. Tears are like water. They are a _____ (not a solid or a gas).

2. The three types of tears are not the same. They _____ in

   purpose and in composition.

3. People usually produce a certain amount of basal tears in a certain

   amount of time: five to ten ounces a day. We produce basal tears at that

   _____ (or speed).

4. When a wind _____ cold air into your eyes, your eyes fill

   with reflex tears.

5. Tears help wash away dust, dirt, sand, or any other _____ that might get into your eyes.

6. When you feel certain emotions, tears may start to _____, like water moving in a river.

7. According to Tom Lutz, people in every culture, at every point _____ history, have cried.

Vocabulary Tip:
Use *throughout* to mean during all of a period of time or in every part of a particular area: *The news spread quickly throughout the community.*

8. People don't all share the same opinions about tears. People hold different _____.

9. Tears are good for your eyes and may be good for your _____ health, too—that is, for your state of mind.

10. There are different substances in the three types of tears. The _____ in emotional tears include a painkiller.

EXPANDING VOCABULARY

Building on the Vocabulary

Studying Collocations: Verbs Used with *View*

The noun **view** has different meanings:

- *View* often means "opinion, belief." When view has this meaning, use it with the verbs *have, hold, share,* and *take: He takes the view that children should be seen and not heard.*

- *View* can also mean "the area someone can see:" You can use *have* with *view* when it has this meaning: *He has a view of the park from his house.*

Complete the following sentences. Make true statements.

1. _____ and I hold similar views on _____.
   (name)

2. From my _____ window, I have a view of _____.
   (room)

Using the Target Vocabulary in New Contexts

A. Complete the sentences with the target words and phrases in the box. There are two extra words.

blew	emotional	liquid	normal
chemicals	flows	materials	notices
differs	go ahead	mental	surface

1. The river _____ to the sea.

2. Only a few people have walked on the _____ of the moon.

3. A strong wind _____ the man's hat off.

4. A good manager _____ when employees make a special effort to do their jobs well.

5. As I listened to him describe the place, I closed my eyes and tried to make a _____ picture of it.

6. It's _____ to feel nervous during a job interview. Everyone does.

7. To build a good house, you need good-quality building _____.

8. _____ and take the last piece of pizza.

9. You can depend on your friends for _____ support in difficult times.

10. Be careful! There are strong _____ in some cleaning products.

> **Vocabulary Tip:**
> The verb *notice* can be used with or without a direct object. Don't use a progressive form of this verb (not "I was noticing her"). *Notice* can also be a noncount noun.

B. Match the beginning and end of each sentence. Write the letters.

_____ 1. Water can take the form of a **liquid**,

_____ 2. I cried **throughout** the movie,

_____ 3. The two companies **differ** in

_____ 4. The unemployment **rate**

a. from beginning to end.

b. fell to 5% in June.

c. a gas, or a solid (ice).

d. how they treat their employees.

C. Write each target word from part B next to its definition.

Target Word	Definition
1. =	be different or not alike
2. =	during all of a period of time
3. =	a substance that can flow and be poured
4. =	the number of times something happens, or the number of examples of something, in a certain time period

DEVELOPING YOUR READING SKILLS

Quoting and Paraphrasing

A. Reread "Tears." Then read the quotations from the text. Choose the correct paraphrase.

1. "While it hasn't been proven, tears may be good not only for our eyes but for our emotional health as well."

   ☐ **a.** No one knows for sure if tears are actually good for our eyes or our emotions.

   ☐ **b.** Tears are good for our eyes and maybe for our emotional health, too.

2. "Emotional tears are the tears we think of most when we use the word *cry*."

   ☐ **a.** The word *cry* generally refers to one kind of tears, emotional tears.

   ☐ **b.** We cry emotional tears when we think of the word *cry*.

3. "Most people are aware of the social rules about when, where, and why it is and isn't acceptable to cry."

   ☐ **a.** Sometimes it's okay to cry, and sometimes it is not, and you have to learn the difference.

   ☐ **b.** Each culture has its rules for when crying is okay, and most members of a culture know its rules.

4. "Some people think it's not just acceptable to cry but actually healthy to let the tears flow."

   ☐ **a.** According to some people, crying is more than just okay—it's good for us.

   ☐ **b.** Crying might not be accepted by some people, but it's bad for you to hold the tears in.

> **Reading Tip:**
> When you reread "Tears," notice *in fact* in line 1. Writers use this phrase to add more information about what was just said, often a surprising detail.

B. Read the questions and the incomplete answers. Complete the answers by copying the exact words the writer used in the text. Use quotation marks (" ") before and after the words you copy.

Writing Tip: Try to answer questions in your own words, but use a quotation when you think the writer's words express an idea in the best way possible.

1. What would happen if we did not have tears in our eyes?

   If we did not have tears in our eyes, _"our eyes would be at risk of_ _infection"_____ .

2. How do tears help us see clearly?

   The holes in the cornea of the eye would make it hard to see, but _____

   _____ .

3. On an average day, how much liquid do our eyes produce just for their own protection?

   Our eyes usually produce basal tears _____

   _____ .

4. Social rules about crying are different for different people. How do they differ?

   The rules are different for adults and children and usually for men and

   women. They also _____

   _____ .

5. What is a possible effect of the painkiller endorphin?

   When endorphin from tears gets into the brain, it might _____

   _____ .

Understanding Major Points

Main Ideas, Major Points, and Supporting Details

There is generally one main idea in a reading passage. The major points in the reading support the main idea, and the details support the major points.

On a piece of paper, write answers to these questions about the major points in the reading. Do not copy sentences from the reading. Use your own words.

1. How do tears help our eyes?
2. When do our eyes produce basal, reflex, and emotional tears?
3. Why do some people believe it is good to cry?

Summarizing

A. Complete the summary of "Tears." Include the answers to the questions below. Try to paraphrase. Use quotation marks as needed.

- What are tears good for?
- Which kinds of tears protect our eyes?
- Which kind of tears do we produce when we cry?
- What do social rules about crying tell us?
- What do some people believe about crying?

The reading "Tears" gives several reasons why tears are good for us.

B. Compare your summary with a partner's. Did you both include the same major points?

CRITICAL THINKING

Discussion

Talk about these questions with a partner.

1. In paragraphs 1 and 8, you see the expression "have a good cry." What is "a good cry" and why is it good? Does this expression refer to basal, reflex, or emotional tears? How do you know?

2. What are the three types of tears? The reading states that they "differ not only in purpose but in composition" (paragraph 3). In this context, *composition* is closest in meaning to:

   a. quality   b. chemistry   c. response

   What difference in the composition of emotional tears does the reading describe? Where do you find this description in the reading?

3. The reading states that tears "help us see the world while at the same time protecting our eyes from it" (paragraph 2). What does this mean? Tell where in the text you find the information to support your answer.

> **Critical Thinking Tip:** Be aware of the writer's **point of view** as you read (what the writer thinks about the topic). Your own opinions may differ from the writer's.

4. According to the reading, "it's normal for men or women to cry at certain times" (paragraph 7). What examples does the writer give? Do you agree with the writer? What examples would you give of "normal" times to cry?

5. In paragraph 7, what example does the writer give of a time when it would *not* be normal or acceptable for an adult to cry? Do you agree with that example? Does your partner agree? How does a person learn the social rules about crying? What does the writer say happens when someone breaks those rules? Do you think that's true? Does your partner agree?

6. a. Working on your own, read the questions in the chart. Check (✓) the situations in which it is okay to cry. Add a situation of your own to the list.

   b. Share your answers with your partner, and ask your partner about the situation you added. Do you and your partner have the same answers? Based on information in paragraph 7, how would you explain why your answers are the same or why they're different?

Is it okay for a person to cry . . .

	It's okay for an adult.	It's okay for a child.
1. at the movies?		
2. when his or her team loses a game?		
3. when something bad happens at work or at school?		
4. when saying good-bye at the airport?		
5. at a religious service for someone who has died?		
6. _____		

7. In the situations in the chart, are there differences between what's acceptable for men and what's acceptable for women? Explain.

WRITING

A. Use the Target Vocabulary: Choose five of the target words or phrases from the chart on page 82. On a piece of paper, use each word or phrase in a sentence and underline it. Find a partner and read each other's sentences.

B. Practice Writing: Choose one of these topics and write a paragraph about it. Then find a partner and read each other's paragraphs.

1. Do you remember crying as a child, or do you remember a recent experience that made you cry? Describe it.

2. Write about one of the opinions you gave when you discussed the situations in question 6 under **Discussion**. Give your reasons for what you believe.

CHAPTER 8

The Power of Touch

A child on his father's lap

LEARNING OUTCOME

❯ Learn about how touch can be good for your health

GETTING READY TO READ

Talk about these questions with a partner.

1. Which of the five senses is most important to you? Number them from 1 (most important) to 5 (least important). Explain the reasons for your choices.

   Hearing ____

   Sight ____

   Smell ____

   Taste ____

   Touch ____

2. Some research shows a relationship between the sense of touch and good health. How do you think touch might be good for children's health? What about the health of adults?

READING

Read to Find Out: What is "the power of touch"?

Look at the picture, words, and definitions next to the reading. Then read without stopping. If you see a new word, try to understand the sentence without it. You will learn the word later.

The Power of Touch

1   Most people today know that babies need to be held. It's through the loving touch of the people who take care of them that babies learn to feel safe in the world. Touch is the first language they understand, and they depend on it for their **physical**, mental, and emotional **development**. What most people don't know is how touch is a **key** to good health for adults, too.

2   A baby's need for touch was not always as well understood as it is today. Back in 1928, a leading psychologist,[1] John B. Watson, wrote that parents should avoid touching their children:

> Never **hug** and kiss them, never let them sit on your lap. If you must, kiss them once on the forehead[2] when they say goodnight. Shake hands with them in the morning. Give them a pat[3] on the head if they have made an extraordinarily[4] good job on a difficult task.

Watson's goal was for parents to **raise** their children to become confident and **independent** adults. We now know that to reach that goal, he should have given the opposite advice.

3   In the 1980s, researchers in the United States started to study the effects of touch on newborn babies. In one study, a group of babies born prematurely[5] received three 15-minute massages in a week. (To give a massage, someone gently **pressed** on the baby's body in a way that helped the baby to relax.) A second group of babies received only the usual medical care for premature babies, which generally included very little touching. The researchers then recorded the babies' weight gains, an important sign of good health in newborns. They found that the babies who had received the massages gained 47 percent more weight than the control group. Over time, similar results in other studies resulted in major changes in how newborns are cared for in U.S. hospitals.

4   Tiffany Field, one of the researchers who worked on that particular study, later had a baby born prematurely. This life-changing experience, and a growing understanding of the **benefits** of touch, led Dr. Field's career in a new direction. In 1992, she founded[6] the Touch Research Institute (the TRI) at the University of Miami School of Medicine, where researchers have done over 100 studies on ways that touch affects

[1] *psychologist* = someone who studies the human mind and how it influences our actions

[2] *forehead*

[3] *a pat* = a friendly act of touching someone with your hand flat

[4] *extraordinarily* = especially great

[5] *born prematurely* = born before the usual, expected time of birth

[6] *founded* = set up (an organization, company, etc. that is expected to last a long time)

health. In further studies on massage, TRI researchers have seen it **reduce** pain and **improve** the health of people with serious medical **conditions** (such as cancer).

5   Massage is not the only kind of touch that's good for people. Studies have shown that when doctors give patients a friendly pat on the back, the patients do better. Hugs from family and friends have health benefits, too. In a study at Carnegie Mellon University, every day for two weeks researchers asked 400 adult volunteers a **set** of questions. They asked about the time the volunteers spent with other people and the number of hugs they got. Then all 400 were exposed to the virus[7] that causes the common cold, after which most of them—78 percent—caught a cold. However, the people who had received more hugs were *less* likely to get sick. When they did get sick, their colds were not as bad.

6   Researchers believe that many of the good effects of touch result from the way it can reduce **stress**. In response to a welcome touch, the human brain experiences an increase in oxytocin (a hormone[8] tied to feelings of love and trust) and a **drop** in cortisol (a stress hormone).

7   Everyone is different in how they feel about hugs, massage, pats on the back, and similar kinds of touch. How comfortable you are with these kinds of touch depends in part on your **culture**. Consider some research done by psychologist Sidney Jourard in the 1960s. He traveled to various countries and studied the conversations of pairs of friends as they sat together in a café. In each place, he watched people for the same amount of time. In England, he saw that friends never touched each other. In the United States, friends touched an average of twice an hour. In France, the picture was very different: friends touched almost every 30 seconds, for an average of 110 times an hour. In Puerto Rico, the number of touches per hour hit 180.

Friends at a café

8   In his research, Jourard was looking at the role of touch in people's social lives. We now know, from further research, that touch has a role in people's health, too, and that it can make a difference for people of all ages.

[7] *were exposed to a virus* = came in contact with a small living thing that makes people sick

[8] *hormone* = a chemical produced in the body that influences its growth, development, and condition

Quick Comprehension Check

A. Read these statements **about the reading**. Circle T (true) or F (false). On the line, write the number of the paragraph with the answer.

1. Touch can be good for the health of both mind and body.   T   F   _____

2. Touch is especially important for babies' good health.   T   F   _____

3. The writer says parents shouldn't hug or kiss their children.   T   F   _____

4. Hugging your friends makes you more likely to catch a cold.   T   F   _____

5. Touch Research Institute scientists study the social effects of touch.   T   F   _____

6. Touch can help people relax.   T   F   _____

B. Work with your class. Share your answers from part A. Go back to the reading to find the reason why a statement is true or false. Correct the false statements.

EXPLORING VOCABULARY

Thinking about the Target Vocabulary

A. Look at the chart with the target vocabulary from "The Power of Touch." Six nouns and two adjectives are missing. Scan the reading to find them, and add them to the correct places in the chart. Use the singular form of any plural noun.

¶	Nouns	Verbs	Adjectives	Other
1				
2		hug		
		raise		
3		press		
4				
		reduce		
		improve		

¶	Nouns	Verbs	Adjectives	Other
5	set			
6				
7	culture			

B. Which words and phrases are new to you? Circle them in the chart. Then find them in the reading. Look at the context. Can you guess the meaning?

Understanding the Target Vocabulary

A. These sentences are **about the reading**. Complete them with the words and phrases in the box.

benefits	culture	drop	independent	reduce
conditions	development	hug	key	stress

1. Babies need the loving touch of their families to help them become strong and healthy in body and mind. A child's _____ depends on that loving touch.

2. Researchers are learning how important touch is for adults, too. It's a _____ to the good health of people of all ages.

3. Psychologist John B. Watson advised parents never to put their arms around their children and hold them to show their love. He said parents shouldn't _____ their children.

4. Watson wanted children to grow up being able to do things for themselves without the help of others. He was afraid that parents' hugs and kisses would keep children from becoming _____.

5. Through her research, Tiffany Field came to understand the many ways that touch helps people. She learned about the _____ of touch for children and adults.

Vocabulary Tip:
Benefit can be a verb as well as a noun. As a verb, it is often followed by *from: Many patients could benefit from the treatment.*

6. Research has shown that massage can help people in pain feel better. It can _____ the pain, making it less strong.

7. Massage can also improve the health of people who have illnesses or health problems of the kind that affect them for a long time or even their entire lives. These _____ include cancer.

8. Researchers say touch can help people worry less about things in their personal lives. It reduces _____ and helps people relax.

9. One benefit of touch is its effect on a certain stress hormone in the human body. It causes a _____ in cortisol, meaning there is less of it.

10. How you feel about handshakes and hugs, or a pat on the arm or the back, depends in part on your _____. It's normal for people from the same large social group to share many of the same ideas and beliefs, including beliefs about touch.

Vocabulary Tip: *Stress* has several meanings, as a noun and a verb. It can also refer to how we pronounce words. See your dictionary for more information.

B. Read each definition and look at the paragraph number. Look back at the reading on pages 91–92 to find the **boldfaced** word to match the definition. Copy it in the chart.

Definition	Paragraph	Target Word
1. related to someone's body (not their mind or emotions)	1	
2. take care of (children) and help them grow	2	
3. push firmly against something	3	
4. make something better	4	
5. a group of similar things that belong together	5	

Vocabulary Tip: The verb *improve* can be transitive (used with a direct object, as in *I want to improve my grades*) or intransitive (without one, as in *The weather is improving*).

EXPANDING ON THE VOCABULARY

Building on the Vocabulary

> ### The Suffix -al
>
> A suffix usually changes a word to another part of speech. You can often tell what part of speech a word is by the form of the word, even if you do not know its meaning.
>
> The suffix -al often changes a noun to an adjective, as in the case of *beneficial, cultural, developmental, emotional, influential,* and *natural.*

Complete the sentence. Use the noun in parentheses or its adjective form.

1. (benefit) Researchers found that massage was _____ for newborn babies.

2. (culture) There are _____ differences in how people view and use touch.

3. (development) As children grow up, they go through different _____ stages.

4. (emotion) Love is a very strong _____.

5. (influence) Tiffany Field is an _____ researcher in her field of study.

6. (nature) Babies want to be held. It's in their _____.

Using the Target Vocabulary in New Contexts

These sentences use the target words in new contexts. Complete them with the words in the box.

condition	improve	physical	reduced
drop	independent	press	set
hugged	key	raised	stress

1. _____ this button to turn on the TV.

2. When he quit smoking, he _____ his risk of certain medical conditions.

3. The managers were worried. They had no explanation for the recent _____ in sales.

Vocabulary Tip:
Drop and *reduction* are synonyms. A drop in something is often a large or sudden reduction.

4. Dad's doctor says he has a serious heart _____ and should see a heart specialist.

5. Are you sleeping well? I know you've been under a lot of _____.

6. I'm taking a course to _____ my Spanish before I go to Mexico.

7. When I said good-bye to my friend at the airport, we _____ each other.

8. As children grow older and learn to do things for themselves, they become more _____.

9. Each culture has its own _____ of values and beliefs.

10. What is the _____ to living a long and healthy life?

11. I was born and _____ in a small town, but I prefer a life in the city.

12. School children in the United States learn about sports and the benefits of exercise in _____ education classes, also called *PE* or *phys ed*.

DEVELOPING YOUR READING SKILLS

Text Features

Uses of Parentheses

Parentheses are punctuation marks that are used when a writer adds information that is useful to the reader but is not key to understanding the main point. If the information were taken out of the sentence, the basic meaning of the sentence would stay the same.

Reason for parentheses	Example
1. A definition	The volunteers in Group A received nicotine gum. (That's chewing gum with nicotine, the drug in tobacco that gives smokers the good feeling they get from smoking.) (page 68)
2. An explanation	In German, for example, *der Mond* (the word for the moon) is masculine but *die Sonne* (the sun) is feminine. (page 26)
3. An example	A placebo is something that seems like a medical treatment (such as a pill or a medical procedure[4]) but that doesn't actually have any *direct* effect on the body. (page 68)
4. An abbreviation	Smith studied engineering at the Massachusetts Institute of Technology (MIT) in the United States, ... (page 134)

Look for these uses of parentheses in "The Power of Touch." For each one, write the paragraph number and complete the notes.

1. To give a definition: In paragraph _____, there's a definition of

   _____.

2. To give an explanation: In paragraph _____, there's an explanation of

   _____.

3. To give an example: In paragraph _____, there's an example of

   _____.

4. To give an abbreviation: In paragraph _____, there's the abbreviation for

   _____.

Understanding Topics and Main Ideas

A. Reread "The Power of Touch." Write the topic of each paragraph.

1. Paragraph 1: _____

2. Paragraph 2: _____

3. Paragraph 3: _____

4. Paragraph 4: _____

5. Paragraph 5: _____

6. Paragraph 6: _____

7. Paragraph 7: _____

8. Paragraph 8: _____

B. What is the main idea of the reading?

_____

_____

Quoting and Paraphrasing

Answer these questions about "The Power of Touch." Try to paraphrase sentences from the reading. If you quote from the reading, use quotation marks around the material you've copied.

1. According to the writer, what do "most people" know today, and what do they not know about touch?

_____

_____

_____

2. What advice did psychologist John B. Watson give parents back in 1928, and why did he give this advice?

_____

_____

_____

3. What was the difference in treatment between the two groups of newborn babies in the study described in paragraph 3?

_____

_____

_____

4. What is the purpose of the TRI?

_____

_____

_____

5. What examples does the reading give of the kinds of touch that can have health benefits?

_____

_____

_____

6. How did psychologist Sidney Jourard study touch, and what did he notice?

_____

_____

_____

> **Reading Tip:**
> When a text describes a scientific study, make sure you understand who did it, why and how they did it, and what they found.

CRITICAL THINKING

Discussion

Talk about these questions in a small group.

1. The writer calls touch "the first language [babies] understand" (paragraph 1). How can touch be a language?

2. What is the goal the reading talks about in paragraph 2? What does the writer mean by saying "to reach that goal, [Watson] should have given the opposite advice"? What would "the opposite advice" say to do? Is the writer stating a fact or expressing an opinion?

3. What did researchers learn from the study described in paragraph 3? What can you infer about the "major changes in how newborns are cared for"—what changed? What information in the paragraph helped you make that inference?

4. According to the study described in paragraph 5, how are hugs good for people? Does this surprise you? Explain why or why not.

5. What is the purpose of paragraph 7? What is the purpose of the entire reading?

WRITING

A. Use the Target Vocabulary: Choose five of the target words or phrases from the chart on pages 93–94. On a piece of paper, use each word or phrase in a sentence and underline it. Find a partner and read each other's sentences.

B. Practice Writing: Choose one of these topics and write a paragraph about it. Then find a partner and read each other's paragraphs.

1. Imagine that you are part of a research team that is re-creating the study by Sidney Jourard that is described in "The Power of Touch." Imagine that you are in a café in your hometown. Describe what you notice. Compare what you've noticed with what you learned from the reading.

2. Return to question 1 under Getting Ready to Read on page 90: *Which of the five senses is most important to you?* Explain how you would answer this question and give your reasons.

Checkpoint

LOOK BACK

A. Think About This

Look back at the *Think About This* question on page 55. Can you answer the health-related questions now?

B. Remember the Readings

What do you want to remember most from the readings in Unit 2? For each chapter, write one sentence about the reading.

Chapter 5: Living to 100 and Beyond

_____

Chapter 6: What Causes the Placebo Effect?

_____

Chapter 7: Tears

_____

Chapter 8: The Power of Touch

_____

REVIEWING VOCABULARY

A. Complete the phrase.

1. Write the adjective *emotional*, *likely*, or *mental*.

   a. the _____ result

   b. an _____ good-bye

   c. _____ health

2. Write the noun *chemistry*, *treatments*, or *views*.

   a. painful _____

   b. normal brain _____

   c. the writer's personal _____

3. Write the adjective *further*, *physical*, or *similar*.

   a. _____ lifestyles

   b. _____ education classes

   c. waiting for _____ developments

B. Complete the sentences with words or phrases from the box. There are two extra words or phrases.

actually	generally	independent	possibly
as well	go ahead	made no difference	recent
break the habit	has nothing to do with	make it	simply

1. Al had an ID that said he was 21, but he was _____ 18.

2. _____ and cry—it's perfectly normal.

3. As a teenager, I looked forward to leaving home and being _____.

4. Sadly, the treatment _____, and the patient got sicker.

5. Our plane leaves in fifteen minutes—will we _____?

6. You can't _____ work eighty hours a week!

7. The new software wasn't the problem—I was. I _____ didn't read the directions!

8. The _____ drop in the temperature has farmers worried about their fruit trees.

9. The average Australian will live a long life, and the average Japanese will _____.

10. *A battery of tests* means "a set of tests," such as medical tests. *Battery* in this phrase _____ the kind of batteries that provide electricity.

EXPANDING VOCABULARY

Transitive and Intransitive Verbs

Some verbs are **transitive**. After a transitive verb, there is a direct object, usually a noun or pronoun. For example, the verb *take* is transitive and needs a direct object: *He took **a pill**. / He took **it**.* (We cannot say *He took.*)

Other verbs are **intransitive**, such as *sleep*. There can be no direct object after *sleep: He slept.* (We cannot say *He slept ~~the baby~~.*)

Some verbs can be used either way—with or without a direct object: *I **drove my car** to the beach* or *I **drove** to the beach.*

Remember that verbs can have more than one meaning, and the meanings of a verb may differ when it's used with and without a direct object, as in these sentences with *drop:*

The baseball player dropped the ball.   (He let it fall.)

The temperature is going to drop tonight.   (It's going to go down.)

A. Underline the verbs in the sentences below. Circle any direct objects after the verbs. Which verbs are transitive, and which are intransitive? Check (✓) your answers.

			Transitive	Intransitive
1.	a.	The sisters <u>hugged</u> when they met.	☐	☑
	b.	I <u>hugged</u> (my son.)	☑	☐
2.	a.	Please don't chew with your mouth open.	☐	☐
	b.	Chew your food well.	☐	☐
3.	a.	They treat many patients with this condition.	☐	☐
	b.	Don't treat me like a child.	☐	☐
4.	a.	Traffic is flowing well.	☐	☐
	b.	Rivers flow to the sea.	☐	☐
5.	a.	Did you notice any changes?	☐	☐
	b.	Mark was silent, but the others didn't notice.	☐	☐
6.	a.	Fill in your name and address on the form.	☐	☐
	b.	Ms. Green is out sick, so I'm filling in.	☐	☐

B. On a piece of paper, write sentences with at least six of the verbs targeted in Unit 2. Mark each verb *T* for transitive or *I* for intransitive.

A PUZZLE

There are 12 target words from Unit 2 in this puzzle. The words go across (→) and down (↓). Find the words and circle them. Then use them to complete the sentences below.

A	X	M	H	K	P	W	D	K	Q
F	R	E	D	U	C	E	E	E	K
F	J	C	Z	V	G	Q	V	Y	J
E	W	N	M	W	T	T	E	Y	M
C	H	E	M	I	C	A	L	S	A
T	H	R	O	U	G	H	O	U	T
X	S	T	R	E	S	S	P	R	E
P	R	O	C	E	S	S	M	F	R
R	E	S	P	O	N	S	E	A	I
J	X	S	T	A	F	F	N	C	A
S	M	N	H	P	V	X	T	E	L

Across

1. The baby slept _____ the trip.

2. It's an expensive project—what can we do to _____ the cost?

3. Everyone's under a lot of _____ at work right now.

4. The hospital doesn't have enough _____, so they're hiring more people.

5. We hope the patient will have a good _____ to the new treatment.

6. Raising a child is a long _____.

7. Oxytocin is a _____ in the brain that affects how we feel.

Down

1. What _____ is the jacket made of?

2. A child psychologist studies children's mental and emotional _____.

3. The wedding will be indoors, so rain won't _____ it.

4. Tears fill in holes in the _____ of the eye.

5. What is the _____ to living a happy life?

BUILDING DICTIONARY SKILLS

Understanding Codes in the Dictionary

Dictionaries use **codes** to give grammatical information about words. The codes shown here come from the *Longman Dictionary of American English*:

[C] = count noun (a noun that generally has both a singular and plural form: *a book / two books, one child / many children*)

[U] = uncountable or noncount noun (one form only: *bread, furniture*)

[T] = transitive verb (followed by a direct object: *buy something, love someone*)

[I] = intransitive verb (does not take a direct object: *He's sleeping. Don't fall!*)

A. Circle the codes in this dictionary entry for the noun *benefit*, and read the definitions and examples.

> **ben·e·fit¹** /ˈbenəfɪt / *n* **1** [C] the money or other advantages that you get from something such as insurance or the government, or as part of your job: *The company provides medical benefits.* | *Social Security benefits.* **2** [C,U] an advantage, improvement, or help that you get from something: *What are the benefits of contact lenses?* | *The new credit cards will be of great benefit to our customers.* **3** [C] a performance, concert, etc. that is done in order to make money for a charity. **4 give someone the benefit of the doubt** to believe or trust someone, even though it is possible that s/he is lying or is wrong: *His story was hard to believe, but I gave him the benefit of the doubt.*

B. How can you use the noun *benefit?* Check (✓) your answers.

☐ in the singular ☐ in the plural ☐ as a noncount noun

C. Look up these nouns in your dictionary. Check (✓) the way or ways you can use each one.

1. increase ☐ in the singular ☐ in the plural ☐ as a noncount noun

2. condition ☐ in the singular ☐ in the plural ☐ as a noncount noun

3. limit ☐ in the singular ☐ in the plural ☐ as a noncount noun

4. liquid ☐ in the singular ☐ in the plural ☐ as a noncount noun

D. Circle the codes in this dictionary entry for the verb *improve*, and read the definitions and examples.

> **im·prove** /ɪmˈpruːv / *v* [I,T] to become better, or to make something better: *Do some exercises to improve your muscle strength.* | *Your math skills have improved.*

E. How can you use the verb *improve?* Check (✓) your answers.

☐ with a direct object following the verb ☐ with no direct object

F. Look up these verbs in your dictionary. Check (✓) the way or ways you can use each one.

1. blow   ☐ with a direct object following the verb   ☐ with no direct object

2. prove   ☐ with a direct object following the verb   ☐ with no direct object

3. differ   ☐ with a direct object following the verb   ☐ with no direct object

4. trick   ☐ with a direct object following the verb   ☐ with no direct object

Vocabulary Self-Test 1

Circle the letter of the word or phrase that best completes each sentence.

1. Consumers are people who buy _____ and services.
   a. liquids   b. goods   c. advertising   d. treatment

2. What _____ him to work so hard?
   a. earned   b. gained   c. dropped   d. drove

3. The boy's parents let him play outside _____ he promises to stay close to home.
   a. as long as   b. in return   c. in charge of   d. besides

4. It was an accident—I didn't _____ to do it.
   a. believe in   b. prove   c. mean   d. appear

5. I couldn't hear the message clearly, but it _____ the weather.
   a. kept up with   b. had something to do with   c. made a living at   d. turned something into

6. Bob wants to drink less soda, but it's hard to _____.
   a. break the habit   b. sign up   c. go ahead   d. make a difference

7. Some jobs may not sound like fun, but they _____ are.
   a. beyond   b. quite   c. as well   d. actually

8. I believe that all children have the _____ to a good education.
   a. volunteer   b. right   c. lifestyle   d. community

9. If we want to learn the game, Robin is _____ to teach us.
   a. normal   b. uncertain   c. willing   d. similar

10. We wanted to go to the party, but we couldn't _____.
    a. make it   b. reduce it   c. set up   d. deal with

11. I know energy from the sun can be turned into electricity, but how? I don't understand the _____.
    a. service   b. set   c. process   d. staff

12. I sent her a text message, and now I'm waiting for her _____.

    a. chemistry   b. culture   c. response   d. surface

13. Some people leave work early to _____ the heavy traffic.

    a. design   b. avoid   c. notice   d. press

14. Dina wants to buy a car, but she has no _____ car in mind.

    a. particular   b. mental   c. key   d. economic

15. It's not _____ a matter of money—there are other reasons, too.

    a. in return   b. generally   c. within   d. simply

16. Do you agree with Roberto's _____ of the problem?

    a. risk   b. material   c. role   d. view

17. Their stores first appeared in the bigger cities but soon _____ throughout the country.

    a. announced   b. raised   c. spread   d. limited

18. The school _____ children with a good hot lunch.

    a. hires   b. provides   c. blows   d. increases

19. If Gail doesn't study, she's _____ to fail the test.

    a. likely   b. developing   c. financial   d. emotional

20. How do you think he'll _____ when he hears the news?

    a. react   b. trick   c. treat   d. flow

21. All professionals should pay attention to new research and

    _____ in their fields.

    a. security   b. qualities   c. hugs   d. developments

22. Police cars are _____ the road, so we'll have to turn around.

    a. blocking   b. employing   c. getting rid of   d. coming up with

23. There are benefits to having a pet _____ simply having fun.

    a. possibly   b. besides   c. throughout   d. forever

24. She's been sick, but I'm happy to report she's _____.

    a. improving   b. affecting   c. differing   d. investing

25. Pay for their employees starts at a _____ of $15.00 an hour.

    a. staff   b. stress   c. condition   d. rate

See the Vocabulary Self-Test Answer Key on page 271.

EXPLORING TECHNOLOGY

THINK ABOUT THIS

How has technology changed the world?

Technology includes all kinds of tools and machines, things as simple as a spoon or as complex as the international space station. It also includes skills, from using fire to making a film. Write examples of important technology in the chart.

Technology That Has Changed the World

CHAPTER 9

A History of Telling Time

Sand falling through an hourglass

LEARNING OUTCOME

> Learn what people throughout history have done to tell time

GETTING READY TO READ

Talk about these questions with your class.

1. How many people in the class wear a watch? What other ways are there to find out the time?

2. How many times a day do you look to see what time it is? What is the average for the class?

   a. 0–5   b. 5–10   c. more than 10

3. Do you agree with either of these ideas? Explain.

   a. Life without clocks would be beautiful.

   b. Life without clocks would be terrible.

READING

Read to Find Out: What has *not* changed in the way that people measure time?

Look at the pictures, words, and definitions next to the reading. Then read without stopping. If you see a new word, try to understand the sentence without it. You will learn the word later.

A History of Telling Time

1 No one knows when people first thought about **measuring** time. We do know that they measured it by the sun, moon, and stars, and that they first divided time into months, seasons, and years. Later, they began dividing the day into parts, like hours and minutes, and they developed simple **technology** to help them do this. Today, we have much more **advanced** ways to tell time, and we can measure even tiny parts of a second. A great many things have changed in how people tell time—but not everything.

2 The Sumerians, who lived in the area of present-day Iraq, were the first to divide the day into parts. Then, five or six thousand years ago, people in North Africa and the Middle East developed ways to tell the time of day. They needed some kind of clock because by then they had organized religious and social activities to **attend**. That meant people needed to plan their days and **set** times for these events.

3 Among the first clocks were Egyptian obelisks.[1] The Egyptians used the movement of an obelisk's **shadow** to divide the day into morning and afternoon. Later, they placed stones on the ground around the obelisk to mark **equal** periods of time during the day, the way that numbers do on the face of a clock. That worked **fairly** well, but people could not carry obelisks with them. They needed something **portable**. So the Egyptians invented a kind of sundial[2] that is now called a shadow clock. It came into use about 3,500 years ago, around 1500 BCE.[3]

4 There were many types of sundials in Egypt and in other areas around the Mediterranean Sea. All of them, of course, depended on the sun, which was no help in telling time at night. Among the first clocks that did not depend on the sun were water clocks. There were various types of these, too. Some were designed so that drops of water would fall at a constant rate (an unchanging speed) from a tiny hole in the bottom of a container. Others were designed to have a container slowly fill with water, again at a constant rate. It took a certain amount of time for the container to fill up or empty out. However, the flow of water was hard to control, so these clocks were not very **accurate**, and people still did not have a clock they could put in their pocket. Hourglasses filled with sand had similar problems.

[1] *an obelisk*

[2] *one kind of sundial*

[3] *BCE* = Before the Common Era (also written *BC*, "before Christ")

5   In the early 1300s, the first mechanical clocks—machines that measured and told the time—appeared in public buildings in Italy. Around 1500, a German inventor, Peter Henlein, invented a mechanical clock that was powered by a spring.[4] Now clocks were getting smaller and easier to carry, but they still were not very accurate. Then in 1656, the Dutch scientist Christiaan Huygens invented a clock that was a big step forward. This was the first pendulum clock.[5] A pendulum moves from side to side, again and again, at a constant rate. Counting the movements of a pendulum was a better way to keep time. Huygens's first pendulum clock was accurate to within one minute a day.

6   Developments in clock technology continued as the **demand** for clocks increased. Clocks were needed for factories, banking, communications, and **transportation**. Today, much of **modern** life happens at high speed and depends on having the **exact** time. We must also have international agreement on what the exact time is.

7   Now we have atomic clocks, the best of which are accurate to about one-tenth of a nanosecond[6] a day. But even with these **high-tech** clocks, we still measure a year by the time it takes the earth to go around the sun, just as people did long, long ago.

8   We say that it takes the earth 365 days for a trip around the sun, but that is not exactly true. A year is actually a little longer—365.242 days (or 365 days and almost six hours). So we generally add a day, February 29, every fourth year, and we call those years *leap years*. However, this creates another problem. The extra hours in four years actually add up to less than one day, so adding a day every fourth year would give us too many days. So when a year ends in –00 (like 1800, 1900, or 2000, for example), we don't always make it a leap year. We do it only when we can evenly divide the year by 400, as in 1600 and 2000. Remember that when you set your watch for the year 2100!

[4] *two springs*

[5] *A grandfather clock is an example of a pendulum clock.*

[6] *a nanosecond =* 1/1,000,000,000 (one-billionth) of a second

Quick Comprehension Check

A. Read these statements **about the reading**. Circle T (true) or F (false). On the line, write the number of the paragraph with the answer.

1. People first measured time by the sun, moon, and stars.   T   F   _____

2. We no longer use the sun in measuring time.   T   F   _____

3. People invented ways to tell time so they would know when to meet.   T   F   _____

4. People didn't have very accurate clocks until about 350 years ago.   T   F   _____

5. Knowing the exact time is more important today than it was long ago.   T   F   _____

6. The earth takes exactly 365 days to circle the sun.   T   F   _____

B. Work with your class. Share your answers from part A. Go back to the reading to find the reason why a statement is true or false. Correct the false statements.

EXPLORING VOCABULARY

Thinking about the Target Vocabulary

A. Look at the chart with the target vocabulary from "A History of Telling Time." Four nouns and five adjectives are missing. Scan the reading to find them, and add them to the correct places in the chart. Use the singular form of any plural noun.

¶	Nouns	Verbs	Adjectives	Other
1		measure		
2		attend		
		set		
3				
				fairly
4			accurate	
6				
7			high-tech	

> **Vocabulary Tip:**
> *Measuring* in paragraph 1 is a **gerund**. A gerund is the *-ing* form of a verb, but it acts like a noun.

B. Which words are new to you? Circle them in the chart. Then find them in the reading. Look at the context. Can you guess the meaning?

Understanding the Target Vocabulary

A. These sentences are **about the reading**. Complete them with the words in the box.

advanced	fairly	set	technology
demand	modern	shadow	transportation
exact	rate		

1. Thousands of years ago, people began developing _____

   for telling time. That is, they developed tools and skills for this

   purpose.

2. The first ways to tell time that people invented were simple

   compared to the ways we use today. Today we have much more

   _____ technology.

3. Six thousand years ago, when people in North Africa and the

   Middle East began to organize religious and social activities, they

   needed to agree on when these events would happen. They had to

   _____ times to come together for these events.

4. The Egyptians were the first to tell time by the movement of an obelisk's

   _____ (a darker area made by blocking sunlight).

5. Using an obelisk to tell time worked _____ well. It wasn't

   great, but it was better than nothing.

6. The need for clocks increased in part because more and more people

   were traveling and sending goods from one place to another. Advances

   in _____ meant that it became more important to know the

   correct time.

7. A sundial will give you a general idea of the time, but today's high-tech

   clocks can tell you the _____ time.

8. The reading says that " _____ life" is fast-moving. This

   phrase refers to the way people live now or have lived in recent times.

Vocabulary Tip:
Technology can also mean "advanced machines and ways of doing things based on science and the use of computers."

114   UNIT 3

B. These sentences are also **about the reading**. What is the meaning of each **boldfaced** word? Circle a, b, or c.

1. We use clocks to **measure** time. *Measure something* means

   a. use and enjoy it.   b. find out the size   c. notice it.
                              or amount of it.

2. If people want to **attend** an event, they have to know what time to be there. *Attend an event* means to

   a. sign up for it.   b. be present for it.   c. organize it.

3. The stones on the ground around an obelisk marked **equal** periods of time. *Equal* means .

   a. daylight.   b. short.   c. the same.

4. Obelisks were not **portable**. *Portable* means

   a. able to be carried.   b. nice to look at.   c. of high quality.

5. Water clocks and hourglasses were not very **accurate**. We call a clock *accurate* when it

   a. costs very little.   b. tells time   c. can be carried
                               correctly.   easily.

6. The **demand** for accurate clocks increased with advances in communications, banking, and transportation. *Demand* means

   a. need.   b. limit.   c. risk.

7. Today we have **high-tech** clocks, like atomic clocks. *High-tech* means

   a. fairly accurate.   b. beautifully   c. using advanced
                              designed.   technology.

EXPANDING VOCABULARY

Building on the Vocabulary

Word Grammar: Using *Port* to Form Words

The **root** of the words *portable* and *transportation* is *port*. It comes from a Latin word meaning "carry." Something that is portable is something you can carry. The verb form is *transport*: *We transported the computers by truck.*

Complete the sentences. Use your own ideas.

1. The first _____ were not portable, but now people can buy

   portable ones.

2. Modern transportation includes _____, _____, and

   _____.

3. In my country, businesses often transport goods by _____.

Using the Target Vocabulary in New Contexts

A. Complete the sentences with the target words in the box. There is one extra word.

advanced	exact	measuring	set
demand	fairly	modern	technologies

1. You won't believe all the things his new phone can do. It is very

   _____.

2. Her Spanish isn't perfect, but she speaks it _____ well.

3. The course is on _____ Chinese history, covering the

   last 75 years.

4. Have you _____ a date for your wedding?

5. Hannah is _____ the flour for a cake she's making. She needs

   2½ cups.

6. Scientists have found that chocolate contains more than 300 chemicals. I

   don't know the _____ number.

7. Some people are slow to accept new _____. They would

   rather continue using the tools that they're used to.

> **Vocabulary Tip:**
> The adjective *advanced* is related to *advance*, which can be a noun (*advances in technology*) or a verb (*trying to advance our understanding of the placebo effect*).

> **Vocabulary Tip:**
> *Technology* is usually a noncount noun. When it is used in the plural, it means "types of technology."

B. Complete the sentences with the words in the box. There are two extra words.

accurate	demand	high-tech	set
attend	equal	modern	shadows

1. _____ grow longer late in the day as the sun gets lower in

   the sky.

2. I do the same work he does, so we should get _____ pay.

   Instead he earns more than I do.

3. A pencil is not a _____ tool. It's a very simple one.

4. He gave the police an _____ report of the accident.

5. The law says children must _____ school until a certain age.

   In most U.S. states, they can't quit school until the age of 16.

6. The price of a product or service is likely to go up if the

   _____ increases but the supply does not.

DEVELOPING YOUR READING SKILLS

Text Organization

A. How is the reading "A History of Telling Time" organized? Check (✓) your answer.

☐ 1. The writer compares and contrasts ways that different cultures measure time.

☐ 2. The writer describes developments in measuring time in chronological order.

☐ 3. The writer presents arguments for and against the idea of measuring time.

> **Vocabulary Tip:** *In chronological order* means in time order, starting with the earliest event.

B. Find the information on these topics in the reading. Number them in chronological order from 1 (the earliest development) to 8 (the most recent).

_____ a. Countries around the world had to agree on the exact time.

_____ b. People measured time by the sun, moon, and stars.

_____ c. Peter Henlein invented a spring-powered clock.

_____ d. The Egyptian shadow clock, the first portable clock, was invented.

_____ e. People used hourglasses.

_____ f. Christiaan Huygens invented a pendulum clock.

_____ g. The first mechanical clocks appeared in public buildings in Italy.

_____ h. The Egyptians built obelisks to help them tell time.

Scanning

Read these statements about the reading. Scan the reading for the information you need to complete them.

1. People in _____ and _____ were the first to develop

   ways to tell the time of day.

2. People started needing clocks and setting times to meet after they

   developed _____ and _____ .

3. Obelisks and _____ depended on the sun.

4. A _____ measured time by filling up a container with water, or

   emptying one out, at a constant rate.

5. The first really accurate clock was a _____ clock, invented in

   the year _____ .

6. The best atomic clocks are accurate to _____ .

7. It takes _____ days and _____ hours for the earth

   to circle the sun.

8. A year with 366 days is called a _____ .

Understanding Reference Words

What do the **boldfaced** reference words mean in these sentences? Look
back at the reading. Write your answers on the lines.

1. Paragraph 2: **They** needed some kind of clock . . . _____

   _____

2. Paragraph 2: . . . and set times for **these** events. _____

   _____

3. Paragraph 4: All of **them**, of course, depended . . . _____

   _____

4. Paragraph 8: However, **this** creates another problem. _____

   _____

5. Paragraph 8: We do **it** only when . . . _____

   _____

> **Reading Tip:**
> Remember: A
> reference word
> usually refers
> the reader back
> to someone
> or something
> already named.

CRITICAL THINKING

Discussion

Talk about these questions in a small group.

1. The reading describes a series of advances, or improvements, in time-telling technology. With each new kind of technology, people were trying to deal with a problem. Complete the chart with information about the limitations of each technology and how people tried to deal with those problems.

Vocabulary Tip: A **solution** to a problem is a way of dealing with the situation to make the problem go away.

Technology	Problem	Solution
The obelisk	not portable	the sundial
The sundial		
The water clock, the hourglass		
The spring-powered mechanical clock		
The pendulum clock		

2. The reading states, "Much of modern life happens at high speed and depends on having the exact time" (paragraph 6). Does the reading give details to support this statement? What examples can you think of to support it?

3. In paragraph 8, the reading states, "However, this creates another problem." What was the first problem? What was the solution to it? What was the new problem? How has that problem been solved?

Critical Thinking Tip: When a writer introduces a problem, read to find out what solution, or solutions, the writer presents.

4. When is it important to be on time? How important is it? If a friend is supposed to meet you, but he or she is late, how long are you likely to wait?

5. Although we need international agreement on what time it is, not everyone marks time by the same calendar. What examples can you give of calendars used by various cultures? What do you know about each one?

WRITING

A. Use the Target Vocabulary: Choose five of the target words or phrases from the chart on page 113. On a piece of paper, use each word or phrase in a sentence and underline it. Find a partner and read each other's sentences.

B. Practice Writing: Choose one of these topics and write a paragraph about it. Then find a partner and read each other's paragraphs.

> **Writing Tip:**
> When you write an opinion paragraph, explain the reasons for your opinion.

1. There are many popular sayings about time in English— for example, "Time is money" and "Time flies when you're having fun." Give your opinion of one of these sayings, or explain a saying from your first language that refers to time.

2. Write about question 4 from **Discussion**: When is it important to be on time? How important is it? If a friend is supposed to meet you, but he or she is late, how long are you likely to wait?

The Screen vs. the Printed Page

LEARNING OUTCOME

❯ Learn about how technology can affect reading and learning

Readers have choices in technology.

GETTING READY TO READ

Talk about these questions with your class.

1. When do you read on a screen? List the kinds of technology you use and the kinds of things you read on a screen (materials for school, text messages, etc.).

2. When do you read on a printed page? List the types of printed materials you read (books, newspapers, etc.) and the kinds of things you read in them (materials for school, news reports, etc.).

3. Sometimes you can choose how to read something—on a screen or on a printed page. When you have a choice, what do you choose? Why?

READING

Read to Find Out: How does reading a text on a screen compare with reading it on paper?

Look at the words and definitions next to the reading. Then read without stopping. If you see a new word, try to understand the sentence without it. You will learn the word later.

The Screen vs. the Printed Page

1   We do a lot of reading on screens these days: on computers, smartphones, and other kinds of **electronic** devices.[1] Is reading on a screen a different experience from reading on a printed page? Most people would say yes, but is it different in a way that matters? **In particular**, are there differences for someone who's reading not just for fun but to learn? Most college students today, **at least** in the United States, are reading some if not all of their course materials on a screen because electronic **resources** have begun to **replace** printed texts. So these students need to know: Is one kind of reading better than the other when it comes to[2] understanding and remembering what you read?

2   Since the 1980s, over a hundred studies have been **carried out** to see if the technology you use changes how you read. Scientists have tried to find whether the brain **responds** differently to onscreen text than to words on paper. **So far**, the research has had mixed results. However, people generally seem to do a little better when they read a text—especially a long one—on a printed page rather than on a screen. That is, they do a little better on tests of how well they have understood and can remember what they read.

3   One reason for this may be the physical properties[3] of books. When you open a book, you see a page on the left and a page on the right. The four corners on each page give you a sense of where you are as you read. It's also easy to see where you're going because at all times, you can see how long the book is and where you are in it. That helps you make a mental map of the text. Every piece of information in the book has its home address, so to speak,[4] and when readers want to return to a particular piece of information, they often remember where in the book it appeared.

4   With an electronic text, **on the other hand**, you can't see the entire text, and you can't make the same kind of mental map. You can use the search function[5] to find a particular phrase, but it's hard to see any **section** of the text in the context of the whole. This may help explain why people reading electronic texts have to use more mental energy, get tired more quickly, and don't remember as much.

[1] *an electronic device* = a hand-held piece of computerized equipment, like a tablet

[2] *when it comes to* = when you are talking about, when you are dealing with

[3] *physical properties* = qualities, features, or characteristics you can see and touch

[4] *so to speak* = used to show you're using words differently from their usual meaning

[5] *search function* = a computer program tool to help you quickly find a word, number, etc.

5   There also seems to be a difference in the attitude[6] that readers bring to reading on a screen. Without knowing it, many people seem not to **take it** as **seriously** as reading on paper. They spend more time scanning rather than reading, and they are more likely to read a text only once. They're also more likely to get distracted.[7] They're less likely to set goals for their reading and less likely to reread the hard parts. These **behaviors** won't help readers understand or remember what they've read.

6   Many students seem to know without being told that reading a printed page gives them something that reading on a screen does not. Studies have shown that many students print out electronic texts when they really need to understand them well. This **practice** may change as technology improves. The experience of reading on a screen may become less tiring, and it may become easier for students to mark up an electronic text the way they mark up a printed page.

7   However, you don't need to wait for technology to improve. You can go ahead and change the things that are within your control—your attitudes and behaviors. Start by giving onscreen text the attention it **deserves** if you are reading to learn. To better understand and remember what you read:

- Plan to reread the text, especially the difficult parts.
- Avoid getting distracted while you're reading, and don't multitask (do more than one thing at the same time).
- As you read, ask yourself questions about what you're learning.
- Take notes while you read and after you finish.

These are tips that apply to any kind of reading—on paper as well as on a screen—**whenever** you're reading to learn.

[6] *attitude* = the opinions and feelings someone usually has about something

[7] *get distracted* = stop paying attention to what you're doing because you notice something else

Quick Comprehension Check

A. Read these statements **about the reading**. Circle T (true) or F (false). On the line, write the number of the paragraph with the answer.

1. Scientists haven't yet studied how different technologies affect reading.   T   F   _____

2. Many materials for U.S. college courses are electronic texts.   T   F   _____

3. People seem to understand and remember electronic texts better.   T   F   _____

4. People seem to be more serious about reading on a screen.   T   F   _____

5. The reading contains advice for reading electronic texts. T F ____

6. The reading advises students to print out all electronic texts. T F ____

B. Work with your class. Share your answers from part A. Go back to the reading to find the reason why a statement is true or false. Correct the false statements.

EXPLORING VOCABULARY

Thinking about the Target Vocabulary

A. Look at the chart with the target vocabulary from "The Screen vs. the Printed Page." Four nouns and four verbs are missing. Scan the reading to find them, and add them to the correct places in the chart. Use the singular form of any plural noun. Use the base form of each verb.

¶	Nouns	Verbs	Adjectives	Other
1			electronic	
				in particular
				at least
2				
				so far
4				on the other hand
5				take (something) seriously
6				
7				
				whenever

B. Which words and phrases are new to you? Circle them in the chart. Then find them in the reading. Look at the context. Can you guess the meaning?

Understanding the Target Vocabulary

A. These sentences are **about the reading**. What is the meaning of each **boldfaced** word or phrase? Circle a, b, or c.

1. The writer of "The Screen vs. the Printed Page" discusses one type of reading **in particular**, reading to learn. *In particular* means

   a. simply.   b. especially.   c. possibly.

2. **So far**, studies on the effects of technology on how we read have had mixed results. *So far* means

   a. in return.   b. as well.   c. until now.

3. The reading describes certain **behaviors** that won't help readers understand or remember what they've read onscreen, such as reading a text only once. A behavior is something that a person

   a. believes.   b. does.   c. has.

4. Many students are in the habit of printing out texts to read rather than just reading them on a screen, but this **practice** may change as technology improves. A practice is something that people

   a. do repeatedly.   b. announce.   c. should avoid.

5. When someone has to read an educational text on a screen, the writer advises giving that text "the attention it **deserves**." If a text deserves attention, it's

   a. important.   b. accurate.   c. uncertain.

> **Vocabulary Tip:** When a person deserves something, the person has earned it by his or her behavior (good or bad): *Their employees deserve better working conditions.*

B. These sentences are also **about the reading**. Complete them with the words and phrases in the box.

at least	electronic	replaced	respond	take it less seriously
carry it out	on the other hand	resources	section	whenever

1. Computers have screens, and so do smartphones and other types of

   _____ devices (all of which operate through the use of a

   computer system).

2. In paragraph 1, the writer wrote "Most college students today" but then

   wanted to correct that phrase, so the writer added "_____

   in the United States" to make the phrase more specific, limiting "most

   college students" to just most *U.S.* college students.

> **Vocabulary Tip:** *Electronic* is often shortened to *e-* and used as a prefix for a noun, as in *email* or *e-commerce* (buying and selling using the Internet).

3. College students have traditionally used printed textbooks, but today, they also have other types of _____ they can use to get information, such as websites and films.

Vocabulary Tip: The reading discusses educational resources. *Resources* is also used in these phrases: *natural resources*, *human resources*, and *financial resources*. See your dictionary for further information.

4. When students use electronic resources instead of printed ones, you can say that the electronic resources have taken the place of—or _____—the printed ones.

5. To find the answer to a question—such as "Is the technology we use affecting how we read?" —researchers often plan and organize a study and then _____.

6. When you see words on paper or on a screen, your brain will _____ to those words, but because of differences in the technologies, your brain's response might not be the same in each case.

7. When you read a book, it's easy to see where you are in the book. _____, when you read an electronic text, it's not so easy.

Vocabulary Tip: Use *on the other hand* to give a second fact or opinion that should be considered as well as the one you have just given.

8. When you are reading a part of a book, it's easy to see the relationship between that part and the whole text. You can see where that part is in the book and how big a part it is. With an electronic text, it's not so easy to see how the _____ you're reading relates to the whole.

9. Researchers have found that students may have a different way of thinking about the reading they do on a screen (compared with the attitude they bring to reading a textbook). Students seem to be a little more relaxed about it. In other words, they _____.

10. The advice the writer gives students for when they do onscreen reading is also good advice for reading in general—that is, at any time, or _____ , students are reading materials for their courses.

EXPANDING VOCABULARY

Building on the Vocabulary

Word Grammar: *Behavior*, *Practice*, and *Habit*

The nouns *behavior*, *practice*, and *habit* all refer to things people do.

- *Behavior* is the most general of the three nouns. It refers to things that a person or animal does.

  The baby-sitter was upset about the children's bad behavior.

  Someone who gets time off for good behavior gets out of prison sooner.

  Misbehavior is behavior that's bad or wrong.

- *Practice*, as used in the reading, refers to something that a person or group does often, especially a chosen way of doing something or a social or religious custom.

  The practice of raising fish for food is called aquaculture.

  Over a long period of time, a common practice can become a custom or a tradition.

- *Habit* refers to something that you do regularly or usually, often without thinking about it because you have done it so many times before. People often judge habits as good or bad.

  It's good to get into the habit of regular exercise.

  Dad's in the habit of salting his food before he even tastes it.

Complete the following sentences. Write *behavior, misbehavior, practice,* or *habit.*

1. Tom wants to break the _____ of eating fast food for lunch

   every day.

2. The parents were pleased with their children's good _____

   during the trip.

3. The new law is designed to end the _____ of paying women less

   than men.

4. Children don't always behave well in class, so teachers-in-training must

   learn how to respond to their _____.

Using the Target Vocabulary in New Contexts

A. Complete the sentences with the target words and phrases in the box. There is one extra word.

at least	in particular	respond	take it seriously
deserves	on the other hand	so far	whenever
electronic	resource		

1. The team is designing a new ad and has come up with several ideas for it _____, but they're still working on more.

2. Today's _____ watches do more than just tell you what time it is.

3. My grade for the course depends on the final exam, so I need to _____.

4. The change would bring certain benefits, but _____, it would have certain costs, so we need to consider both.

5. Your idea _____ serious consideration, and I promise to think about it.

6. Spring is a wonderful season to visit that region, the month of May _____.

7. There's no major difference between the two products, _____ as far as I know.

8. Try using this website for your research—it's an excellent _____.

9. _____ someone invests money, they want to know the rate of return on their investment—that is, how much they can hope to gain over a particular amount of time.

B. Match the beginning and end of each sentence. Write the letters.

_____ 1. We have a plan, and now we just need to

_____ 2. My computer was old, so I bought a new one to

_____ 3. First-class passengers on a plane sit in

_____ 4. I can't control their behavior; I can only control how I

a. **respond** to it.

b. **replace** it.

c. **carry** it **out**.

d. the front **section** of it.

C. Write each target word or phrase from part B next to its definition.

Target Word or Phrase		Definition
1.	=	put something new in place of (another thing)
2.	=	one of the parts that something is divided into
3.	=	do something in reaction to what has been said or done
4.	=	do something that needs planning and organizing

DEVELOPING YOUR READING SKILLS

Text Organization

How is the reading "The Screen vs. the Printed Page" organized? Check (✓) your answer.

☐ 1. The writer describes developments in reading technology in chronological order.

☐ 2. The writer reports on research findings and then gives advice based on them.

☐ 3. The writer presents arguments for and against students reading texts on a screen.

> **Reading Tip:**
> Notice how a text is organized. It can help you understand the main idea and the writer's purpose.

Supporting Details

Write two statements below with details that support each of the major points below. Use your own words whenever possible.

1. Researchers have been studying reading on a screen vs. reading on the printed page.

   They have done more than 100 studies since the 1980s.

   The results of the research have been mixed, but the printed page seems

   to make it a little easier to understand and remember what you read.

2. The physical properties of books might have something to do with making printed texts a little easier to understand and remember.

   _____

   _____

   _____

3. People seem to behave differently when they read electronic texts compared with printed texts.

   _____

   _____

   _____

4. There are things students can do to improve how well they understand and remember electronic texts.

   _____

   _____

   _____

Summarizing

A. Complete the summary of "The Screen vs. the Printed Page." Include the answers to the questions below. Try to paraphrase. Use quotation marks as needed.

   What have researchers found, in general?

   What might be one reason for the difference?

   What difference in attitude have researchers noticed?

   What reading tips does the writer offer?

> According to "The Screen vs. the Printed Page,"
> researchers have been studying whether people read,
> understand, and remember information in the same way
> when the text is on a screen instead of a printed page.

B. Compare your summary with a partner's. Do your summaries include the same reading tips?

CRITICAL THINKING

Discussion

Talk about these questions in a small group.

1. What is the writer's purpose in writing "The Screen vs. the Printed Page"?

2. The writer states that "most people" would say that reading on a screen is "a different experience from reading on a printed page" (paragraph 1). Is it different for you? If so, how is it different? Consider the answers you gave to the questions on page 121 about the types of materials you read using electronic devices and the types you read in books or other printed materials.

3. Have the results of all the studies described in paragraph 2 been clear and consistent? That is, have they been the same every time? How do you know? Does the writer expect that future studies will continue to show similar results? How do you know?

4. Check (✓) your answer: In paragraph 3, the writer compares the text in a book to

    ☐ **a.** an electronic text.

    ☐ **b.** a room in a house.

    ☐ **c.** an area you travel across.

    How do you know? For what purpose does the writer make this comparison?

> **Critical Thinking Tip:** The purpose of a comparison may be to help the reader by showing how something new is similar to something familiar and well understood.

5. In paragraph 5, what attitude towards reading onscreen text does the writer describe? According to the writer, what problem behaviors does this attitude lead to? In your opinion, why would a reader be more likely to get distracted while reading on a screen? List as many reasons as you can, based on your own experience.

6. The reading says that as technology improves, "it may become easier for students to mark up an electronic text the way they mark up a printed page" (paragraph 6). What is the purpose of marking up a text? In what ways can someone mark up printed pages? In what ways can someone mark up electronic texts? How do *you* mark up a text—printed or electronic—when you are reading to learn?

WRITING

A. Use the Target Vocabulary: Choose five of the target words or phrases from the chart on page 124. On a piece of paper, use each word or phrase in a sentence and underline it. Find a partner and read each other's sentences.

B. Practice Writing: Choose one of these topics and write a paragraph about it. Then find a partner and read each other's paragraphs.

1. Which piece of advice the writer gives for reading electronic texts do you think is most important? Why? Which one is the most difficult to do? Why?

2. What's different when you read to learn compared with how you read outside of school? How are the materials you read different? How is your behavior different?

Writing Tip:
Before you write a comparison, get ready to write by making a chart with two columns. At the top, write the two things you're going to compare. Make notes comparing them side by side.

CHAPTER 11

Appropriate Technologies

LEARNING OUTCOME

❯ Learn about technology for developing countries

Keeping vegetables fresh in a cooler made from two clay pots with wet sand in between*

GETTING READY TO READ

Talk about these questions with a partner.

1. What percentage of the people in the world do you think have no electricity?

   a. less than 10%   b. about 18%   c. about 33%

2. Do you know the phrases *developed countries* and *developing countries*?

   Read the definitions and list some examples of each.

   developed countries = countries with many industries, comfortable living for most people, and (usually) governments chosen by the people

   Examples: _____

   _____

   developing countries = countries without much industry that are working to improve their people's lives

   Examples: _____

   _____

* Developed by Mohammed Bah Abba of Nigeria for use in hot, dry places with no electricity.

READING

Look at the pictures, words, and definitions next to the reading. Then read without stopping. If you see a new word, try to understand the sentence without it. You will learn the word later.

Appropriate Technologies

1   You are probably reading this book in a developed country. So when you hear the word *technology*, you are likely to think of computers, high-tech phones, cars, and so on. People who live in such countries can look forward to new and better **models** of all these products each year. Modern technology has made life in developed countries much easier. Technology can make life easier in developing countries, too, but it has to be technology of another kind because the needs in those countries are very different. About 1.2 billion people—almost one-fifth of the people on Earth—don't even have electricity. What they need is technology that is **appropriate** for their situations. That is, they need technology that will help them meet basic needs for food, water, clothes, housing, health services, and ways to make a living.

2   The phrase *appropriate technologies* means types of technology that

-   use materials available in the local area;
-   can be understood, built, and repaired by the people who use them;
-   bring communities together to **solve** local problems.

3   Some appropriate technologies are beautifully simple. For example, a project in Sri Lanka is using sunlight to make drinking water safe. Clear bottles are filled with water and placed in the sun for six hours. That is usually enough time for the sun to heat the water and kill germs.[1] If the weather is cool or cloudy, it takes two days. This **method** has been proven to help people stay healthier.

4   Amy Smith is a U.S. inventor with a passion[2] for designing appropriate technologies. Smith studied **engineering** at Massachusetts Institute of Technology (MIT) and then spent four years in Botswana. She taught math, science, and English there, and she trained farmers to take care of bees so they could get honey[3] from them. In Africa, she **realized** that she could help people more by using her skills as an engineer. Smith said, "The longer I was there, the more I realized there were **plenty** of inventions that could improve the quality of life."

[1] *germs* = very small living things that can make a person sick

[2] *a passion* = a strong love

[3] *bees produce honey*

5   So Smith went back to MIT and started working on low-tech inventions. Her first great invention was a screenless hammermill. A hammermill is a machine that grinds **grain** into flour. Usually a hammermill needs a metal screen[4] to separate the flour from the unwanted parts of the grain. But screens often break, and they are hard to replace, so regular hammermills are not much use in **rural** Africa. Women there often end up grinding grain by hand and spending hours each day doing it. Smith's invention does not need a screen. It is cheap to build, simple to use, easy to repair, and it does not need electricity. With this machine, a woman can grind as much grain in a minute as she used to do in an hour.

[4] *a screen* = a wire net that lets only air or very small things pass through

Grinding grain by hand

Amy Smith's screenless hammermill

6   Smith's invention has been a great success in Africa, but some other ideas that people have tried have not done so well. In northern Ghana, another project designed to help women failed partly for cultural reasons. The women in that area do most of the farming, and they spend a lot of time and energy walking to and from their farms. Most of the time, they carry heavy **loads** on their heads. They are very much in need of a better way to transport farm products, tools, water, and so on. Because bicycles are popular in the region, a bicycle trailer seemed to be a good solution to the problem. The trailer was like a shopping cart[5] but had two wheels and was **attached** to the back of a bike. However, the idea didn't work. For one thing, it's the men in northern Ghana, not the women, who own and ride bicycles. In addition, the type of bicycle offered to the women was a bicycle with a crossbar.[6] A woman wearing a dress, as is traditional there, cannot ride such a bicycle. For these reasons, the idea of using a bicycle trailer failed.

[5] *a shopping cart*

[6] *a bicycle with a crossbar*

7   Amy Smith and others continue to work on new technologies that are appropriate for developing countries. However, they must try to develop technologies that don't depend on electricity, since so many of these countries don't have it. Everyone would **be better off** if they had not only good low-tech technologies but also electricity. That would open the door to advances in education and communication, and it would let doctors store medicines that must stay cold. It's true that the **production** of electricity sometimes causes **pollution**, but creative[7]

[7] *creative* = very good at thinking of new ideas and ways to do things

engineers could solve that problem. They could find ways to produce it without hurting **the environment**, perhaps by using energy from the sun, wind, or water.

8   Of course, the problems of developing nations cannot all be solved by thinkers like Amy Smith, but many can. As she says, "Technology isn't the only solution, but it can certainly be part of the solution."

Quick Comprehension Check

A. Read these statements **about the reading**. Circle T (true) or F (false). On the line, write the number of the paragraph with the answer.

1. *Appropriate technologies* means the most modern, high-tech machines.   T   F   _____
2. The same technology will not work everywhere.   T   F   _____
3. Amy Smith is an engineer and an inventor.   T   F   _____
4. Culture can influence how people use or feel about new technology.   T   F   _____
5. Only a few people in the world still don't have electricity.   T   F   _____
6. Electricity would not help developing countries.   T   F   _____

B. Work with your class. Share your answers from part A. Go back to the reading to find the reason why a statement is true or false. Correct the false statements.

EXPLORING VOCABULARY

Thinking about the Target Vocabulary

A. Look at the chart with the target vocabulary from "Appropriate Technologies." Nine nouns are missing. Scan the reading to find them, and add them to the correct places in the chart. Use the singular form of any plural noun.

¶	Nouns	Verbs	Adjectives	Other
1				
			appropriate	
2		solve		
3				

¶	Nouns	Verbs	Adjectives	Other
4				
		realize		
5				
			rural	
6				
		attach		
7				be better off

B. Which words and phrases are new to you? Circle them in the chart. Then find them in the reading. Look at the context. Can you guess the meaning?

Understanding the Target Vocabulary

A. These sentences are **about the reading**. What is the meaning of each **boldfaced** word or phrase? Circle a, b, or c.

1. Each year, carmakers produce new **models** of cars. *Models* means

   a. customers. b. habits. c. types or designs.

2. When the people in a community share a problem, they need to work together to **solve** it. When you solve a problem, you

   a. find an answer to it. b. increase it. c. first notice it.

3. Some people in Sri Lanka use a simple **method** for making their drinking water safe. *Method* means

   a. a planned way of doing something b. an explanation for something. c. a bad habit.

4. After living and working in Botswana for a while, Amy Smith **realized** that she could use her skills to invent new machines and processes. When you realize something, you

   a. truly deserve it. b. suddenly understand it. c. completely block it.

5. Smith realized there were **plenty of** inventions that could improve the lives of Africans. If you have plenty of something, you have

a. a small amount of it. b. enough or more than enough of it. c. an exact amount of it.

6. There is little modern technology in **rural** Africa. *Rural* means relating to

a. country areas, not the city. b. expensive goods. c. high-tech inventions.

7. Someone in Ghana tried to solve a problem by **attaching** trailers to back of bicycles. When you attach one thing to another, you

a. replace them. b. connect them. c. trick them.

8. Water power is often used in the **production** of electricity. *The production of something* means

a. the investment in it. b. the influence of it. c. the process for making it.

9. Clean ways to make electricity do not hurt **the environment**. *The environment* means

a. all our land, water, and air. b. people's lifestyles. c. types of transportation.

> **Vocabulary Tip:**
> *The environment* has a particular meaning, but you can use *environment* to mean the people and things around you, as in *a happy home environment*.

B. Read each definition and look at the paragraph number. Look back at the reading on pages 134–136 to find the **boldfaced** target word or phrase to match the definition. Write it in the chart.

> **Vocabulary Tip:**
> Engineering is a kind of professional work. It includes chemical, civil, electrical, or mechanical engineering. The person who does this work is an engineer.

Definition	Paragraph	Target Word or Phrase
1. right for a certain purpose, situation, or time	1	
2. the work of designing and building machines, roads, bridges, etc.	4	
3. seeds of plants such as rice, corn, or wheat that are used for food	5	
4. amounts of things that are carried by a person, animal, truck, etc.	6	
5. be richer, more comfortable, or more successful	7	
6. dangerous amounts of dirt or chemicals in the air, water, etc.	7	

EXPANDING VOCABULARY

Building on the Vocabulary

Word Grammar: The Suffix -tion

The suffix -tion is often used to make a verb into a noun. Study these examples. Notice that all these verbs drop the final –e before adding the suffix, and sometimes there are other spelling changes, too.

Check your dictionary when you aren't sure if a verb has a related noun form.

Verb	Noun
pollute	pollution
produce	production
realize	realization
solve	solution

Complete the sentences. Use the nouns and verbs from the chart.

1. When you _____ a problem, you come up with a

   _____.

2. When we _____ the air, water, or land, we create environmental

   _____.

3. "_____" can mean the process of making or growing things, or

   it can mean the amount of things that you _____.

4. If you _____ something that you weren't aware of before, then

   you suddenly come to a _____.

Using the Target Vocabulary in New Contexts

Complete the sentences with the target words in the box. There is one extra word.

appropriate	engineering	method	realize
attach	grain	models	rural
be better off	loads	plenty	the environment

1. He lives on a farm in a quiet _____ area.

2. Whole _____ breads are better for you because they use every part of the seed.

3. You can get a TV at SuperBuy. There are lots of _____ to choose from.

4. I like her _____ of cooking rice. It has just a few simple steps.

5. There's no need to rush—we have _____ of time.

6. If there are no seats on the bus, then we'd _____ waiting for the next one.

7. The company had to stop using chemicals that were bad for _____.

8. It's important to wear something _____ to a job interview.

9. Students often carry heavy _____ of books in backpacks.

10. When I send an email or a text message to a friend, I sometimes _____ a photo.

11. The work of designing computer hardware and software is called computer _____.

> **Vocabulary Tip:** The opposite of *rural* is *urban*: Urban areas usually have better public transportation than rural areas.

DEVELOPING YOUR READING SKILLS

Problem and Solution

Reread "Appropriate Technologies." Underline each problem and each solution described in the text. Then use information from the text to complete the chart.

Reading Tip: Before you reread, review the reading tips in the passage on page 123.

Problem	Solution Described	Has the problem been solved?	
		Yes	No
1. basic needs not met in developing countries	*appropriate technologies*		✓
2. unsafe drinking water in Sri Lanka			
3. long hours grinding grain in rural Africa			
4. no transportation for farmers in Ghana			
5. little electricity in developing nations			

Cause and Effect

Complete each sentence about the reading.

1. Developing countries need appropriate technologies because _____

   _____.

2. People in Sri Lanka put bottles of water in the sun because _____

   _____.

3. Amy Smith's screenless hammermill can be called an appropriate

   technology because _____

   _____.

4. The women in Ghana did not use the bicycle trailers because _____

   _____.

Supporting Details

Write two statements with details that support each of the major points below.

1. *Technology* means different things to people depending on where they live.

   To people in developing countries, technology means ways to meet

   basic needs.

   To people in developed countries, technology means high-tech

   inventions like computers and cars.

2. Appropriate technologies do not depend on high-tech machines or processes.

   _____

   _____

   _____

   _____.

3. Bringing electricity to developing countries could have both good and bad effects.

   _____

   _____

   _____

   _____.

4. Technology can make people's lives easier.

   _____

   _____

   _____

   _____.

CRITICAL THINKING

Discussion

Talk about these questions in a small group.

1. What are people's basic needs, as described in the reading? How would electricity help people in developing countries meet those needs? What technology does the writer say would help them? What other technology would you add to the list?

2. The reading gives three examples of efforts to use appropriate technology. In which two cases did the technology succeed? Why did it succeed? Where did it fail? What made the difference between success and failure?

3. How did Amy Smith know that women in rural Africa had a problem that she might be able to solve? How would you describe Amy Smith? Cite evidence from the reading to support your ideas.

Critical Thinking Tip: Make inferences about people you read about. Think about what they say and do, and try to understand the reasons for their actions.

4. In paragraph 8, the writer states, "Of course, the problems of developing nations cannot all be solved by thinkers like Amy Smith, but many can." Is this a fact or an opinion? Why does the writer say "Of course?" In the following sentence, the writer quotes Amy Smith. The sentence begins, "As she says." Why does the writer use this phrase?

5. Fill in the chart with examples of modern technology that you use. Write what people had to do before the invention of each type of technology.

Modern Technology	In the Past
1. dishwashers	People washed dishes by hand.
2.	
3.	
4.	
5.	

6. Consider each of the types of technology in your chart. Which ones would you miss the most and the least if you didn't have them? Why?

WRITING

A. Use the Target Vocabulary: Choose five of the target words or phrases from the chart on pages 136–137. On a piece of paper, use each word or phrase in a sentence and underline it. Find a partner and read each other's sentences.

B. Practice Writing: Choose one of these topics and write a paragraph about it. Then find a partner and read each other's paragraphs.

1. Return to question 6 under **Discussion**: *Consider each of the types of technology in your chart.* Write about the one you would miss the most or the one you would miss the least if you didn't have it. Explain why.

2. Write a summary of the project that failed in Northern Ghana. Imagine that you were part of the team working on this project, and describe what you would try next.

Writing Tip: When you give more than one reason for something, consider giving your most important reason last for a stronger effect on the reader.

CHAPTER 12

Technology in Science Fiction

Space travelers

LEARNING OUTCOME

❯ Learn about technology predicted by science fiction writers

GETTING READY TO READ

Talk about these questions with your class.

1. *Science fiction* means stories about future developments in science and technology and their effects on people. Sometimes these stories include travel by spaceship.[1] There have been many popular science-fiction movies set in outer space, such as *Star Wars*. What others can you name?

2. a. Look at the illustration above. What is happening in the picture?

   b. An artist created this illustration long before the age of space travel. How well did the artist imagine the future? Explain.

[1] *a spaceship*

READING

Look at the pictures, words, and definitions next to the reading. Then read without stopping. If you see a new word, try to understand the sentence without it. You will learn the word later.

Technology in Science Fiction

1   Facts are pieces of information we can show to be true. When we read history, we want to know the facts—what really happened. Fiction is the opposite. Writers of fiction **make up** stories. These stories tell about people and events that come from the writer's **imagination**. Science fiction writers imagine not only people and events but, perhaps most importantly, technology. They often write about the effects of that technology on a person, a group, or **society**. These writers usually **set** their stories in the future. Some of them have **predicted** technology that seemed impossible at the time but really does **exist** today.

2   An Englishwoman named Mary Shelley was one of the first writers of science fiction. In 1818, she wrote the book *Frankenstein*, which tells the story of a young scientist, Dr. Frankenstein, who wants to create a human life. He puts together parts of dead people's bodies and then uses electricity to bring the creature[1] to life. However, he cannot control the creature, and it kills him. Since then, the idea of a "mad scientist" (someone who tries to use science and technology to gain power) has been very popular in science fiction, especially in science fiction movies.

[1] *a creature = a living thing (but not a plant)*

3   In 1863, the French writer Jules Verne finished his first novel, *Cinq Semaines en Ballon* (*Five Weeks in a Balloon*), one of his many great science fiction **adventure** stories. It tells of three men traveling across Africa by hot-air balloon.[2] Readers loved it, but many were **confused**: Was it fact or fiction? The story sounded unlikely, but the writer's **style** and the **scientific** details made it seem true.

[2] *a hot-air balloon*

4   Later that same year, Jules Verne wrote *Paris au Vingtième Siècle* (*Paris in the Twentieth Century*), a story he set in the 1960s, almost 100 years into the future. This story has **descriptions** of high-speed trains, gas-powered cars, electronic devices, skyscrapers,[3] and modern methods of communication. Verne imagined all these things at a time when **neither** he **nor** anyone else in Paris had even a radio! In another book, *De la Terre à la Lune* (*From the Earth to the Moon*, 1865), he predicted that people would travel into outer space and walk on the moon, a prediction that came true on July 20, 1969. Verne even got some

[3] *a skyscraper = an extremely tall building*

of the details right. Both in his book and in real life, there were three astronauts[4] making the flight to the moon, their spaceship **took off** from Florida, and they came down in the Pacific Ocean on their return.

5   Space travel continued to be a popular subject for science fiction in the twentieth **century**. The best writers based the science and technology in their stories on a real understanding of the science and technology of their time. Computers, robots,[5] and genetic engineering[6] all appeared in the pages of science fiction long before they appeared in the news.

6   The following quotation comes from a story by the great science fiction writer Isaac Asimov. He wrote these words in 1954. When you read them, remember that at that time, there were no home computers. In fact, the few computers that existed were as big as some people's homes. In this story, called "The Fun They Had," Asimov describes a child of the future using a personal computer to learn math:

7   Margie went into the schoolroom. It was right next to her bedroom, and the mechanical teacher was on and waiting for her. . . .

8   The screen was lit up, and it said: "Today's arithmetic lesson is on the addition of proper fractions. Please insert yesterday's homework in the proper slot."

9   Margie did so with a sigh. She was thinking about the old schools they had when her grandfather's grandfather was a little boy. All the kids from the whole neighborhood came, laughing and shouting in the schoolyard, sitting together in the schoolroom. . . .

10   And the teachers were people. . . .

11   Back in 1954, readers probably found Asimov's story hard to believe. Today, his ideas do not seem so strange, do they? Asimov, Jules Verne, and others made some accurate predictions. Does that suggest that we should pay more attention to what sci-fi writers are saying today about the world of tomorrow? Perhaps, but we should also remember that such predictions have been wrong more often than right. Here we are in the twenty-first century without flying cars or vacations on the moon, and **in spite of** computers, the Internet, and online courses, people still do go to school.

[4] *an astronaut* = someone who travels and works in outer space

[5] *a robot*

[6] *genetic engineering* = the science of changing the genes of living things

Quick Comprehension Check

A. Read these statements **about the reading**. Circle T (true) or F (false). On the line, write the number of the paragraph with the answer.

1. People began writing science fiction in the 1900s.   T   F   ____

2. Science fiction is often about the technology of the future.   T   F   ____

3. The predictions of science fiction writers have generally been correct.   T   F   ____

4. The story of Frankenstein describes an appropriate use of technology.   T   F   ____

5. Jules Verne imagined technology that was later invented.   T   F   ____

6. More than sixty years ago, one writer imagined computers replacing schools and teachers.   T   F   ____

B. Work with your class. Share your answers from part A. Go back to the reading to find the reason why a statement is true or false. Correct the false statements.

EXPLORING VOCABULARY

Thinking about the Target Vocabulary

A. Look at the chart with the target vocabulary from "Technology in Science Fiction." Six nouns and two adjectives are missing. Scan the reading to find them, and add them to the correct places in the chart. Use the singular form of any plural noun.

¶	Nouns	Verbs	Adjectives	Other
1		make up		
		set		
		predict		
		exist		

¶	Nouns	Verbs	Adjectives	Other
3				
4				
				neither … nor
		take off		
5				
11				in spite of

B. Which words or phrases are new to you? Circle them in the chart. Then find them in the reading. Look at the context. Can you guess the meaning?

Understanding the Target Vocabulary

A. These sentences are **about the reading**. Complete them with the words and phrases in the box.

description	imagination	neither … nor	scientific	style
exist	in spite of	predicted	set	took off

1. The people and events in fiction come from the writer's

   _____ (his or her ability to think of new ideas or form

   mental pictures).

2. Science fiction writers sometimes have their stories take place in the

   present, but they have often _____ them in the future,

   sometimes with the action happening in outer space.

3. Writers have imagined technologies of the future and described them

   in their stories. They have _____ technologies that had

   not yet been invented.

Vocabulary Tip:
The noun form of *predict* is *prediction*: *Good readers make predictions, before they read and as they read, about what the text will say.*

4. There were no computers or robots when science fiction writers first described them in their stories. Of course, computers and robots do _____ today.

5. The way that Jules Verne wrote and told his stories—in other words, his _____ of writing—made them seem true.

6. Verne made readers believe his stories by including information about science. His stories were full of _____ details that sounded true.

7. Verne wrote a story in which he described Paris 100 years into the future. In the story, he gave a _____ of what Paris would be like at that time.

8. Verne used his imagination to write about advanced technology. He didn't have any such technology himself. In fact, _____ he _____ anyone in Paris had even a simple radio, much less a phone or a car.

9. In both the book *From the Earth to the Moon* (published in 1865) and in real life (the United States' Apollo 11 mission of 1969), the astronauts _____ from Florida. That is, their spaceships went up into the air from Florida.

10. Some people expected computers to replace teachers and classrooms. However, computers have not done that. _____ computers, people still go to school.

> **Vocabulary Tip:**
> Use *in spite of* + something that could have a negative effect or block an action or event: *We went for a walk in spite of the rain.*

B. These sentences are also **about the reading**. What is the meaning of each **boldfaced** word or phrase? Circle a, b, or c.

1. Writers of history shouldn't **make things up**, but writers of science fiction always do. *Make something up* means

   a. report it.　　　b. invent it.　　　c. prove it.

2. Science fiction often deals with the effects of future technology on **society**. *Society* means

   a. the author.　　　b. machines.　　　c. people in general.

3. Jules Verne's science fiction stories are full of danger and **adventure**. *Adventure* means
   a. rural communities. b. goods and services. c. exciting experiences.

4. Readers of *Five Weeks in a Balloon* were **confused**. *They were confused* means that they
   a. didn't know what to believe. b. didn't like the book. c. didn't want the story to end.

Vocabulary Tip:
Use *confused* to describe how someone feels: *His listeners felt confused.* Use *confusing* to describe the thing that confuses: *a confusing explanation.*

5. Science fiction books and movies were popular during the twentieth **century**. A century is
   a. a period of 100 years. b. a lifetime. c. a lifestyle.

EXPANDING VOCABULARY

Building on the Vocabulary

Word Grammar: *In Spite of* and *Despite*

The phrase ***in spite of*** and the preposition ***despite*** are synonyms. After either one, you can use:

- a noun: *The soccer game continued in spite of the rain and wind.*
- a pronoun: *We knew the risks but went ahead with the plan despite them.*
- a gerund (the *-ing* form of a verb used as a noun): *I went to class in spite of feeling sick.*

Write three statements using *in spite of* and *despite*.

1. _____.

2. _____.

3. _____.

Using the Target Vocabulary in New Contexts

A. Complete the sentences with the target words in the box. There are two extra words.

adventure	descriptions	made up	society
century	exists	predicted	style
confused	imagination	set	took off

1. Jules Verne died in 1905, more than a _____ ago.

2. The actor didn't like his name, so he _____ another.

3. Some people enjoy taking risks. They want exciting experiences. They go looking for _____.

4. We _____ that they would solve the problem, and they soon did.

5. She told her students to use their _____ to find a solution.

6. The time and place where a film or story is _____—that is, when and where the action takes place—is called its setting.

7. _____ expects people to obey the law and respect the rights of others.

8. The twins look so much alike that I can't be sure who's who. I get _____.

9. We've solved the problem. It no longer _____.

10. The plane _____ from Madrid several hours ago. In a little while, it will land in Mexico City.

Vocabulary Tip:
Imagination and the verb *imagine* are related to the adjective *imaginary*, meaning "not real, existing only in the mind:" *Children sometimes have imaginary friends.*

B. Match the beginning and end of each sentence. Write the letters.

____ 1. I like the **style** of

____ 2. H₂O is a **scientific**

____ 3. We gave the police a full **description**

____ 4. Sales have **neither** increased **nor**

a. expression meaning water.

b. of the car that hit ours.

c. decreased—they've stayed exactly the same.

d. that jacket but not the color.

C. Write each target word from part B next to its definition.

Target Word		Definition
1.	=	not (this) and not (that) either
2.	=	the way something is made or done
3.	=	relating to science or using its methods
4.	=	a piece of writing or speech giving details of what someone or something is like

DEVELOPING YOUR READING SKILLS

Scanning

Scan the reading to find the titles below. Number them in chronological order. Add the author's name and the date for each work.

Title	Author	Date
a. "The Fun They Had"		
b. *Cinq Semaines en Ballon (Five Weeks in a Balloon)*		
c. *Paris au Vingtième Siècle (Paris in the Twentieth Century)*		
d. *De la Terre à la Lune (From the Earth to the Moon)*		
e. *Frankenstein*		

> **Writing Tip:**
> Use italics for titles of books and films (or underline them if you are writing by hand). Use quotation marks around titles of stories or articles.

Paraphrasing

Reread "Technology in Science Fiction." Then read the quotations from the text. Choose the correct paraphrase.

1. "Science fiction writers imagine not only people and events but, perhaps most importantly, technology" (paragraph 1).
   - ☐ a. Science fiction writers make up stories, but a key thing they do is think of new technology.
   - ☐ b. Science fiction is the most important way that we learn about people, events, and technology of the future.

2. "Some of them have predicted technology that seemed impossible at the time but really does exist today" (paragraph 1).
   - ☐ a. Today we have technology that was impossible even to imagine in the past.
   - ☐ b. Some sci-fi writers have been very good at imagining and predicting future technology.

3. "The story sounded unlikely, but the writer's style and the scientific details made it seem true" (paragraph 3).
   - ☐ a. Jules Verne's writing style and use of scientific details made readers wonder if his story could actually be true.
   - ☐ b. Readers didn't like Jules Verne's story, but they believed it because of the style and the scientific details.

4. "Here we are in the twenty-first century without flying cars or vacations on the moon . . ." (paragraph 11).

    ☐ a. Twenty-first century technology so far has been a disappointment in many ways.

    ☐ b. Many predictions that science fiction writers have made have not come true.

Summarizing

A. Complete the summary of "Technology in Science Fiction." Include answers to the following questions.

- Who was one of the first writers of science fiction?
- Who was Jules Verne?
- What were some of the things that Jules Verne accurately predicted in his stories?
- What happened with science fiction during the twentieth century?

> The reading "Technology in Science Fiction" starts with a definition of "science fiction." Science fiction stories come from the writer's imagination, they often deal with the effects of technology on people, and they are usually set in the future.

B. Compare your summary with a partner's. Do you agree on what happened with science fiction during the twentieth century?

CRITICAL THINKING

Talk about these questions in a small group.

1. In paragraph 1, the reading states that science fiction writers often write about the effects of technology "on a person, a group, or society." What examples of this type of science fiction are described in the reading? In those stories, who is affected by a particular type of technology, and how are they affected?

2. In 1863, readers were confused by Jules Verne's story about three adventurers crossing Africa by hot-air balloon. Readers didn't know whether to believe it. According to the writer, why were they confused? Do you think that someone reading science fiction today would feel the same confusion, about what was fact and what was fiction? Explain.

3. The title of Isaac Asimov's story is "The Fun They Had." Who are "They?" How do you know? How does this title help the reader understand what is happening in the story?

4. The paragraphs from "The Fun They Had" contain words that you may not know. Answer these questions about the story using the context to guess word meanings.

   a. The reading states, "Asimov describes a child of the future using a personal computer to learn math." On the computer screen, Margie can read these words:

      Today's arithmetic lesson is on the addition of proper fractions.

      Which words are related to math?

   b. The computer tells Margie to "insert yesterday's homework in the proper slot." A slot is a long, narrow opening in a surface. (We sometimes put letters into a mail slot or money into a coin slot.) What is the meaning of *insert*? What about *proper*?

   c. Margie put her homework into the computer "with a sigh." What is the meaning of *sigh*?

      ☐ a big smile   ☐ an angry word   ☐ a sad or tired sound

5. How does Margie feel about the way education has changed since the school days of her grandfather's grandfather? What clues does Asimov give the reader? How do you feel about the ways technology has affected your experience as a student?

6. In paragraph 11, what predictions does the writer list that have *not* come true? Are any of them predictions you wish would come true? Explain.

> **Critical Thinking Tip:** Writers sometimes don't give information openly but rather give the reader clues (pieces of information that help you guess the truth) so the reader can make inferences.

WRITING

A. Use the Target Vocabulary: Choose five of the target words or phrases from the chart on pages 147–148. On a piece of paper, use each word or phrase in a sentence and underline it. Find a partner and read each other's sentences.

B. Practice Writing: Choose one of these topics and write a paragraph about it. Then find a partner and read each other's paragraphs.

   1. Do you like to read science fiction, or do you enjoy watching science fiction movies, either in English or in your first language? Explain how you feel about science fiction, with examples of stories or books you've read or films you've seen.

   2. Become a science fiction writer! Imagine your life thirty years from now. Think especially about the technology you will use every day. Describe something from your daily life.

> **Writing Tip:** When you write about your life in the future, start by explaining the setting: What year is it? Where are you living?

UNIT 3

Checkpoint

LOOK BACK

A. Think About This

Look back at your answers to the *Think About This* question on page 109:
How has technology changed the world?

Do you want to change your answer? Do you want to add anything new?

B. Remember the Readings

What do you want to remember most from the readings in Unit 3? For each
chapter, write one sentence about the reading.

Chapter 9: A History of Telling Time

_____

Chapter 10: The Screen vs. the Printed Page

_____

Chapter 11: Appropriate Technologies

_____

Chapter 12: Technology in Science Fiction

_____

REVIEWING VOCABULARY

Complete the phrase.

1. Write the noun *grain*, *methods*, or *shadows*.

   a. _____ of transportation

   b. fields of _____

   c. long _____ at the end of the day

2. Write the verb *attend*, *carry out*, *make up*, or *predict*.

   a. _____ stories

   b. _____ a class

   c. _____ the future

   d. _____ further research

3. Write the adjective *exact*, *modern*, or *rural*.

   a. a _____ area

   b. the _____ time

   c. _____ society

4. Write the noun *adventure*, *description*, or *technology*.

   a. a detailed _____

   b. an exciting _____

   c. advanced _____

EXPANDING VOCABULARY

Antonyms

Antonyms are words with opposite meanings, like *always* and *never, help* and *hurt,* or *break* and *repair.*

Sometimes a word takes a prefix that creates an antonym, like *agree* / **dis**agree and *happy* / **un**happy. These prefixes, *dis-* and *un-,* mean "not." Other prefixes that often mean "not" are *in-* and *ab-*.

Use one word from each pair of adjective antonyms to complete the sentences.

accurate	inaccurate
appropriate	inappropriate
equal	unequal
normal	abnormal
predictable	unpredictable
similar	dissimilar

1. It's easy to guess what John is going to say or do. He's highly

   _____ .

2. You can't wear that shirt to your job interview! It's _____ .

3. Older men often lose their hair, but hair loss in a child is _____ .

4. The report was full of mistakes. It was highly _____ .

5. He broke the candy bar into two _____ parts and gave me the

   smaller one.

6. The scientists expected _____ results, and they were right: The

   numbers were almost exactly the same.

A PUZZLE

Complete the sentences with words you studied in Chapters 9–12. Write the words in the puzzle.

Across

2. He often exchanges his phone for a newer _____.

3. Let's _____ a date to have lunch together.

6. Should I _____ a photo to my job application?

7. Cars pollute, so they're bad for the _____.

9. You two are sisters? I didn't _____ that.

10. Please explain again. I'm _____.

11. Yoko got her hair cut in a new _____.

12. The staff did such a great job, they all _____ a pay raise.

Down

1. A laptop computer is smaller and more _____ than a desktop model.

3. Our seats for the play are in the orchestra _____ , close to the stage.

4. Neither Sam nor Pat was able to _____ the problem. Maybe you can help.

5. Students do well in school _____ they take their work seriously.

8. High-tech clocks _____ time very accurately.

10. We're now in the twenty-first _____.

BUILDING DICTIONARY SKILLS

Words with Multiple Meanings

Look at the dictionary entries below. Then read each sentence and write the number of the meaning.

> **fair·ly** /ˈfɛrli/ *adv* **1** more than a little, but much less than very: *She speaks English fairly well.* | *The recipe is fairly simple.* **2** in a way that is fair and reasonable: *I felt that I hadn't been treated fairly.*

1. ____ a. Do they treat their employees fairly?

   ____ b. It was a fairly traditional wedding.

> **take off**
> **1 take** sth ↔ **off** to remove something [≠ **put on**]: *Your name has been taken off the list.* | *Take your shoes off in the house.* **2** if an aircraft takes off, it rises into the air from the ground **3** *informal* to leave a place: *We packed everything in the car and took off.* **4 take time/a day/a week etc. off** also **take time, etc. off work** to not go to work for a period of time: *I'm taking some time off work to go to the wedding.* **5** to suddenly become successful: *He died just as his film career was taking off.*

2. ____ a. The plane took off on time.

   ____ b. He was here a moment ago, but then he took off.

   ____ c. She took a month off after having her baby.

> **load¹** /loʊd/ *n* [C] **1** a large quantity of something that is carried by person, a vehicle, etc.: *a ship carrying a full load of fuel and supplies.* **2 carload/truck load etc.** the largest amount or number that a car, etc. can carry: *a busload of kids.* **3** the amount of work that a machine or a person has to do: *a light/heavy work load.* **4** a quantity of clothes that are washed at the same time: *Can you do a load of clothes later today?*

3. ____ a. Her business partner is sick, so her work load has increased.

   ____ b. There's already a load in the washing machine.

   ____ c. That's a heavy load of books in your backpack!

> **de·mand¹** / dɪˈmɑːnd / dɪˈmænd / *n* **1** [sing, U] the need or desire people have for particular goods or services, and their willingness to buy them → SUPPLY: *Demand for the new model is outstripping supply.* | *Nurses are in great demand (= wanted by a lot of people) these days.* | *The factory will have to increase production to meet demand.* **2** [C] a strong request that shows you believe you have the right to get what you ask for: *Union members will strike until the company agrees to their demands.* **3 demands** [plural] the difficult or annoying things that you need to do: *women dealing with the demands of family and career* | *The school makes heavy demands on its teachers.*

4. ____ a. The demands of the job were too much for him, so he quit.

   ____ b. How can we meet the demand for electricity without causing pollution?

   ____ c. They've agreed to discuss the workers' demands for safer working conditions.

re·source / rɪˈzɔːs, -ˈsɔːs / ˈriːsɔːrs / n **1** [C usually plural] something such as land, minerals, or natural energy that exists in a country and can be used in order to increase its wealth: ***natural resources*** *such as timber and oil*. **2** [C] something that can be used in order to make a job or activity easier: *an electronic resource for lesson plans*. **3 resources** [plural] all of the money, property, skill, etc. that you have available to use: *the organization's financial resources* →
HUMAN RESOURCES

5. ____ **a.** All students should get to know the resources available at the university library.

____ **b.** John came from a family with very limited resources.

____ **c.** A nonrenewable resource is a resource that cannot be easily replaced as it is consumed, such as oil, natural gas, and coal.

least / liːst / *determiner, pron.* [the superlative of "little"] **1 at least a)** not less than a particular number or amount: *The storm lasted at least two hours.* **b)** used when mentioned an advantage to show that a situation is not as bad as it seems: *Well, at least you got your money back.* **c)** said when you want to correct or change something you have just said: *His name is Jerry. At least, I think it is.* **d)** even if nothing else is said or done: *Will you at least say you're sorry?*

6. ____ **a.** You'd be better off getting another job—at least, that's *my* opinion.

____ **b.** If you don't have time to call, at least send me a text.

____ **c.** I was disappointed in my grade, but at least I passed the exam.

____ **d.** They have several children—at least three, I believe.

UNIT 4

THE ENVIRONMENT

THINK ABOUT THIS

What kinds of stories about the environment are in the news these days?

Check ✔ your answers, and add ideas of your own.

- [ ] Stories about climate and weather
- [ ] Stories about the ocean
- [ ] Stories about air quality
- [ ] Stories about plant and animal life
- [ ] Other: _____

CHAPTER 13

Small Ride, Big Trouble

LEARNING OUTCOME

❯ Learn about pollution from two-stroke engines

Driving a tuk-tuk in the streets of Bangkok

GETTING READY TO READ

Talk about these questions with your class.

1. What do these words mean: *a pollutant*, *pollute*, and *polluted?* Match them with their definitions:

   a. _____ = *v.* to make air, water, soil, etc., dangerously dirty and not good enough for people to use

   b. _____ = *adj.* dangerously dirty and unhealthy (used to describe air, water, or soil)

   c. _____ = *n.* a substance that is produced by factories, cars, etc., and that makes air, water, or soil, etc., dangerously dirty

2. How many different kinds of pollution can you name? Are any of them a problem where you live?

3. Look at the photo above. What kind of pollution does it suggest?

READING

Read to Find Out: Does the reading offer a solution to the problem of air pollution?

Look at the pictures, words, and definitions next to the reading. Then read without stopping. If you see a new word, try to understand the sentence without it. You will learn the word later.

Small Ride, Big Trouble

1   Mary Jane Ortega, the mayor of San Fernando City in the Philippines, knew that her city was choking.[1] The cause? Air pollution, especially pollution from two- and three-wheeled **vehicles** like scooters,[2] motorcycles, and *tuk-tuks*.[3]

2   The World Health Organization **estimates** that air pollution kills two million people a year. While big vehicles often get the **blame** for it, much of the blame in Asia really belongs to the "little guys." Small vehicles with two-stroke **engines** put out huge amounts of dangerous gases and oily black smoke. Cars, with their bigger, four-stroke engines, are actually cleaner and do less **harm** to the environment. In fact, one two-stroke engine vehicle can produce as much pollution as fifty cars.

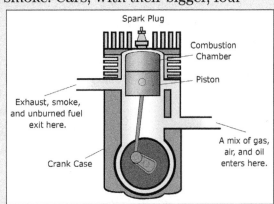
A diagram of a two-stroke engine*

3   Mayor Ortega thought that the solution was to get rid of the two-strokes. She offered **interest**-free **loans** to help people pay for new vehicles with four-stroke engines. Within three years, there were 400 of them on the streets of San Fernando. But there were still more than 800 of the two-strokes. Even with a loan, the change to a four-stroke was just too expensive for many people. (Two-stroke engines are lighter and simpler, so they are less expensive to buy and **maintain**.) Another problem was that the people who did change to a four-stroke were selling their old two-stroke to someone else in the city. The loans had led to no **decrease** in either the number of two-strokes or the amount of pollution. San Fernando needed another solution, and it had to be cheap.

* Go online and search "two-stroke engine animation" to see how a two-stroke engine works.

[1] *choking* = unable to breathe because there is not enough air

[2] *a scooter* = a small motorcycle

[3] *a tuk-tuk* See the photo on page 162.

4   **Meanwhile**, in Colorado (USA), a team of college students were trying to win a **competition**. They were developing a clean, two-stroke-engine snowmobile[4] for use in Yellowstone National Park. The team built a winning snowmobile that led to the start-up of a nonprofit business, Envirofit.

5   Using technology developed for the snowmobile, Envirofit came up with a way to retrofit two-stroke engines. *Retrofit* means to improve a machine by putting new and better parts in it (after it is already made). The company designed a retrofit kit—a set of parts and tools for people to use on their own two-stroke engines. Using the kit could both reduce the pollutants in the exhaust[5] and help the engine make better use of **fuel**.

6   The company sent kits to the Philippines to be tested by thirteen taxi drivers. Each driver had a three-wheeled motorbike with a sidecar for **passengers**. After eight months, the results were great. Using the kits had cut both pollution (by more than 70 percent) and the waste of gas and oil. Saving money on fuel turned the taxi drivers into believers. They found that using the kit could mean increasing their **income** by as much as a third. Right away, they started to spread the word[6] among other drivers.

7   Rolando Santiago, president of a taxi drivers' organization, was one of the first drivers to retrofit his engine. He says, "After six months of using the kit, my extra income helped me save for a matching house grant.[7] I rebuilt my home and my neighbor's home, which provided better housing for six families." Santiago's story gives one example of how better air can lead to a lot of other better things.

8   Few two-stroke-engine vehicles are in use in the United States. However, the United States has good reason to care about the harm these vehicles do. Pollution pays no attention to **borders** between countries or continents. For that reason, the U.S. government has spent thousands of dollars on kits for cities in India and other parts of Asia that have major air pollution problems. Pollution in India or the Philippines is not just their national problem, and pollution in Asia is not just Asia's problem.

[4] *a snowmobile*

[5] *exhaust* = the gas produced by a working machine

[6] *spread the word* = tell others the news

[7] *a grant* = an amount of money given (by the government or an organization) for a particular purpose

Quick Comprehension Check

A. Read these statements **about the reading**. Circle T (true) or F (false). On the line, write the number of the paragraph with the answer.

1. Two-stroke engines cause major air pollution. T F _____
2. Four-stroke engines cause twice as much pollution as two-strokes. T F _____
3. Two-stroke engines are cheaper than four-stroke engines. T F _____
4. You can fix a two-stroke so it causes less pollution. T F _____
5. The taxi drivers who tried the kits were happy with them. T F _____
6. Two-stroke engines are used only in the Philippines. T F _____

B. Work with your class. Share your answers from part A. Go back to the reading to find the reason why a statement is true or false. Correct the false statements.

EXPLORING VOCABULARY

Thinking about the Target Vocabulary

A. Look at the chart with the target vocabulary from "Small Ride, Big Trouble." Eight nouns are missing. Scan the reading to find them, and add them to the correct places in the chart. Use the singular form of any plural noun.

¶	Nouns	Verbs	Adjectives	Other
1				
2		estimate		
3	interest			
	loan			
		maintain		

¶	Nouns	Verbs	Adjectives	Other
4				meanwhile
5	fuel			
6				
8	border			

B. Which words are new to you? Circle them in the chart. Then find them in the reading. Look at the context. Can you guess the meaning?

Understanding the Target Vocabulary

A. These sentences are **about the reading**. Complete them with the words in the box.

blame	decrease	fuel	income	meanwhile
borders	estimate	harm	loan	vehicles

1. Things that are used to carry people and goods from one place to another—like cars, scooters, buses, and trucks—are called

   _____.

2. Many people believe that big vehicles—trucks, buses, and cars—cause more pollution than small ones. These big vehicles get the

   _____ for air pollution. However, small vehicles with

   two-stroke engines are actually worse.

   > **Vocabulary Tip:**
   > *Blame* can also be a verb. The verb is always transitive, so use it with a direct object (+ *for*): *Don't blame me for what happened—I had nothing to do with it.*

3. The World Health Organization cannot say exactly how many

   people die from air pollution, but they _____, or

   guess, that the number is about 2 million a year.

4. Two-stroke engines are worse for air quality than four-stroke engines.

   They do more _____ to the environment.

5. People in San Fernando City got money to buy new four-stroke vehicles. Over time, they had to pay the money back. The money was not a gift. It was a _____.

6. Unfortunately, the loans did not result in fewer two-stroke-engine vehicles. The loans did not lead to a _____ in the number of two-strokes.

> **Vocabulary Tip:**
> *Decrease* can also be a verb. It can be transitive (*How can I decrease the stress in my life?*) or intransitive (*The unemployment rate has decreased*).

7. Two things were happening at the same time. In San Fernando City, people were dealing with air pollution from two-strokes. _____, in Colorado, a team of U.S. college students was developing a clean two-stroke engine.

8. The taxi drivers' three-wheeled motorbikes burn gasoline to produce energy. Gasoline is one kind of _____. Others are wood, gas, and coal.

9. The Envirofit retrofit kit helped the Philippine taxi drivers earn more money. They were able to increase their _____.

10. Air pollution doesn't care about the lines that divide one country from another. Air pollution does not respect _____.

B. Read each definition and look at the paragraph number. Look back at the reading on pages 163–164 to find the **boldfaced** word to match the definition. Write it in the chart.

Definition	Paragraph	Target Word
1. the parts of vehicles or machines that produce power to make them move	2	
2. money that you pay for the use of a loan	3	
3. keep something in good condition	3	
4. a situation in which people or groups try to beat each other to win something	4	
5. people who are traveling in a car, bus, plane, etc., but are not driving it	6	

EXPANDING VOCABULARY

Building on the Vocabulary

> **Word Grammar: Words Related to Money**
>
> These words all relate to money:
>
> *borrow*   *v.* to take money or something else to use and give back later: *Dan borrowed a book from me. —borrower n.*
>
> *interest*   *n.* **1** the extra money you must pay back when you borrow money: *What rate of interest did you pay on the loan?* **2** the money a bank pays you when you keep money in an account there: *The more you save, the more interest you'll earn.*
>
> *lend*   *v.* to let someone borrow money or something else: *Could you lend me a pen?* (simple past: *lent*) *—lender n.*
>
> *loan*   *n.* an amount of money you get to use for a period of time: *a student loan, a new car loan*

Complete the sentences with *borrowed, interest, lenders, lent,* and *loans.*

1. Jack _____ some money to his brother but never got it back.

2. Paula _____ money from the bank to start her business.

3. How much interest do you have to pay on your _____?

4. Banks are the major _____ in the housing market.

5. Be careful how you use credit cards: the _____ rate can be over

    20 percent.

Using the Target Vocabulary in New Contexts

A. These sentences use the target words **in new contexts**. What is the meaning of each **boldfaced** word? Circle a, b, or c.

1. The painter **estimated** that the job would take three days. *Estimated* means

    a. promised.   b. doubted.   c. guessed.

> **Vocabulary Tip:**
> *Estimate* can also be a noun: *A rough estimate is a guess that may not be very accurate.*

2. We were working hard to clear away the snow. **Meanwhile**, another storm was coming our way. *Meanwhile* means

    a. earlier.   b. at the same time.   c. afterwards.

3. This cough medicine may not help, but it won't do you any **harm**. If something does harm, it

    a. causes trouble or injury.   b. improves a situation.   c. helps something last.

4. Your food is **fuel** for your body. A fuel is something that
   a. makes you gain weight.
   b. makes you sick.
   c. produces heat or energy.

5. Your car will last longer if you **maintain** it. *Maintain it* means
   a. drive it slowly.
   b. take care of it.
   c. not use it.

6. A **decrease** in production costs can bring a company an increase in profits. If there is a decrease in something, there is
   a. less of it.
   b. plenty of it.
   c. more of it.

B. Complete the sentences with the target words in the box. There is one extra word.

blame	competition	fuels	passengers
border	engine	income	vehicles

1. Solar-powered _____ run on energy from the sun.

2. Please turn off the car while you wait. Don't leave the _____ running.

3. You must show your passport if you want to cross the _____.

4. Who won first place in the piano _____?

5. If you accept the _____ for something that went wrong, you take responsibility for it.

6. First-class _____ on an airplane have more comfortable seats.

7. I have to pay _____ tax on the money I earned last year.

> **Vocabulary Tip:** When you learn a new word, try to learn the other words in its family. *Competition* is related to the verb *compete*, the noun *competitor*, and the adjective *competitive*.

DEVELOPING YOUR READING SKILLS

Main Ideas

A. Which sentence best states the main idea of "Small Ride, Big Trouble"?
   ☐ 1. Private companies are better at solving problems than governments are.
   ☐ 2. New technology can help solve problems like air pollution.
   ☐ 3. Two-stroke engines are to blame for a lot of air pollution.

B. Which statement best describes the writer's point of view?

☐ 1. The writer thinks you have to pay people if you want them to stop polluting.

☐ 2. The writer thinks people everywhere should know and care about air pollution in Asia.

☐ 3. The writer thinks competitions are the best way to figure out how to stop pollution.

Reading Tip: Remember, the writer's point of view means the writer's opinion. Notice when the writer gives an opinion, and ask yourself, "Do I agree?"

Cause and Effect

> **Using *Because* and *Because Of***
>
> *Because* and *because of* are used differently in sentences.
>
> • Use **because** + a subject and a verb.
>
> subject   + verb
>
> *Many people prefer motorcycles to cars **because** motorcycles do not cost as much.*
>
> • Use **because of** + a noun or noun phrase only (no verb).
>
> noun phrase
>
> *Many people prefer motorcycles to cars **because of** <u>the cost</u>.*

A. Complete each sentence **about the reading**. Use *because* or *because of.*

1. The World Health Organization estimates that two million people die

   each year _____

   _____.

2. San Fernando City had a bad problem with air pollution _____

   _____.

3. Two-stroke engines are worse than four-stroke engines _____

   _____.

B. Find two more cause-effect relationships in the reading. Write two sentences with *because* or *because of.*

1. _____

   _____

2. _____

   _____

Problem and Solution

Complete the chart with information from the reading.

Problem	Solutions Tried	Results
bad air quality—pollution from two-stroke engines	1.	
	2.	

CRITICAL THINKING

Discussion

Talk about these questions in a small group.

1. The reading says that the mayor of San Fernando City "knew that her city was choking" (paragraph 1). Is it actually possible for a city to choke? What does the writer mean? By using *choking*, what is the writer comparing the city to?

2. In paragraph 3, you read about Mayor Ortega's idea for a solution. What was the problem? Where in the reading is it described? Why did the mayor think that interest-free loans would be the solution? What was the result of the program? What do you think the mayor could have done differently?

3. What does it mean to say that Envirofit is a "nonprofit business?" Who started this particular nonprofit? What was the relationship between the snowmobile mentioned in paragraph 4 and the kits sent to the Philippines?

4. What do you think about the drivers of two-stroke-engine vehicles described in the reading? Choose one, or add your own idea, and explain your choice.

    a. They don't realize that they are polluting the air.

    b. They know they're polluting the air but they don't care.

    c. _____

5. In paragraph 8, the writer says that "pollution in Asia is not just Asia's problem." Whose problem does the writer think it is? How do you know? Cite evidence from the text.

> **Critical Thinking Tip:** The **literal meaning** of words is their usual, most basic sense. Writers also use words to suggest how one thing is like another, as in "her city was choking." That kind of comparison is a **metaphor**.

6. Do you agree with the conclusion of Santiago's story in paragraph 7 that better air leads to other better things? How did it help Santiago? Could it help you? If so, how?

WRITING

A. Use the Target Vocabulary: Choose five of the target words or phrases from the chart on pages 165–166. On a piece of paper, use each word or phrase in a sentence and underline it. Find a partner and read each other's sentences.

B. Practice Writing: Choose one of these topics and write a paragraph about it. Then find a partner and read each other's paragraphs.

1. If people are doing something that causes pollution, how do you get them to change? Give examples, from the reading and your own experience, to support your ideas.

2. Does a sense of responsibility for the environment affect the choices you make in your everyday life? For example, does it affect the kinds of transportation you use or the foods you eat? Explain your answer.

> **Writing Tip:**
> When you write a paragraph that has a list or series (of ideas, reasons, causes, etc.), transition words help guide the reader, such as *first (of all)*, *next, in addition*, and *most importantly*.

CHAPTER 14

Your Trees, My Trees, Our Trees

Enjoying the shade

GETTING READY TO READ

Talk about these questions with a partner.

1. What products can you think of that come from trees? Make a list.

2. Which statement do you think is true? Circle the letter.

    a. There are more trees than human beings on Earth.

    b. There are more human beings than trees on Earth.

3. Which number do you think most closely matches the number of trees on Earth? Check (✓) your answer.

    ☐ a. three million (3,000,000)

    ☐ b. three billion (3,000,000,000)

    ☐ c. three trillion (3,000,000,000,000)

READING

Read to Find Out: Do we have enough trees?

Look at the picture, words, and definitions next to the reading. Then read without stopping. If you see a new word, try to understand the sentence without it. You will learn the word later.

Your Trees, My Trees, Our Trees

1   Trees can be very beautiful, but they do much more than just look nice and give us **shade** for picnics.[1] In fact, trees are so **valuable** that it's hard to see how we could exist without them.

2   First, trees supply us with **oxygen**. When we breathe in air, our bodies use the oxygen from it, and then we breathe out **carbon dioxide**. Trees do the opposite—they take in carbon dioxide and put oxygen into the air—making them wonderful partners for us. They use the carbon to produce wood and leaves. Keeping that carbon out of the air is a good thing because carbon dioxide is a greenhouse gas. Greenhouse gases keep heat from escaping into space and may cause Earth to get too hot.

3   Second, trees help clean up the environment. For example, they take pollutants out of the air, both dangerous gases (like carbon monoxide[2]) and dust we don't want to breathe in. According to the International Society of Arboriculture (ISA), in one year, the average tree takes four to five kilograms of pollution from the air. Trees clean the **soil** as well. Sometimes they pull pollutants out of the soil and store them, and sometimes they actually change pollutants so that they do less harm. Trees can also help with urban noise pollution, blocking noise that comes from city traffic, airports, and so on.

4   The list of benefits from trees goes on and on, but let's return to our first one: the effect of trees on our oxygen supply. ISA estimates that one acre[3] of forest puts out four tons of oxygen a year. That, they say, is enough to meet the needs of 18 people. So, if one acre of forest is enough for 18 of us, how many acres does it take to meet the oxygen needs of the whole world? And is the number of trees **keeping up with** the **population** as it grows each year?

5   Ecology[4] professor Nalini Nadkarni wondered about this, so she **looked into** how many trees there are in the world. She knew that scientists had estimated the number of trees by looking at photos of Earth taken by satellites.[5] As of 2005, that estimate was about 400 billion trees. Nadkarni then wondered how many trees that meant per person. To get an answer, she divided the number of trees by the world's population at that time, and she found that there were 61 trees per person.

[1] *a picnic* = a meal eaten outdoors, as in a park

[2] *carbon monoxide* = a poisonous gas produced by engines burning gasoline

[3] *an acre* = a measure of land (about 4,047 square meters)

[4] *ecology* = the study of plants, animals, people, and the environment

[5] *a satellite* = a machine circling Earth in space to send/receive information

6   Was that good news or bad? Nadkarni started thinking about how many trees she herself would **consume** in her lifetime. One of her students reported that each year, the average American uses the amount of wood in a 100-foot-tall tree that is 18 inches in **diameter**. Nadkarni thought about all the things she uses that are made from wood, or from other tree-based products (such as **rubber**), like newspapers, magazines, movie tickets, birthday cards, pencils, **ink**, rubber boots, furniture, wooden chopsticks[6] . . . .

7   Chopsticks? Nadkarni herself probably does not use a great number of those. However, she learned that every year, the Japanese throw away over 20 billion pairs of them. These chopsticks, called *wari-bashi* ("little quick ones"), are made of wood that comes from Vietnam, Malaysia, Thailand, the United States, and Canada. The Chinese throw away even more of them: 450 billion pair a year. That equals about 25 million trees. Every year.

8   Nadkarni does not tell this story to make chopstick users or anyone else feel bad. She says, "I don't want people to feel guilty[7] about their relationships with trees and say, 'Oh, I can never touch another tree-created product again!'" She does want people to feel **grateful** that trees are such a wonderful resource and to understand that trees are a **renewable** resource. We can plant more.

9   In 2007, a nine-year-old boy in Germany decided to do that. Felix Finkbeiner wanted to follow the example of Wangari Maathai of Kenya (she was responsible for getting 30 million trees planted in Africa over 30 years), so he started Plant-for-the-Planet. Since then, children around the world have **gotten involved** with this organization and planted billions of trees.

10 According to a study completed in 2015, people are planting about five billion trees a year. The same study also provided a more accurate tree count: we actually have more than three trillion trees on Earth, more than seven times as many as the earlier estimate. Both facts are very encouraging,[8] aren't they? However, the same study provided some troubling facts: there used to be twice as many trees on Earth as we have now, and each year, *15 billion* are being cut down. At that rate, in 300 years, there won't be any trees left.

[6] *chopsticks*

[7] *guilty* = feeling bad because you've done something you know is wrong

[8] *encouraging* = giving hope and confidence about the future

Quick Comprehension Check

A. Read these statements **about the reading**. Circle T (true) or F (false). On the line, write the number of the paragraph with the answer.

1. Trees improve air quality.   T   F   _____
2. Trees and humans are in competition for air.   T   F   _____
3. Trees are good for the environment in several ways.   T   F   _____
4. Professor Nadkarni says everyone must stop using
   tree-based products.   T   F   _____
5. A 2015 study provided both good news and bad.   T   F   _____
6. We're planting more trees than we're using.   T   F   _____

B. Work with your class. Share your answers from part A. Go back to the reading to find the reason why a statement is true or false. Correct the false statements.

EXPLORING VOCABULARY

Thinking about the Target Vocabulary

A. Look at the chart with the target vocabulary from "Your Trees, My Trees, Our Trees." Seven nouns and two adjectives are missing. Scan the reading to find them, and add them to the correct places in the chart. Use the singular form of any plural noun.

¶	Nouns	Verbs	Adjectives	Other
1	shade			
			valuable	
2				
3				
4		keep up with		
5		look into		
6		consume		

¶	Nouns	Verbs	Adjectives	Other
8				
9				get involved

B. Which words and phrases are new to you? Circle them in the chart. Then find them in the reading. Look at the context. Can you guess the meaning?

Understanding the Target Vocabulary

A. Complete these sentences **about the reading**. Use the target words and phrases in the box.

carbon dioxide	ink	oxygen	shade
diameter	keeping up with	rubber	soil

1. A cooler area of shadow, created by a tree blocking the sun, for example, is called _____.

2. The gas in the air that is needed by all living things is _____. Its chemical symbol is O.

3. The gas that people and animals breathe out is _____. Its chemical symbol is CO_2.

4. The substance that trees and other plants grow in is _____. It is also sometimes called *earth* or *dirt*.

5. The number of people in the world is increasing. Is the number of trees increasing as fast as the number of people? Are trees _____ us?

   Vocabulary Tip: Use *keep up + with +* someone/something else, or use *keep up* alone when the meaning is clear: *He walked so fast I couldn't keep up.*

6. You can measure a tree by how tall it is and by how wide it is—its _____ (a line drawn from one side of a circle to the other, through the center).

7. Certain trees contain a liquid that is used to make such things as car tires, rain boots, and basketballs. This material is called _____.

8. The liquid in a pen, or a colored substance in a computer printer, is called _____.

B. These sentences are **about the reading**. What is the meaning of each **boldfaced** word or phrase? Circle a, b, or c.

1. The reading gives several reasons why trees are very **valuable**. *Valuable* means

   a. worth a lot.   b. nice to look at.   c. increasing in number.

2. Which is greater, the number of trees in the world or the human **population**? *Population* means the number of

   a. products made from something.   b. benefits from something.   c. living things in an area.

3. Professor Nadkarni wanted information about the world's tree population, so she **looked into** it. *Looked into* means

   a. researched.   b. decreased.   c. estimated.

4. We **consume** trees in many ways—as paper, furniture, and chopsticks, to name just a few. When you consume something, you

   a. maintain it.   b. respond to it.   c. use it until it's gone.

5. Professor Nadkarni wants people to be **grateful** that we have trees. *Grateful* means

   a. careful.   b. thankful.   c. awful.

6. Trees are a **renewable** resource. If a resource is renewable, then we

   a. can replace it so it doesn't disappear.   b. should avoid using it.   c. are better off without it.

7. Children can **get involved** in Plant-for-the-Planet and plant trees to help the environment. If you get involved in (or with) an organization or activity, you

   a. take it too seriously.   b. get rid of it.   c. have something to do with it.

> **Vocabulary Tip:**
> The adjective *valuable* is related to *value*, which can be a noun or a verb. The verb means "think something is important:" *I value her friendship.* See your dictionary for the meanings of the noun.

EXPANDING VOCABULARY

Building on the Vocabulary

Studying Collocations: Using *Involve*

If an activity or a situation **involves** something, then that thing is a part or a result of the activity or situation.

Running your own business usually involves working long hours.

Involve is often used in the phrases *be involved* or *get involved*, often followed by *in* or *with* + object. These phrases mean "be, or become, connected to an event or activity in some way."

*They're always arguing. I try not to **get involved.***

*Three vehicles **were involved in** the accident.*

*She**'s actively involved with** the organization.*

Be/get involved (with) can also mean "be in a romantic relationship."

*Dan and his girlfriend have **been involved** for about six months.*

Rewrite each sentence using *involve* or *be/get involved* (+ *in/with*).

1. Travel is part of Ann's new job.

    Ann's new job involves travel.

2. I want to start doing something to help with saving the environment.

    _____

3. Soccer teams from around the world had roles in the competition.

    _____

4. Everyone warned her not to have anything to do with him.

    _____

5. I realize that solving the problem will demand imagination and hard work.

    _____

Using the Target Vocabulary in New Contexts

A. Complete the sentences with the target words and phrases in the box. There is one extra word or phrase.

consume	get involved	keep up with	renewable
diameter	grateful	look into	valuable

1. The boy was often absent, so it was hard for him to _____ the other students, and he felt he was getting left behind.

2. I don't know much about getting a bank loan, so I'll have to _____ it if I want to buy a car or a house.

3. Your support has made a big difference, and I'm very _____ . Thank you!

4. A smaller vehicle will generally _____ less fuel.

5. A soccer ball is about 10 inches in _____.

6. A thing can be _____ because it's worth a lot of money or because it's very useful to someone, like an experience or some good advice.

7. Oil is not a _____ resource—we cannot make more of it.

> **Vocabulary Tip:**
> *Consume* can mean "use (time, energy, materials)" or "eat or drink," but the noun *consumer* has a very specific meaning: "someone who buys and uses products and services."

B. Complete the sentences with the target words and phrases in the box. There is one extra word.

carbon dioxide	ink	population	shade
diameter	oxygen	rubber	soil

1. When a patient has trouble breathing, a doctor may give him or her _____.

2. Air is made up of 78 percent nitrogen, 21 percent oxygen, and other gases including _____.

3. Before they had pens, people had to use a brush and _____ to write Chinese characters.

4. On a sunny day, it is cooler under a tree, in the _____.

5. Rich _____ is good for growing plants.

6. In some countries, the birthrate is low but the _____ is

    growing because people are living longer.

7. _____ is a useful material for things that need to be waterproof.

DEVELOPING YOUR READING SKILLS

Main Ideas

A. What is the main idea of "Your Trees, My Trees, Our Trees"? Write one sentence.

_____

_____

> **Reading Tip:** You may find that by rereading the introduction and conclusion of a text (the first and last paragraphs), you can check your understanding of the main idea.

B. Which of the following sentences would be the most appropriate way to end the reading? Check (✓) your answer.

☐ 1. Trees are too valuable for us to let that happen.

☐ 2. Luckily, that's not going to happen.

☐ 3. New technology may solve that problem.

Supporting Details

Write at least two statements with details that support each of the major points below.

1. Trees are good for the environment.

    _____

    _____

    _____

2. We all depend on trees.

    _____

    _____

    _____

3. We are consuming trees faster than we are replacing them.

    _____

    _____

    _____

4. Some people are trying to make a difference.

_____

_____

_____

Fact vs. Opinion

A. Decide if each statement is a fact or an opinion and circle Fact or Opinion. Base your answers on information from the reading.

1.	Trees have many benefits for human beings.	Fact	Opinion
2.	Trees help limit greenhouse gases.	Fact	Opinion
3.	Having 61 trees per person is not enough.	Fact	Opinion
4.	People in developed countries use many tree-based products.	Fact	Opinion
5.	We should not feel guilty about using trees.	Fact	Opinion
6.	We can replace the trees we use.	Fact	Opinion

B. Write two sentences.

1. Write another fact about trees. If you use information from the reading, write a paraphrase or use quotation marks as needed.

_____

_____

2. Write an opinion of your own about trees.

_____

_____

CRITICAL THINKING

Discussion

Talk about these questions with your class.

1. What was the writer's purpose in writing "Your Trees, My Trees, Our Trees?"

2. The reading presents a set of reasons why trees are valuable. Underline them. Which is the strongest reason? What reasons could you add that are _not_ in the reading?

3. Which of these words is closest in meaning to _troubling_ in paragraph 10:

   a. willing   b. worrying   c. confusing

   How can a reader figure out the meaning from the context?

> **Critical Thinking Tip:** When a writer presents a set of reasons to show that something is true or untrue, right or wrong, the writer is **making an argument**. The writer wants to get readers to agree.

4. Which questions did Professor Nadkarni ask, either directly or indirectly? Check (✓) your answers.

   ☐ a. How many trees are there in the world?

   ☐ b. How does the number of trees compare to the number of people?

   ☐ c. How many trees will she use up in her lifetime?

   ☐ d. Should she try to use fewer things made from wood and other tree-based products?

   Explain your answers. Which questions does the reading answer? Where do you find those answers?

5. In paragraph 4, the writer asks if the number of trees is keeping up with the population as it grows each year. Does the reading answer this question? If so, where do you find the information? Is there a problem, and if so, what is the solution?

WRITING

A. Use the Target Vocabulary: Choose five of the target words or phrases from the chart on pages 176–177. On a piece of paper, use each word or phrase in a sentence and underline it. Find a partner and read each other's sentences.

B. Practice Writing: Choose one of these topics and write a paragraph about it. Then find a partner and read each other's paragraphs.

1. Think of a time when you became aware of a problem and, as a result, you changed your behavior. Describe that experience. What did you learn, and how did you change?

2. Professor Nadkarni feels grateful for trees. Name something, or someone, that you feel grateful for, and tell why.

> **Writing Tip:** A **topic sentence** at the beginning of a paragraph lets the reader know what the main idea of the paragraph will be. It may be easier to write your topic sentence *after* you draft your paragraph.

CHAPTER 15

Would You Eat Bugs to Save the World?

Fried grasshoppers

GETTING READY TO READ

Read the statements below and circle True or False. Then compare your answers with those of the class.

1.	People in my country eat some types of insects.	True	False
2.	I have seen people eat insects.	True	False
3.	I have eaten insects.	True	False
4.	I would be willing to try eating insects.	True	False
5.	The insects in the photo look good to eat.	True	False

READING

Read to Find Out: How would you "save the world" by eating insects?

Look at the pictures, words, and definitions next to the reading. Then read without stopping. If you see a new word, try to understand the sentence without it. You will learn the word later.

Would You Eat Bugs to Save the World?

1   Do you find it hard to imagine eating an insect? Perhaps you are saying to yourself, "Never in a million years would I eat bugs!" Or perhaps you are one of the many people who like to snack on chocolate-covered grasshoppers.[1]

[1] *a grasshopper*

2   Human beings have eaten insects for thousands of years, and not just when they were **forced** to. The Romans ate them, and many modern cultures also consider them food. According to the United Nations (UN), people today eat over 1,400 species[2] of insects. They eat them in 29 countries in Asia, 36 countries in Africa, and 23 in the Americas. No doubt some of these people eat insects because they will go hungry **unless** they do, but many of them eat insects because they like the taste. Now there is another good reason to eat insects: to help the environment.

[2] *a species* = a particular kind of plant or animal

3   David Gracer eats insects, and he thinks you should, too. He **has set out** to **educate** people in the United States about eating them, especially in place of beef, chicken, and pork. He says the major reason to eat less of those foods is that **current** methods of raising livestock—animals such as cows, chickens, and pigs—use 30 percent of all the land on Earth and have a terrible effect on the environment. According to Gracer, a 2006 UN report made clear just how bad the situation is: Raising livestock is causing much of our water pollution, **destroying** large areas of land, and adding to global warming.[3] This is true for both huge factory farms and places where farmers can afford only a few animals. According to the report, raising cattle[4] produces more greenhouse gases[5] than cars and all other forms of transportation.

[3] *global warming* = an increase in world temperatures

[4] *cattle*

[5] *greenhouse gases* = gases that keep heat from escaping into space, like carbon dioxide

4   Raising insects, on the other hand, would cause far fewer **environmental** problems. At present, most edible[6] insects are not raised but rather harvested—that is, people go out into the forest to find them. All anyone needs to do is collect them and cook them. However, increased demand has led some farmers to start raising them, as in Thailand, where many types of insects are popular snacks.

[6] *edible* = safe to eat

5   David Gracer also points out some of the benefits that insects offer as food. For example, if you are trying to lose weight, you might like to know that grasshoppers contain only one-third the fat found in beef. Insects are also a good **source** of **protein**. Dried insects often have twice the protein of fresh fish.

6   **In terms of** protein, insects again compare well with beef. For every pound of grain that insects eat, they create far more protein than cattle do. Cattle have to eat several pounds of grain to produce just one pound of beef. In other words, cattle are not adding to the world's food supply— they are *subtracting* from it. Cattle also **require** huge amounts of another valuable resource: water. It takes 1,847 gallons of water to produce a pound of beef. (That will get you only three or four hamburgers.)

7   The idea of insects as food has the support of **experts**, such as Robert Kok, who teaches bioresource engineering[7] at McGill University in Montreal. Professor Kok sees insects as a great source of protein. He has long spoken **in favor of** farming them, although he's not sure many Canadians **are open to** the idea. Nutrition[8] professor Marion Nestle of New York University would agree with him about the benefits of insects as food. However, she also thinks that before most North Americans would eat them, they would have to be very, very hungry.

8   For now, David Gracer will continue to **speak out**—at schools and on TV and radio—on why people should eat insects. He realizes change will come slowly, if at all, but he hopes one day to import[9] and sell edible insects, like the Mexican grasshoppers called *chapulines*. He won't try to make a living at it, however. He says, "If I did this for a living, my family and I would be eating bugs all the time."

[7] *bioresource engineering* = applying technology to problems in food production

[8] *nutrition* = getting the right foods for good health and growth

[9] *import* = bring something into a country (to sell it)

Quick Comprehension Check

A. Read these statements **about the reading**. Circle T (true) or F (false). On the line, write the number of the paragraph with the answer.

1. Members of many cultures around the world eat insects.   T   F   _____

2. Most North Americans seem willing to eat insects.   T   F   _____

3. David Gracer is trying to stop people from using insects as food.   T   F   _____

4. Raising farm animals for meat is bad for the environment.   T   F   _____

5. Insects have little real value as food.   T   F   _____

6. Gracer earns a good living selling insects for food.   T   F   _____

B. Work with your class. Share your answers from part A. Go back to the reading to find the reason why a statement is true or false. Correct the false statements.

EXPLORING VOCABULARY

Thinking about the Target Vocabulary

A. Look at the chart with the target vocabulary from "Would You Eat Bugs to Save the World?" Three nouns and six verbs are missing. Scan the reading to find them, and add them to the correct places in the chart. Use the singular form of any plural noun. Use the base form of each verb.

¶	Nouns	Verbs	Adjectives	Other
2				
				unless
3				
			current	
4			environmental	
5				
6				in terms of
7				
				in favor of
				be open to
8				

B. Which words and phrases are new to you? Circle them in the chart. Then find them in the reading. Look at the context. Can you guess the meaning?

Understanding the Target Vocabulary

A. These sentences are **about the reading**. Complete them with the words and phrases in the box.

are open to	destroy	in favor of	protein	speaking out
current	forced	in terms of	source	unless

1. Some people have eaten insects because they chose to, others because conditions _____ them to. In other words, there was nothing else to eat, so they had to eat insects to live.

2. Some people will go hungry if they don't eat insects. They will have nothing to eat _____ they eat insects.

> **Vocabulary Tip:**
> Use *force + someone + to + verb: Bad weather forced them to delay the baseball game.*

3. Many people are unhappy about the ways that cows, chickens, and pigs are raised for food today. For one thing, the _____ methods of raising livestock (the methods in use at present) have a terrible effect on the environment.

4. Because about 30 percent of all the land on Earth is used to raise livestock, it's important to consider the methods used. Current methods can _____ large areas of land. They make the land unusable by polluting the soil and water.

5. People get their food from plants as well as from animals. For some people, another good food _____ is insects.

> **Vocabulary Tip:**
> Use *source + of: the main source of income / energy / air pollution.*

6. Insects, just like beef and fish, are a source of _____. This is a substance that is also found in eggs, beans, and milk. It helps the human body grow.

7. Insects are better than beef when you consider them _____ protein—that is, when you think about them in that way.

8. Professor Robert Kok and other experts support the idea of farming insects. They are _____ this idea.

9. Professors Kok and Nestle doubt that North Americans are willing

   to think about eating insects. They don't think North Americans

   _____ that idea.

10. David Gracer will continue to speak in public about why people should

    raise insects for food instead of cattle, chicken, or pigs. He will go on

    _____ about this because it's something he strongly believes in.

B. Read each definition and look at the paragraph number. Look back at the reading on pages 185–186 to find the **boldfaced** word or phrase to match the definition. Write it in the chart.

Definition	Paragraph	Target Word or Phrase
1. start (doing something, with a particular purpose or a goal in mind)	3	
2. teach	3	
3. relating to or affecting the land, air, or water on Earth	4	
4. need, demand	6	
5. people who know a lot about a subject from long study or experience	7	

EXPANDING VOCABULARY

Building on the Vocabulary

Word Grammar: *Unless*

Unless often has the same meaning as *if . . . not*. For example, these two sentences have the same meaning:

   *I won't eat a grasshopper **unless** you eat one, too.* =

   *I won't eat a grasshopper **if** you **don't** eat one, too.*

Use *unless* to refer to future conditions only. (Use *if . . . not* to refer to the past: *I wouldn't have known class was cancelled **if** you **hadn't** called me.*)

Complete the sentences.

1. I'll be in class on _____ unless _____

   _____.

2. I won't _____ unless _____

   _____.

Using the Target Vocabulary in New Contexts

A. What is the meaning of each **boldfaced** word or phrase? Circle a, b, or c.

1. What—or who—would be a good **source** of information about renewable energy? A source is a person, place, or thing that

   a. supplies something.
   b. deserves something.
   c. causes harm.

2. Bad weather **forced** the airport to close. If you force people to do something, you

   a. let them do it.
   b. make them do it.
   c. ask them to do it.

3. More and more people are **speaking out** about climate change. When someone speaks out, they

   a. talk in a loud voice.
   b. give their opinion.
   c. ask questions.

   Vocabulary Tip: After *speak out*, you can use *against* or *in favor of* + object: *I didn't support the plan and spoke out against it.*

4. I haven't made up my mind. **I'm open to** suggestions. *To be open to something* means to be

   a. in need of it.
   b. in charge of it.
   c. willing to consider it.

5. That car is too big, but **in terms of** passenger comfort, it's great. *In terms of* means

   a. in spite of.
   b. on the subject of.
   c. getting rid of.

6. Storing video on my computer **requires** a lot of memory. *Require something* means

   a. create it.
   b. need it.
   c. attend it.

7. Go online to find out about **current** weather conditions. *Current* means

   a. fast-moving.
   b. uncertain.
   c. present.

   Vocabulary Tip: The phrase *current events* means "important things happening in the world:" *We depend on the news media to inform us about current events.*

B. Complete the sentences with the target words and phrases in the box. There is one extra word.

destroyed	environmentally	in favor of	set out
educated	experts	protein	sources

1. Things such as soaps and containers that do less harm to the environment are called " _____ friendly."

2. Your body uses _____ from your food to make the red blood cells that carry oxygen.

3. Nobody wants air pollution. Everybody is _____ getting rid of it.

4. When someone says that a fire consumed a building, they mean that the fire _____ it.

5. We don't completely understand the problem, so we're depending on the _____ to come up with a solution.

6. In 1519, Ferdinand Magellan left Spain with five ships. He _____ to sail around the world.

7. Good science fiction really makes the reader think. Some sci-fi writers have _____ their readers about technology and its effects on society.

DEVELOPING YOUR READING SKILLS

Understanding Main Ideas, Major Points, and Supporting Details

The Main Idea, Major Points, and Supporting Details

A reading generally has

- one main idea
- several major points to support the main idea
- supporting details to support each major point

Use a graphic organizer to help you remember and understand the information in a text. Look at the **concept map** below. It's a useful organizer to show relationships among ideas in a text.

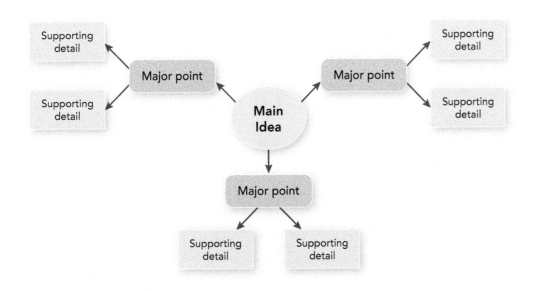

A. Reread "Would You Eat Bugs to Save the World?" and then choose the main idea.

☐ 1. Eating insects has a long and respectable history.

☐ 2. David Gracer wants people to change their eating habits.

☐ 3. It could be good for the environment if more people ate insects.

B. Which three sentences state major points of the reading, and which ones give supporting details? Write *MP* (major point) or *SD* (supporting detail).

_MP_ 1. Eating insects is normal in many cultures.

_____ 2. People around the world eat over 1,400 species of insects.

_____ 3. There are over 80 countries where people eat insects.

_____ 4. Raising livestock, such as cows or pigs, does harm to the environment.

_____ 5. A UN report said raising cattle is to blame for a lot of greenhouse gases.

_____ 6. It takes 1,847 gallons of water to produce a pound of beef.

_____ 7. Grasshoppers have much less fat than beef.

_____ 8. Insects can be a good source of protein.

_____ 9. Insects have many benefits as food.

C. On a piece of paper, draw a concept map. Write notes in the map to show the main idea, three major points, and at least three supporting details from the reading.

Using Graphic Organizers

Using a Venn Diagram

Using a **Venn diagram** to record information from a text can make it easy to see what two people, things, events, or ideas have in common and what the differences between them are. In the left side of the diagram, write points that are true for only one of the two; on the right, list points that are true only for the other. In the area in the middle, write what is true for both of them.

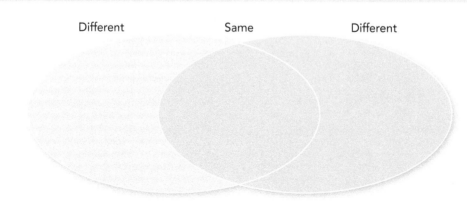

Different   Same   Different

On a piece of paper, draw a Venn diagram. Label the left side "Cattle" and the right side "Insects." Write notes in the spaces on the left and right to show the differences between them that you read about in the text. In the space in the middle, show what they have in common.

Reading Tip: When you take notes about a reading, drawing a chart or diagram can help you organize and remember the key points and how they relate to each other.

Fact vs. Opinion

Decide if each statement is a fact or an opinion and circle Fact or Opinion. Base your answers on information from the reading.

1. Some people like the taste of insects.   Fact   Opinion
2. David Gracer is trying to educate people about food.   Fact   Opinion
3. People should stop raising cattle.   Fact   Opinion
4. Producing beef requires too much grain and water.   Fact   Opinion
5. Insects are rich in protein.   Fact   Opinion
6. Professor Robert Kok thinks people should raise insects.   Fact   Opinion

CRITICAL THINKING

Discussion

Talk about these questions in a small group.

1. Find the phrase *never in a million years* in paragraph 1. What does it mean? Why does the writer use this phrase? How would *you* answer the question in the title of this chapter?

2. What is the purpose of paragraph 2? Check (✔) your answer.
   - ☐ a. To show that eating insects is a common practice.
   - ☐ b. To show that increasing numbers of people are eating insects.
   - ☐ c. To show why everyone should try eating insects.

   Explain why you chose your answer.

Critical Thinking Tip: Understanding the purpose of each paragraph will help you follow a writer's argument and decide if you do or do not agree.

3. In paragraph 6, find the words "they are *subtracting* from it." What does *subtracting* mean? Who is subtracting from what? Why is this word in italics in the sentence?

4. What is the purpose of paragraph 7? Check (✔) your answer.
   - ☐ a. To offer another solution to the problem.
   - ☐ b. To describe new reasons to eat insects.
   - ☐ c. To provide more support for Gracer's ideas.

   Explain why you chose your answer.

5. According to the text, what is David Gracer's main reason for saying people should eat insects? How does he support his argument? Does he succeed in getting you to agree with him about the problem? Do you agree with him about the solution? Explain.

6. A person who is optimistic about the future believes that good things are going to happen. A person who is pessimistic believes the opposite. Are Robert Kok and Marion Nestle optimistic about people in North America eating insects? Use information from the reading to support your answer. Is David Gracer optimistic? Explain what he means when he says, "If I did this for a living, my family and I would be eating bugs all the time" (paragraph 8).

WRITING

A. Use the Target Vocabulary: Choose five of the target words or phrases from the chart on page 187. On a piece of paper, use each word or phrase in a sentence and underline it. Find a partner and read each other's sentences.

B. Practice Writing: Choose one of these topics and write a paragraph about it. Then find a partner and read each other's paragraphs.

1. Write a short letter to David Gracer. Tell him what you think of his efforts to educate people about eating insects.

2. Describe a time when you spoke out about something you believed in. What were you speaking out about, what was the situation, and how did people respond?

> **Writing Tip:** If you write to someone about something they have said, be sure to include the source (that is, name the place where you found the information).

CHAPTER 16

A Small Creature with a Big Job

A beekeeper and his honeybees

LEARNING OUTCOME

> Learn about how people depend on bees

GETTING READY TO READ

Talk about these questions with your class.

1. What do you see happening in the photo above?
2. What do you know about bees? Give some facts about what they do. What do you think is the "big job" mentioned in the title?

A honeybee collecting pollen

Wild bees and their hive

READING

Read to Find Out: What has been happening to bees?

Look at the picture, words, and definitions next to the reading. Then read without stopping. If you see a new word, try to understand the sentence without it. You will learn the word later.

A Small Creature with a Big Job

1　Have you ever watched a bee at work on a flower? It wastes no time as it packs pollen onto its back legs to carry off to the hive. On their travels, bees carry pollen from flower to flower, pollinating[1] the plants, a process which allows the plants to produce fruit. The bee and the plant are partners in this process, each **essential** to the other—and to us.

2　One-third of the food we eat comes from plants that need animals to pollinate them. Birds do some of this work, but insects do most of it, and most of those insects are bees. In the United States, bees pollinate 75 percent of all the fruits, vegetables, and nuts that growers produce. Without the services of bees, we would have no tomatoes, soybeans, apples, or pears, to name just a few bee-pollinated plants. If anything happened to the world's bee populations, that would be bad news for anyone who eats fruits or vegetables anywhere. If that includes you, then you need to know that bees today—in North America, Europe, and Asia—are facing many **threats**.

3　Jeff Anderson knows a great deal about those threats. He has been a beekeeper for 30 years, ever since he married a beekeeper's daughter and went into the family business. Each year, he travels the United States with his honeybees, spending the spring among California fruit trees and summers in the fields of Minnesota. He's continuing a long tradition of beekeepers who move their hives with the seasons so their bees can **hunt** for new sources of pollen. In ancient[2] Egypt, beekeepers would transport their bees down the Nile River to find flowering **crops**. In North America, beekeepers over the years have traveled by covered wagon,[3] riverboat, and train. Transporting hives long distances became much easier with the development of major highways in the 1940s.

4　Around that same time, another change **occurred**. Traveling beekeepers in North America were used to paying farmers to let them place hives on their land. However, wild bees started disappearing, until finally there were no longer enough wild bees left to pollinate the farmers' crops. That meant the farmers had to **call on** the beekeepers' bees to do the job instead. Then the farmers started paying the beekeepers.

[1] *pollinate* = make a flower or plant produce seeds by giving it pollen

[2] *ancient* = existing very far back in history

[3] *a covered wagon*

5 The wild bees were disappearing because of changes in land use and methods of farming. As more and more land was developed for housing, there were fewer and fewer flowering plants to feed wild bees. **Agriculture** was changing, too, with the introduction of new **pesticides**. Wild bees were carrying pollen with pesticides home to their hives and killing off entire populations.

6 North America is home to **at least** 4,500 different kinds of bees. The bees that Jeff Anderson and other beekeepers work with are European honeybees, which were brought over from Europe about 400 years ago. Their numbers have been dropping, too, and Anderson says it keeps getting harder to raise healthy honeybees. In the 1980s, honeybees came under attack from two types of parasites[4] that were new to North America. Honeybees have been hurt by pesticides and diseases[5], too. In the spring of 2005, U.S. beekeepers found that one-third of their honeybees had died during the winter, much more than is normal. From 2015 to 2016, in spite of ever increasing efforts to protect honeybee populations, U.S. beekeepers lost over 40 percent of their bees. The reasons are still not fully understood.

[4] *a parasite* = an animal that lives on another and gets food from it

[5] *disease* = a kind of sickness affecting people, animals, or plants

7 Saving wild bees may be the best hope for the long-term health of crops that depend on bees. However, wild bees face a problem that has to do with the way that farmland is managed. For example, one of the most **productive** farm regions in North America is California's Central Valley, **yet** this area is not at all welcoming to wild bees. Too little of the land is in its natural state. Farmers and homeowners there have put the land to their own uses and gotten rid of weeds (wild plants growing where they aren't wanted), which are rich sources of pollen for wild bees. Bee experts know that wild bees do best when farmers avoid chemical pesticides and leave some land in its natural state. Farmers and other big landowners—and anyone with a garden—must do whatever they can to protect wild bees.

8 The disappearing bee is only one of the many environmental **crises** in the news today. But while there *are* serious problems with our environment, there are also many good people working hard to solve them. Douglas Barasch, editor of the environmental magazine *OnEarth*, knows that news about the environment often sounds bad, and it can make people anxious.[6] Yet he is not anxious. Why not? Experience tells him that within each problem **lies** its solution. He is always meeting people who, when they see something "broken," **immediately** see an opportunity. They see a chance to fix something and make it better, whether it's a **motor** to be improved or a forest to be restored.[7] In the case of the honeybee, perhaps there are laws that need to be changed. One thing is clear: We'll have to figure out how to save the bee's way of life if we want to save our own.

[6] *anxious* = very worried

[7] *restored* = put back into good condition

Quick Comprehension Check

A. Read these statements **about the reading**. Circle T (true) or F (false). On the line, write the number of the paragraph with the answer.

1. A beekeeper is a place where honeybees live.   T   F   _____

2. Traveling beekeepers are not welcomed by farmers.   T   F   _____

3. Large numbers of bees have been dying.   T   F   _____

4. Modern farming methods have harmed bee populations.   T   F   _____

5. Changes in land use are needed to protect bees.   T   F   _____

6. No one who cares about the environment has any hope these days.   T   F   _____

B. Work with your class. Share your answers from part A. Go back to the reading to find the reason why a statement is true or false. Correct the false statements.

EXPLORING VOCABULARY

Thinking about the Target Vocabulary

A. Look at the chart with the target vocabulary from "A Small Creature with a Big Job." Four nouns, four verbs, and two adjectives are missing. Scan the reading to find them, and add them to the correct places in the chart. Use the singular form of any plural noun. Use the base form of each verb.

¶	Nouns	Verbs	Adjectives	Other
1				
2				
3				
4				
5	agriculture			
	pesticide			
6				at least
7				
				yet

¶	Nouns	Verbs	Adjectives	Other
8				
				immediately

Vocabulary Tip:
The singular form of *crises* is *crisis*.

B. Which words and phrases are new to you? Circle them in the chart. Then find them in the reading. Look at the context. Can you guess the meaning?

Understanding the Target Vocabulary

A. These sentences are **about the reading**. What is the meaning of each **boldfaced** word? Circle a, b, or c.

1. Bees and bee-pollinated plants are **essential** to each other. *Essential* means

   a. quite similar.   b. very important.   c. portable.

Vocabulary Tip:
Essential can also be a noun (usually plural). *The essentials* means "the most basic and important facts." *Tell me just the essentials of what happened.*

2. Traveling beekeepers move to places where their bees can **hunt** for new sources of pollen. *Hunt* means

   a. estimate.   b. look for.   c. require.

3. Some areas of farmland are very successful, **yet** wild bees cannot live there. *Yet* in this sentence means

   a. because.   b. unless.   c. but.

4. The loss of bees is a **crisis** because many fruits and vegetables depend on bees for pollination. A crisis is

   a. a very bad situation that might get worse.   b. a chance to make some money.   c. a story about a new development.

5. Douglas Barasch believes that the solution to each environmental problem **lies** within it. In this sentence, *lies* means

   a. maintains.   b. deserves.   c. can be found.

6. When some people see an environmental problem, they **immediately** see a chance to do some good. *Immediately* means

   a. right away.   b. naturally.   c. gratefully.

7. "A **motor** to be improved" is an example of something that needs to be fixed. A motor is

   a. a kind of bee.   b. an engine.   c. an event.

B. Complete these sentences **about the reading**. Use the words and phrases in the box.

agriculture	call on	occurred	productive
at least	crops	pesticides	threats

1. Bees today are facing many _____ that could do them serious harm.

   > **Vocabulary Tip:** *Threat* is related to the verb *threaten. Threaten* can mean "to say you will cause someone harm if they don't do what you want" (*The workers threatened to quit*) or "to be likely to destroy something" (*A storm is threatening the island*).

2. Some farmers make a living by raising vegetables, grains, or fruit. The products that farmers grow for sale are their _____.

3. In the 1940s, changes in transportation happened in the United States, and a change also _____ in the relationship between farmers and traveling beekeepers.

4. After wild bees started disappearing, there weren't enough of them to pollinate crops. Since then, farmers have had to _____ the European honeybee to get the job done.

5. The science and work of farming is called _____.

6. Farmers often use chemicals to kill insects that would destroy their crops. These chemicals are called _____.

7. There are many kinds of bees in North America—_____ 4,500 kinds. There may be more than 4,500 but not fewer.

8. California's Central Valley is famous in North America because so many crops grow there. It is a very _____ farm region.

   > **Vocabulary Tip:** *Productive* is related to the verb *produce* and the nouns *product*, *producer*, and *produce*, pronounced PRO-duce, meaning "fruits and vegetables to be sold."

EXPANDING VOCABULARY

Building on the Vocabulary

Word Grammar: *Occur, Take Place,* and *Happen*

The verbs **occur**, **take place**, and **happen** have similar meanings.

- *Occur* means "happen" but is more formal. Use it to report past, unplanned events: *The accident occurred at 11:25 p.m. at Main Street and Broadway. Occur to* (someone) means "come into someone's mind, often suddenly:" *It occurred to me that I needed to call him.*

- *Take place* means "happen" but is used for planned events, not usually for things that happen by chance: *The wedding will take place in June.*

- *Happen* is used more often than the other verbs, usually for unplanned events: *What happened to your eye?*

Circle the correct verb to use in each sentence.

1. Our monthly meetings always (occur / take place) in the school library.

2. I don't understand what's (occurring / happening).

3. When did the accident (occur / take place)?

4. It didn't (occur / happen) to me to check the pockets before washing my jeans.

Using the Target Vocabulary in New Contexts

A. Complete the sentences with the target words and phrases in the box. There is one extra word.

agriculture	crises	hunt	motor	threat
at least	crop	immediately	pesticides	yet

1. Gardeners use many methods for getting rid of harmful insects, including natural _____, which do not contain chemicals.

2. I don't know how many tree-based products I use, but I could probably think of _____ twenty-five.

3. The predicted ice storm presents a serious _____ to apple trees in the region.

4. An engine generally uses fuel, while a _____ can also be electric.

5. I hope to repay the loan _____, or at least very soon, because the interest starts adding up right away.

6. My grandfather forgets where he left his glasses, and then we all have to _____ for them.

Vocabulary Tip: *Hunt* also means "to chase animals and birds to catch or kill them:" *It's against the law to hunt some kinds of animals.*

7. The phrase a bumper _____ means a very large amount of fruit or vegetables produced in one season.

8. People who choose to study _____ may be planning to raise crops or livestock.

9. Experts say that insects can be good sources of protein, _____ many people are simply not open to the idea of eating them.

B. Read these sentences. Write the **boldfaced** target words or phrases next to their definitions.

a. The experts predicted an economic **crisis**.

b. A good diet is **essential** for good health.

c. The manager knew who the most **productive** employees were.

Vocabulary Tip: *Call on* can also mean "ask (a student, an employee in a meeting, etc.) to speak:" *Maria raised her hand and the teacher called on her.*

d. The president **called on** everyone to avoid wasting electricity and fuel.

e. The engineer believed the answers **lay** in developing appropriate technologies.

Target Word or Phrase		Definition
1.	=	existed or could be found
2.	=	needed, highly important
3.	=	getting a lot of work done
4.	=	a time when a situation is very bad or dangerous
5.	=	formally asked someone to do something or to accept a responsibility

DEVELOPING YOUR READING SKILLS

Understanding Main Ideas, Major Points, and Supporting Details

Reread "A Small Creature with a Big Job" and answer these questions.

1. What is the main idea of "A Small Creature with a Big Job"?

_____

_____

2. Which four sentences state major points of the reading, and which ones give supporting details? Write *MP* (major point) or *SD* (supporting detail).

_____ a. Bees play an important part in the lives of many plants.

_____ b. There are at least 4,500 kinds of bees in North America.

_____ c. U.S. agriculture depends on the services of beekeepers and their honeybees.

_____ d. Beekeepers today are finding it difficult to raise healthy bees.

_____ e. Apples, pears, and other fruit need bees to carry pollen from flower to flower.

_____ f. Surprisingly, California's rich Central Valley is not a great place for wild bees.

_____ g. Both wild bees and honeybees are in danger.

_____ h. Farmers and gardeners don't like weeds, but bees do.

Text Organization

Number these events in chronological order, from 1 (the earliest) to 7 (the most recent).

> **Reading Tip:** Make sure you understand the chronological order of events. It may help you see cause and effect relationships among them.

_____ a. U.S. land was taken for housing and highways, and new pesticides came into use.

_____ b. Beekeepers in ancient Egypt transported their hives down the Nile River.

_____ c. Two new types of parasites attacked honeybees in North America.

_____ d. The European honeybee was imported into the United States.

_____ e. Wild bees began to disappear.

_____ f. U.S. beekeepers lost almost half of their bees during the winter.

_____ g. Farmers started paying traveling beekeepers for the services of their honeybees.

Cause and Effect

Complete each sentence about the reading. Use *because* or *because of.*

1. Beekeepers like Jeff Anderson travel _____

   _____

2. U.S. farmers started depending on beekeepers _____

   _____

3. Bees have been disappearing _____

   _____

4. The disappearance of bees matters _____

   _____

5. Leaving land in its natural state is a good idea _____

   _____

CRITICAL THINKING

Talk about these questions in a small group.

1. In paragraph 1, find the phrase *partners in this process.* Who are the partners, and what do they do for each other? How are these partners "essential . . . to us"?

2. The reading describes the disappearance of both wild bees and beekeepers' honeybees. Is it normal for some honeybees to die during the winter? How do you know? Review the reasons given in the reading for the drop in the bee population. Which of them are natural causes, and which ones are people to blame for?

3. In paragraph 8, you read, "Douglas Barasch, editor of the environmental magazine *OnEarth*, knows that news about the environment often sounds bad, and it can make people anxious." Do you agree that news about the environment is often bad news? Do news stories about the environment make you anxious? Why isn't Douglas Barasch anxious? What do you think the writer's purpose is in describing Barasch's experience and his point of view?

   > **Critical Thinking Tip:** Citing experts is one method that writers use to try to make an argument stronger.

4. In paragraph 8, the writer states that "perhaps there are laws that need to be changed." What would be the purpose of changing laws? Using information from the text, suggest what new laws might help improve the situation. Then reread the last sentence of paragraph 8. What does the writer mean? Where else in the text does the writer refer to our way of life?

5. The chapters in this unit talk about air pollution in Asia, the decrease in the world's tree population, ways that food production is harming the environment, and the disappearance of bees. What do these topics have in common? When you think about them, how do you feel about the future? Explain.

WRITING

A. Use the Target Vocabulary: Choose five of the target words or phrases from the chart on pages 198–199. On a piece of paper, use each word or phrase in a sentence and underline it. Find a partner and read each other's sentences.

B. Practice Writing: Choose one of these topics and write a paragraph about it. Then find a partner and read each other's paragraphs.

1. An optimist is a person who believes that good things will happen. A pessimist is the opposite. When you think about environmental problems you've read or heard about, which are you? Explain.

2. Do you prefer an urban or a rural environment? Or some other kind of environment? Explain what you prefer and why.

Writing Tip: If you find you're always repeating the same words, use your dictionary to find synonyms. Check definitions, sample sentences, and usage notes for the new words.

Checkpoint

LOOK BACK

A. Think About This

Look back at your answers to the *Think About This* question on page 161: *What kinds of stories about the environment are in the news these days?*

Do you want to change any of your answers? Do you want to add anything new?

B. Remember the Readings

What do you want to remember most from the readings in Unit 4? For each chapter, write one sentence about the reading.

Chapter 13: Small Ride, Big Trouble

_____

Chapter 14: Your Trees, My Trees, Our Trees

_____

Chapter 15: Would You Eat Bugs to Save the World?

_____

Chapter 16: A Small Creature with a Big Job

_____

REVIEWING VOCABULARY

A. Think about the meanings of the words in each group below. Cross out the one word that does not belong in the group.

1. engine   vehicle   motor   protein
2. educator   passenger   border   expert
3. valuable   harm   threat   crisis
4. soil   ink   pesticide agriculture
5. diameter   loan   income   interest

B. Complete each sentence with a phrase from the box. There is one extra phrase.

at least	carbon dioxide	keep up with	speak out
be open to	in favor of	look into	
call on	in terms of	set out	

1. The chemical symbol for _____ is CO_2.

2. Most people were too afraid of the government to _____.

3. I don't know the answer to your question, but I'll _____ it and let you know.

4. Georgia managed to do everything she _____ to do.

5. Has the boss already made a decision, or will he _____ other ideas?

6. There are lots of products made of rubber. I'm sure you could list _____ ten.

7. The United Nations must _____ all its member nations for support.

8. It is still a developing country, but it is rich _____ its natural resources.

9. So much is happening in the world that it's hard for me to _____ current events.

EXPANDING VOCABULARY

Word Families

Use words from the six word families to complete the sentences below. Use your dictionary if you have questions about word meanings.

	Nouns	Verbs	Adjectives	Other
1	competition competitor	compete	competitive	competitively
2	destruction	destroy	destructive	destructively
3	gratitude		grateful	gratefully
4	product production	produce	productive	productively
5	renewal	renew	renewable	
6	requirement	require	required	

1. a. The advertising business is highly _____.

   b. Who won the _____?

2. a. Farmers use pesticides for fear that insects will _____ their

      crops.

   b. Who is to blame for the _____ of the rainforest?

3. a. I _____ accepted her offer of a loan.

   b. We'd like to get him a gift, to express our _____ for his

      support.

4. a. The most _____ employees are the ones who get the most

      work done.

   b. New technology has helped farmers use their land more

      _____.

5. a. *Urban* _____ means the process of remaking poor areas of

      cities by building new housing, stores, etc.

   b. _____ energy includes solar power, for example.

6. a. Some U.S. college students have to meet a foreign language _____ before they can graduate.

   b. All living things _____ oxygen.

A PUZZLE

There are 12 target words from Unit 4 in this puzzle. The words go across (→) and down (↓). Find the words and circle them. Then use them to complete the sentences below. (Note: The words in the sentences are not in the same order as the words in the puzzle.)

X	E	Z	F	O	R	C	E	R	P	X
H	S	X	U	N	L	E	S	S	O	J
R	T	K	E	Z	J	X	W	G	P	Z
A	I	X	L	X	W	K	Z	S	U	Q
I	M	M	E	D	I	A	T	E	L	Y
S	A	E	S	S	E	N	T	I	A	L
E	T	X	C	Z	X	V	Q	X	T	Y
D	E	C	R	E	A	S	E	K	I	E
K	X	V	Q	X	W	J	X	Z	O	T
Z	J	X	Z	C	U	R	R	E	N	T
M	E	A	N	W	H	I	L	E	Q	X

Across

1. We'll eat outside _____ it rains.
2. Air and water are not just valuable—they are _____.
3. We must act _____ to deal with this threat.
4. The politicians kept on talking, and _____, the crisis grew.
5. No one can _____ him to do what he does not want to do.
6. The company cut workers' pay to bring about a _____ in its production costs.
7. I read the newspaper to educate myself on _____ events.

Down

1. Heating _____ costs have risen.
2. There are over six billion people in the world, and the _____ is still growing.
3. He didn't want to get involved, _____ he felt that he should.
4. The soil was rich, and they _____ good crops there.
5. I don't know how much it cost, but I would _____ about $100.

BUILDING DICTIONARY SKILLS

Words with Multiple Meanings

Look at the dictionary entries below. Then read each sentence and write the number of the meaning.

---

main·tain /meɪnˈteɪn/ *v* [T] **1** to make something continue in the same way or at the same standard as before: *The U.S. and Britain have maintained close ties.* | *It is important to maintain a healthy weight.* **2** to keep something in good condition by taking care of it: *It costs a lot of money to maintain a big house.* **3** to strongly express an opinion or attitude: *I've always **maintained that** any changes in the law will hurt the poor more than the rich.* | *From the beginning James has maintained his innocence.*

---

1. _____ a. The owner of the apartment building is responsible for maintaining it.

   _____ b. Experts maintain that insects can be good sources of protein.

   _____ c. They maintained a close friendship for the rest of their lives.

---

shade¹ /ʃeɪd/ *n* **1** [singular, U] an area that is cooler, and darker because the light of the sun cannot reach it [→SHADOW]: *Let's find a table **in the shade*** | *boys sitting **in the shade of** a tree.* **2** [C] something that reduces or blocks light, especially a cover that you pull across a window. **3** [C] a particular degree of a color: *a darker **shade of** red.* **4 shades** [plural] *informal* SUNGLASSES **5 shade of meaning/opinion etc.** a meaning, etc. that is slightly different from other ones: *The word can have many **shades** of meaning depending on the context.*

---

2. _____ a. We pull down the shades at night.

   _____ b. It will be cooler in the shade.

   _____ c. I like that shade of blue.

   _____ d. People will argue over the shades of meaning in the president's statement.

---

lie¹ /laɪ/ *v* (past tense **lay** /leɪ/, past participle **lain** /leɪn/, present participle **lying**) [I] **1 a)** to be in a position in which your body is flat on the floor, a bed, etc.: *We **lay on** the beach all day.* | *I lay awake worrying.* **b)** *also* **lie down** to put yourself in this position: *I'm going upstairs to lie down.* **2** to be in a particular place or position: *The town **lies to** the east of the lake.* **3** used to say where something such as a reason or an answer can be found: *"The secret of freedom lies in educating people ...."* **4** to be or remain in a particular condition or position: *After the war, the city **lay in ruins**.*

---

3. _____ a. I spread my beach towel on the sand and lay down for a nap.

   _____ b. For over 40 years, the photos lay forgotten in an old suitcase.

   _____ c. Rio de Janeiro lies on the coast of Brazil.

   _____ d. The solution lies in developing renewable energy sources.

Vocabulary Self-Test 2

Circle the letter of the word or phrase that best completes each sentence.

1. A news reporter must have many _____ of information.

   a. crops   b. sources   c. proteins   d. threats

2. A message appeared on my computer screen saying that a problem

   had _____.

   a. attached   b. occurred   c. solved   d. harmed

3. When you quote, you must use the _____ words someone said
   or wrote.

   a. portable   b. valuable   c. renewable   d. exact

4. Your computer printer isn't broken—it just needs _____.

   a. behavior   b. rubber   c. ink   d. fuel

5. Olga is in Dallas to _____ a meeting.

   a. attend   b. consume   c. destroy   d. exist

6. There has been an increase in the _____ for these electronic
   devices. Everybody wants one.

   a. blame   b. shade   c. demand   d. load

7. We plan to go ahead with our trip _____ the bad weather
   they're predicting.

   a. in spite of   b. in terms of   c. unless   d. meanwhile

8. Many people who once used dangerous chemicals in their yards and

   gardens have stopped that _____.

   a. engineering   b. grain   c. adventure   d. practice

9. I didn't _____ how late it was until I noticed your watch.

    a. lie   b. pollute   c. realize   d. set

10. You'll find fruit and vegetables in the produce _____ of the supermarket.

    a. diameter   b. border   c. shadow   d. section

11. When you go for a job interview, it's important to wear the _____ kind of clothes.

    a. electronic   b. modern   c. appropriate d. portable

12. A travel writer must write detailed _____ of places.

    a. decreases   b. descriptions c. experts   d. styles

13. I don't want to get _____ in their argument about who's to blame.

    a. advanced   b. involved   c. educated   d. replaced

14. They are now _____ that the flight will arrive thirty minutes late.

    a. speaking out b. estimating   c. improving   d. forcing

15. To write science fiction adventure stories, you need a good

    _____.

    a. motor   b. passenger   c. imagination d. interest

16. Do you agree that we should judge a _____ by how it treats its weakest members—children, old people, and the sick?

    a. method   b. resource   c. crisis   d. society

17. A business must keep _____ records of all costs, profits, and losses.

    a. confused   b. accurate   c. grateful   d. equal

18. It's a wonderful plan, but will they be able to _____?

    a. carry it out b. make it up   c. keep up with it d. call on it

19. Would you say that water is our most important natural _____?

    a. carbon dioxide b. resource   c. soil   d. agriculture

20. As an inventor of appropriate technologies, Mark _____ to prove that he could make a difference, and he did.

    a. maintained   b. predicted   c. hunted   d. set out

21. My father was not an emotional man, _____ his tears flowed that day.

    a. yet   b. fairly   c. neither   d. at least

22. Most people I know share my opinion. _____, that's what they tell me. Maybe they're just being polite.

    a. So far   b. At least   c. In particular   d. On the other hand

23. The _____ method means doing careful testing and record keeping.

    a. essential   b. scientific   c. rural   d. productive

24. You can see all the latest _____ at the auto show.

    a. pesticides   b. loans   c. centuries   d. models

25. A fire _____ three things: heat, fuel, and oxygen.

    a. deserves   b. takes off   c. sets   d. requires

26. Trees take in carbon dioxide and use it in the _____ of wood and leaves.

    a. income   b. plenty   c. production   d. competition

27. Members of _____ groups have spoken out against the plan to destroy the forest so as to build houses on the mountainside.

    a. current   b. environmental c. advanced   d. high-tech

28. Maria was in love, but her friends disliked the man and told each other that she would _____ finding someone else.

    a. be better off   b. look into   c. be open to   d. be in favor of

29. In most cars, the _____ is in the front of the vehicle.

    a. transportation b. population   c. engine   d. technology

See the Answer Key on page 271.

ECONOMICS

THINK ABOUT THIS

When you hear the words *the economy*—for example, from a TV news reporter—what topics do you think the reporter might talk about?

Make a list of topics related to the economy.

_____

_____

_____

_____

CHAPTER 17

Economics— What's It All About?

Home buyers

GETTING READY TO READ

Read the definition of *economy*. Then talk about the questions with your class.

> **e·con·o·my** / ɪˈkɒnəmi / ɪˈkɑ / *n* (plural **economies**) [C] the way that money, businesses, and products are organized in a particular country, area, etc.: *the U.S. economy* | *adding jobs to the* **local economy** | *the* **global**/**world** *economy.*

1. How would you describe the current condition of your country's economy? The world economy? Your local economy?

2. Look at the photo above. What does it have to do with the economy?

READING

Read to Find Out: According to the reading, how do economists view the world?

Look at the words and definitions next to the reading. Then read without stopping. If you see a new word, try to understand the sentence without it. You will learn the word later.

Economics—What's It All About?

1   What do you think of when you hear the word **economics**? Perhaps the front page of a newspaper, where you might see stories about employment, or interest rates, or a national **debt** on the **rise**. Many people find that such stories use terms they don't understand. They find economics confusing, yet they feel they need to know something about it. We all do. **After all**, economics is about us. In the words of Canadian economist Jim Stanford, "Economics is about who does what, who gets what, and what they do with it."

2   When we talk about economics, we are talking about ourselves as workers, consumers, savers, and investors. The results of our **individual** and collective[1] decisions in those roles make up the economy. Our individual decisions include such things as what products to buy, what work to do, and how much to invest in our education. To get the things we need and want, we need to use our resources—our money, time, and skills—and those resources are limited. That forces us to make choices.

[1] *collective = shared or done by all the members of a group*

3   Economist Pearl Claunch explains, "The economist's special way of looking at the world involves looking at the costs and benefits of making any decision or choice. Economics says that **since** everything interesting in life is **scarce**, choices have to be made. And choices involve costs as well as benefits. So if you want to make wise choices, you should use a benefit/cost **approach**."

4   This method of decision-making, also called *cost-benefit analysis*, is often used by governments in deciding how to use their financial resources. Take the case of a decision about whether to build a highway. Officials[2] would estimate the costs of the project (in taxpayer money, for example) and compare them with the benefits (to highway users, for example). We can use the same approach in deciding how we spend our own money, or our time.

[2] *an official = someone with a responsible job in an organization or government*

5   However, the costs of buying or doing something includes more than just the price we pay in dollars or euros or yen. When we choose one thing over another thing we also want (because we can't have both), then we lose the **opportunity** to get that other thing. Economists have a term for this **loss**: opportunity cost. When you have a limited amount

of money and you choose to spend it on a pizza instead of a movie, you have lost the chance to see the film. The opportunity cost of getting the pizza is not getting to see the movie.

6   To return to the example of the highway: When the government considers the cost to taxpayers, it must consider more than the price of **labor** and materials. Tax money is a scarce resource, and the government could use that money elsewhere.[3] In other words, what is the opportunity cost of building the highway? In addition, there are environmental costs to consider, such as the loss of fields or forests. There may also be costs to people whose **property** lies in the way of the highway.

[3] *elsewhere* = in some other place

7   Spending decisions are only part of the government's role in the economy. One of its most basic responsibilities is creating currency (the economist's term for money), which lets us make **trades** for goods and services. Imagine if we had to **exchange** goods and services without the use of money, the way people did before money was invented. How would you pay your school for your classes? You could offer to trade the school some of your belongings[4] or do a job for them, but you might not have anything the school needed. Even if you did, you would waste a lot of time negotiating[5] the trade. Money, on the other hand, lets us buy and sell goods and services quickly and easily.

[4] *belongings* = things that someone owns

[5] *negotiate* = discuss in order to reach an agreement

8   Most people agree that the government plays an essential role in creating and regulating[6] money. However, other parts of its role in the economy lead to much disagreement. Our individual values make us judge government actions differently, just as our values lead us to different choices in our own lives. We study the costs and benefits of government actions; we debate[7] what is and is not **necessary**. We all have opinions about who should do what, who should get what, and what they should do with it, and that is what economics is all about.

[6] *regulate* = control an activity or process, usually by having rules

[7] *debate* = discuss something so as to make a decision about it

Quick Comprehension Check

A. Read these statements **about the reading**. Circle T (true) or F (false). On the line, write the number of the paragraph with the answer.

1. Economics is about what governments do.   T   F   _____

2. Your personal resources include your time and
   skills.   T   F   _____

3. Our limited resources force us to make choices.   T   F   _____

4. Economists value a particular decision-making
   method.   T   F   _____

5. The government has one basic role in the economy.   T   F   _____

6. The cost of something can mean more than its price.   T   F   _____

B. Work with your class. Share your answers from part A. Go back to the reading to find the reason why a statement is true or false. Correct the false statements.

EXPLORING VOCABULARY

Thinking about the Target Vocabulary

A. Look at the chart with the target vocabulary from "Economics—What's It All About?" Nine nouns are missing. Scan the reading to find them, and add them to the correct places in the chart. Use the singular form of any plural noun.

¶	Nouns	Verbs	Adjectives	Other
1				
				after all
2			individual	
3				since
			scarce	
5				
6				
7				
		exchange		
8			necessary	

B. Which words and phrases are new to you? Circle them in the chart. Then find them in the reading. Look at the context. Can you guess the meaning?

Understanding the Target Vocabulary

A. Complete these sentences **about the reading**. Use the words in the box.

after all	economics	loss	property
debt	exchange	opportunity	scarce

1. The study of the ways that money, goods, and services are produced and used is called _____.

2. All the money that a national government has borrowed (that is, all the money it has received as loans, both from its own people and from foreign governments) is called the national _____.

3. Many people believe they should learn about economics because " _____, economics is about us" (paragraph 1)—in other words, because we need to remember that fact (that economics is about us).

   > **Vocabulary Tip:**
   > Use *after all* to introduce a fact you think should be considered because it will help to explain what you just said.

4. Economists say we must make choices because everything of value is _____, meaning that it exists in a limited supply.

5. Because of your limited resources, when you choose to do or buy one thing, you generally lose the chance, or _____, to do or buy something else.

6. When you lose something, you experience a _____.

7. If someone's land lies in the way of a highway, that means the highway would cross that person's _____.

   > **Vocabulary Tip:**
   > The verb *lose*, the noun *loss*, and the adjective *lost* belong to the same word family.

8. Money makes it easier to _____ goods and services— to give one thing and get something else in return.

B. These sentences are also **about the reading**. What is the meaning of each **boldfaced** word or phrase? Circle a, b, or c.

1. Some people worry about a **rise** in their country's national debt. A rise in something means it is

   a. decreasing. b. improving. c. going up.

Vocabulary Tip: Use *on the rise* to describe something that's increasing: *Interest rates are on the rise*. *Rise* as a verb has many meanings, including "move up:" *The sun rises in the east.*

2. We make some decisions in life as a part of a group, but we also make our own **individual** decisions. *Individual* means

   a. separate from others. b. volunteer. c. emotional.

3. We have to make choices **since** we cannot have everything. *Since* in this context means

   a. starting when. b. in the past. c. because.

4. Economist Pearl Claunch believes in and advises a certain **approach** to decision making. *An approach to something* means

   a. a threat to doing it. b. a method of doing it. c. a result of doing it.

5. Whether you build a highway or a house, it involves costs for both **labor** and materials. *Labor* means

   a. time. b. work. c. taxes.

6. When the members of a society want to do some kind of business with one another, money makes it easier for them to make **trades**. A trade is

   a. a threat. b. an exchange. c. a prediction.

7. We may not all agree on which government actions are **necessary** and which ones are not important. *Necessary* means

   a. needed. b. modern. c. complex.

EXPANDING VOCABULARY

Building on the Vocabulary

Word Grammar: *Economics* and Its Word Family

The noun **economics** is a noncount noun. When *economics* is the subject of a verb, the verb is singular: *Economics **is** one of my favorite subjects.* (The same is true of the nouns *mathematics*, *physics*, *politics*, and *news*.)

The adjectives **economic** and **economical** have different meanings.

- *Economic* means "relating to economics and trade": *The country is heading for an **economic** crisis.*

- *Economical* means "using money or other resources carefully, without waste:" *A smaller car is more **economical** because it can go farther on less fuel.*

The adverb form of both *economic* and *economical* is **economically**.

Circle the correct word to complete the sentence.

1. The (economic / economics) teacher called on the first student who raised his hand.

2. The unemployment rate has dropped because of strong (economic / economical) growth.

3. Economics (is / are) one of the social sciences, like history and sociology.

4. It'll be more (economic / economical) to buy a whole pizza and share it. Buying individual slices costs more.

5. (Economic / Economics) conditions are improving.

6. Heating our house cost a lot last winter. How can we do it more (economical / economically)?

Using the Target Vocabulary in New Contexts

A. Complete the sentences with the target words in the box. There is one extra word.

approach	exchange	labor	property
debt	individual	opportunity	since

1. When you have to learn new vocabulary, what's your _____ to learning the new words?

2. The word "_____" can refer to land but also to anything you own.

3. The program gives foreign students in France the _____ to live with a French family.

4. _____ his injuries aren't serious, the doctors are letting the man go home.

5. I have Canadian dollars and I need Japanese yen. Can you _____ foreign money at the airport?

6. He keeps buying things on this credit card and getting deeper in _____.

Vocabulary Tip: *Exchange* is more formal than *trade*. As a verb, it takes a direct object (*We exchanged phone numbers*). As a noun, it has several meanings; see your dictionary.

7. When I had my car fixed, they charged me by the hour for the

   _____.

B. Complete the sentences with the target words in the box. There is one extra word.

after all	individual	necessary	scarce
economics	loss	rise	trade

1. The closing of the factory meant the _____ of over 300 jobs.

2. A cake serves several people, while cupcakes are _____ servings.

3. Let's ask Dave to explain cost-benefit analysis. _____, he teaches economics.

4. I thought that was a required course, but it's not actually _____.

5. Wild bees have been disappearing, and they are now _____ in many places.

6. Because of the increase in fuel costs, we should expect a _____ in home heating bills.

7. Ann liked her sister's blue sweater, and her sister liked Ann's new earrings, so they made a _____.

Reading Tip: When you see *after all* at the end of a sentence, it can mean "in spite of what you expected or thought was true:" *I took an umbrella with me, but then I didn't need it after all.*

Vocabulary Tip: *Trade* can also be a verb (*the boys traded bikes*) and a noncount noun meaning "the activity of buying and selling between countries" (*international trade, unfair trade practices*).

DEVELOPING YOUR READING SKILLS

Understanding Main Ideas, Major Points, and Supporting Details

A. Reread "Economics—What's It All About?" and then answer the question, what is the main idea of "Economics—What's It All About?" Check (✓) your answer.

☐ 1. News stories about economics are confusing for most people but not if you learn a few key words.

☐ 2. We all need to know something about economics because it's about us, the choices we have, and the decisions we make.

☐ 3. The government's role in the economy is to consider the costs and benefits of how it's going to spend the taxpayers' money.

B. Write at least two statements with details that support each of the major points below. Use information from the reading.

1. When you talk about economics, you're talking about people's decisions.

_____

_____

_____

2. Every choice involves costs as well as benefits.

_____

_____

_____

3. You can do a cost-benefit analysis in many different types of situations.

_____

_____

_____

4. A national government has different roles in the economy of the country.

_____

_____

_____

Cause and Effect

Complete each sentence using _because (of)_ + information from the reading. Try to paraphrase.

1. People may feel confused when they read or hear economic news _____

_____

_____

2. When planning a building project, government officials must consider more

than just the costs of labor and materials _____

_____

_____

3. Governments create currency _____

_____

_____

4. People disagree on the role of the government in the economy _____

_____

_____

Understanding the Writer's Purpose

Circle a or b to complete the sentence with the writer's purpose.

1. The writer quotes economist Jim Stanford in the introduction . . .
   a. to make the reader feel the subject will not be hard to understand.
   b. to introduce some of the particular vocabulary that economists use.
2. The writer quotes economist Pearl Claunch . . .
   a. to introduce the different roles people play in the economy.
   b. to show how an economist thinks and looks at the world.
3. The writer talks about pizza and a movie . . .
   a. to give the reader some decision-making advice.
   b. to give the reader a real-world example of an economic idea.
4. The writer includes the last sentence . . .
   a. to remind the reader of Stanford's definition of economics.
   b. to show that no one agrees on what *economics* means.

CRITICAL THINKING

Discussion

Talk about these questions with a partner and then with your whole class.

1. In paragraph 2, what examples does the writer give of individual decisions that people make? What examples can you give of collective decisions made by the people of a country? What about decisions that are neither individual nor collective?
2. How does the reading explain the phrase *opportunity cost?* What is the opportunity cost of being a student?

3. In paragraph 8, the word *values* is closest in meaning to:

a. experts or advisors   b. ideas about what's important   c. predictions about the future

Explain how the context led you to your answer. What do a person's values have to do with the economy?

4. On a piece of paper, draw a chart with two columns. Write *Costs* and *Benefits* at the top. Then do a cost-benefit analysis of studying English. Compare your analysis with your partner's. Which costs and benefits are the same for both of you? Which ones are different?

Critical Thinking Tip: A chart with two columns, and a heading at the top of each one, is called a **T-Chart**. This type of graphic organizer is useful for comparing two sets of ideas.

WRITING

A. Use the Target Vocabulary: Choose five of the target words or phrases from the chart on page 219. On a piece of paper, use each word or phrase in a sentence and underline it. Find a partner and read each other's sentences.

B. Practice Writing: Choose one of these topics and write a paragraph about it. Then find a partner and read each other's paragraphs.

1. Describe the cost-benefit analysis you did for question 4 under **Discussion:** *What are the costs and benefits of studying English?*

2. Think about decisions made by your national government on where to spend money (or not spend money). These decisions show what is most valued. Think of a specific way in which your personal values differ from the values expressed by the government in its decisions. Describe what you think your government should do differently.

Writing Tip: Begin and end a pros-and-cons paragraph or essay with your own opinion. In the body of the essay, present the opposite arguments and explain why you disagree with them.

CHAPTER 18

Supply and Demand

Fresh strawberries

LEARNING OUTCOME

❯ Learn about two basic laws of economics

GETTING READY TO READ

Talk about these questions with a partner.

1. Choose one of the products below, one that you both have experience buying. Have you seen the price of this product go up and down? What makes the price change from time to time?

   ☐ fresh fruit

   ☐ shoes

   ☐ plane tickets

2. How do changes in the price affect your decisions about buying the product?

3. How much would you pay for the box of strawberries in the photo?

READING

Look at the words and definitions next to the reading and the illustrations that follow it. Then read without stopping. If you see a new word, try to understand the sentence without it. You will learn the word later.

Supply and Demand

Introduction

1   The most basic laws in economics are the laws of supply and demand. *Demand* means how much of a product or service people want to buy. *Supply* means how much of that product or service is available for sale or can be produced. Understanding these laws is essential to understanding how markets work. That's because almost every transaction[1] between a buyer and a seller is the result of how these two laws affect each other.

[1] *transaction* = a business deal, such as buying and selling something

Setting Prices

2   The laws of supply and demand explain how prices for goods and services are set. When demand is high, producers see an opportunity for profit. They can charge high prices, **as** they're producing goods to meet a demand. So if many consumers want fresh strawberries, for example, growers have reason to increase the supply. That's the law of supply at work. However, the law of demand says that when the price of something goes *too* high, fewer consumers will buy it. So if strawberries get too expensive, some shoppers will buy another fruit instead, and the demand for strawberries will drop. When the demand for strawberries is low, or when people aren't willing to pay a good price for them, growers reduce production.

3   The goal of producers is to set a price low enough to **bring in** the number of sales they need but high enough to make a profit. That price—the point where the **quantity** that consumers want to buy equals the quantity that sellers want to produce—is called the equilibrium price. It's the point where there's a **balance** between supply and demand.

4   Notice in the diagram that as the cost of a box of strawberries rises, the supply goes up. But the demand for strawberries increases only as the cost drops. The point where the two lines **cross** is the equilibrium price.

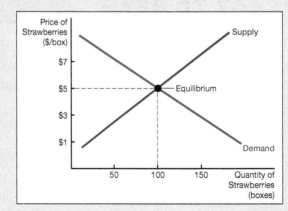

Imbalances Between Supply and Demand

5 Two other important **terms** are *surplus* and *shortage*. When the supply is higher than the demand, producers have more of a good or service than consumers want. In that case, the difference between the supply and the demand is called a surplus. A surplus can mean anything from extra strawberries that no one is buying to extra workers that no one is hiring. When the opposite happens, the difference between supply and demand is called a shortage. A shortage means there isn't enough of something to meet the demand. For example, imagine a company producing a new toy, one that quickly becomes more popular than expected. It flies off the shelf, the company can't produce enough to keep up with the demand, and stores **run out**. The result is a shortage of the toy (and some unhappy children).

Other Factors Affecting Demand

6 The example of the popular toy **brings up** another point about demand: Many factors[2] **other than** price can play a role in how much of a demand there is for a product or service. How did this particular toy get to be so popular? Perhaps there was an especially **effective** ad on TV that sparked[3] demand, or word of mouth might have done the trick.[4] Then, as demand increased, the toy became scarce. When something is scarce, it often seems more **attractive**, which further **drives up** demand.

7 We know that a change in price can affect demand, but other factors influence *how much* effect it will have. In the case of fresh strawberries, shoppers might easily change their minds about buying them if the price goes up a dollar. After all, there are close substitutes[5] for strawberries—other kinds of fruit are available, too. On the other hand, we can **assume** that a one-dollar increase in the price of gas will make little difference in demand, as people will still need to drive to work or school or the doctor's office, and there's no close substitute for gas. Some drivers could use public transportation instead, but many could not, or would not. Here we see another **significant** factor in how much a change in price will affect demand: Is the demand for a *necessity* (something people must have) or a *luxury* (something expensive you buy for pleasure[6])? For most drivers, gas is a necessity. The demand for a necessity is less likely to rise or fall in response to a change in price than the demand for a luxury, like fresh strawberries or expensive toys.

Conclusion

8 **To sum up**, the law of demand says that if the price for a good or service goes down, people will buy more, and if it goes up, people will buy less. The law of supply says that if the price goes up, producers will produce more, and if it goes down, they'll produce less. However, these two laws don't tell the whole story. Nothing about economics is that simple!

[2] *factors* = things that can influence or cause a situation

[3] *sparked* = was the cause of, started (something) happening

[4] *done the trick* = done what was necessary to get a good result

[5] *close substitutes* = similar things that can replace things that aren't available

[6] *pleasure* = feelings of happiness and enjoyment

Quick Comprehension Check

A. Read these statements **about the reading**. Circle T (true) or F (false). On the line, write the number of the paragraph with the answer.

1. The laws of supply and demand work independently of each other.   T   F   _____

2. *Supply* means how much people want to buy something.   T   F   _____

3. A low supply of something often results in a surplus.   T   F   _____

4. A change in price might or might not affect demand.   T   F   _____

5. Price is just one of the things that affect demand.   T   F   _____

6. When something is scarce, people are less interested in buying it.   T   F   _____

B. Work with your class. Share your answers from part A. Go back to the reading to find the reason why a statement is true or false. Correct the false statements.

EXPLORING VOCABULARY

Thinking about the Target Vocabulary

A. Look at the chart with the target vocabulary from "Supply and Demand." Six verbs and three adjectives are missing. Scan the reading to find them, and add them to the correct places in the chart. Use the base form of each verb.

¶	Nouns	Verbs	Adjectives	Other
2				as
3	quantity			
	balance			
4				
5	term			
6				
			other than	

¶	Nouns	Verbs	Adjectives	Other
7				
8				to sum up

B. Which words and phrases are new to you? Circle them in the chart. Then find them in the reading. Look at the context. Can you guess the meaning?

Understanding the Target Vocabulary

A. These sentences are **about the reading**. Complete them with the target words and phrases in the box.

assume	balance	effective	significant
attractive	crosses	run out	to sum up

1. When the demand for a product is at the same level as the supply of the product, then we can say that there's a _____ between supply and demand.

2. In the diagram on page 228, the line for supply (which increases as the price goes up) _____ the line for demand (which increases as the price drops). The point where that happens is the equilibrium price, where there's a balance between supply and demand.

3. If a store sells all it has of a particular product and has no more of it, then the store has _____.

4. If an ad is successful—that is, if it gets the result that the seller was hoping for—then we can say the ad is _____.

5. When something is scarce, only a lucky few can have it. That may make other people want it more. It becomes more _____ to them just because it's scarce.

Vocabulary Tip: Use *run out* alone or *run out of* + object: *Chocolate is the shop's most popular ice cream flavor, so they sometimes run out of it.*

6. Sometimes we accept something as true without having actually proved that it is. For example, we _____ that an increase in the price of gas won't have a big influence on the demand because for most drivers, gas is a necessity.

7. Many factors can affect demand. Some of them we hardly notice, while other factors are more important, like the difference between necessities and luxuries. That is a _____ factor.

8. The text gives a lot of information about supply and demand. _____, the laws of supply and demand affect how prices are set, how much of a product or service people will buy, and how much sellers will produce.

> **Vocabulary Tip:** Use *To sum up* near the end of a talk or a piece of writing to introduce a summary of the information you have presented.

B. What is the meaning of each **boldfaced** word or phrase? Circle a, b, or c.

1. When demand for something is high, producers will produce more, **as** there's a good chance they can make a profit. In this context, *as* means

   a. when, whenever.   b. because, since.   c. but, yet.

> **Vocabulary Tip:** *As* is used in the text to introduce the reason for a situation (see paragraph 2) and also to mean "at the same time as" (*as the cost of a box of strawberries rises*).

2. If a seller sets a low price for a product or service, that will probably **bring in** more sales. If something brings in sales or profits, then it

   a. produces or earns them.   b. blocks or limits them.   c. reduces or decreases them.

3. The equilibrium price is the point where the **quantity** that consumers want to buy equals the quantity that sellers want to produce. *Quantity* means

   a. loss.   b. stress.   c. amount.

4. The writer explains the economic **terms** *surplus* and *shortage*. In this context, *terms* means

   a. periods of time.   b. words or phrases.   c. resources.

5. By discussing the toy that quickly became very popular, the writer **brought up** another point about demand—that it can be affected by many factors. *Bring something up* means to

   a. be in favor of it.   b. destroy it.   c. start talking about it.

6. The demand for a product or service can rise or fall for reasons **other than** changes in price. *Other than* means

   a. in addition to.   b. essential to.   c. in charge of.

7. If a product or service is scarce and becomes very attractive, that can **drive up** the demand for it. If something drives up demand (or drives up the price of something), then it
   a. forces it up.   b. comes up with it.   c. keeps up with it.

EXPANDING VOCABULARY

Building on the Vocabulary

Word Grammar: Prefixes Meaning *Not*

Many words can take on an opposite meaning by adding a prefix that means "not." These prefixes include:

un-	attractive/unattractive, necessary/unnecessary, productive/unproductive
in-	effective/ineffective, significant/insignificant, appropriate/inappropriate
im-	balance/imbalance, possible/impossible
non-	essential/nonessential, traditional/nontraditional
dis-	similar/dissimilar, organized/disorganized

Add the correct prefix to *attractive, balance, effective, organized,* and *significant* to form a word with the opposite meaning. Use the new words to complete the sentences.

1. I'm sorry to report that when the medicine was tested, it proved to be

   _____ against the virus.

2. Sam and Pat thought their house was an _____ color, so they

   wanted to paint it a different color.

3. The increase in the bee population is so small that it won't make any

   difference. It's an _____ increase.

4. The boss didn't have a good plan for how to set up and run the meeting, so it

   was very _____.

5. When there is a difference in the value of a country's exports (sales to other

   countries) and its imports (what it buys from other countries), there is a

   trade _____.

Using the Target Vocabulary in New Contexts

Complete the sentences with the target words and phrases in the box. There is one extra word.

as	bring in	drives up	runs out of
assume	brings up	other than	terms
balance	crosses	quantity	to sum up

1. I found the reading difficult because I didn't understand many of the scientific _____.

2. He doesn't want to talk about it, so no one _____ the subject.

3. There's a fish market at the corner where High Street _____ Main.

4. An increase in gas prices _____ the cost of transportation, which then affects the costs of many other goods and services.

5. The company hoped their new ads would _____ new clients.

6. My sister has stopped using credit cards, _____ she has too much credit card debt.

7. He often forgets to buy milk on his way home from work, so he _____ it again and again.

8. When the ship went down, a huge _____ of oil ended up in the sea.

9. What do you consider "necessities," _____ food, water, and clothing?

10. _____, those are the three main reasons for the company's financial losses.

11. I invited Tom to the meeting, but he hasn't responded. I still think we can _____ that he'll come, as he usually does.

> **Vocabulary Tip:**
> Use *term* to refer to a word or phrase used for a specific subject, profession, or type of language: *"Currency" is the economic term for money.*

DEVELOPING YOUR READING SKILLS

The Main Idea

Reread "Supply and Demand." What is the main idea of the text? Check (✓) your answer.

☐ 1. Every government has to write its own laws of supply and demand.

☐ 2. To understand economics, you need to understand the laws of supply and demand.

☐ 3. The laws of supply and demand explain everything that happens in the economy.

Understanding Text Features

Subheadings

The reading "Supply and Demand" is divided into sections. Each section has its own title, or **subheading**. Look at the subheadings of a text before you read it to see how the information in the text is organized. Subheadings tell you what to expect in each section of the text and help you make predictions as you read.

Reading Tip:
When you make predictions about a text before you read, and then check after you read whether they were correct, you can get a deeper understanding of the text.

Match the five subheadings from "Supply and Demand" with the main ideas of the five sections of the text. Write the letters.

____ 1. Introduction

____ 2. Setting Prices

____ 3. Imbalances Between Supply and Demand

____ 4. Other Factors Affecting Demand

____ 5. Conclusion

a. Surpluses and shortages result from differences between supply and demand.

b. The laws of supply and demand are key, but they don't explain everything about the economy.

c. Supply, demand, and pricing all affect what gets bought and sold.

d. Changes in price aren't the only thing affecting the demand for a product or service.

e. The laws of supply and demand help explain how the economy works.

Major Points and Supporting Details

A. Answer the questions about major points in the text.

1. What does the law of demand say?

   _____

   _____

2. What does the law of supply say?

   _____

   _____

3. What is the difference between a surplus and a shortage?

   _____

   _____

Writing Tip: Remember to use quotation marks when you copy part or all of a sentence from a text.

B. Are these statements about the reading true or false? If the reading doesn't give the information, check (✓) *It doesn't say.*

	True	False	It doesn't say.
1. Changes in price can cause changes in demand.	☐	☐	☐
2. The price of fresh fruit is always changing.	☐	☐	☐
3. Shortages are more common than surpluses.	☐	☐	☐
4. Consumers are happy when there are shortages.	☐	☐	☐
5. Effective ads can drive up demand.	☐	☐	☐
6. Economists say there are substitutes for strawberries.	☐	☐	☐
7. Most drivers consider gas a luxury.	☐	☐	☐
8. Economists think it's easy to predict what consumers will do.	☐	☐	☐

CRITICAL THINKING

Discussion

Talk about these questions in a small group.

1. In paragraph 2, the reading discusses people producing goods "to meet a demand." In this context, *meet* is closest in meaning to

   a. reduce.   **b.** match.   **c.** raise.

   Explain your answer using information from the text.

2. Look at the diagram on page 228. Imagine that strawberries were priced at $10.00/box. What would happen? Use information from the reading to explain. In your answer, try to use economic terms from the reading, such as *consumer, demand, supply, shortage,* and *surplus.*

Reading Tip: When there's a diagram with a reading, take the time to study it. It can help you better understand the text.

3. In paragraph 5, you read, "It flies off the shelf, . . ." In this sentence, what is *it?* What does it mean to fly off the shelf? According to the reading, what has caused this situation? What other factors can you think of that may have led to this situation?

4. The reading makes a general statement about the law of demand: "when the price of something goes *too* high, fewer consumers will buy it" (paragraph 2). What exception to this rule is described in the text? (An *exception to a rule* is an event or situation that is different from what normally happens.) Does the reading describe any exception to the law of supply? Can you imagine a case when the price of something goes up but producers don't want to produce more?

5. According to the reading, the laws of supply and demand predict what consumers will do in certain situations. What information can you find in the text that is true for you and your personal decisions as a consumer? Does the reading describe any differences among consumers? What differences among people do *you* think affect how they behave as consumers?

WRITING

A. Use the Target Vocabulary: Choose five of the target words or phrases from the chart on pages 230–231. On a piece of paper, use each word or phrase in a sentence and underline it. Find a partner and read each other's sentences.

B. Practice Writing: Choose one of these topics and write a paragraph about it. Then find a partner and read each other's paragraphs.

1. Choose a statement, or an idea, about consumer behavior from the reading, and explain how it does or does not describe your own behavior as a consumer.

2. A *necessity* is often used to mean something that everyone needs in order to live, while a *luxury* is used to mean something pleasurable that no one actually needs. However, we all have our own ideas about what we see as necessities and luxuries in our lives. Choose something that you consider a necessity or a luxury but which you think most other people would see differently. Explain its role in your life.

Behavioral Economics

How to decide?

GETTING READY TO READ

Read the statements and circle True or False. Then share your answers with a partner and give examples.

1.	I sometimes buy things I don't need.	True	False
2.	Sometimes I make poor decisions about buying things.	True	False
3.	"Two for the price of one" is always a good deal.	True	False
4.	I'll usually say yes to something that's free.	True	False
5.	Higher prices mean better quality.	True	False

READING

Read to Find Out: What are behavioral economists discovering about consumers?

Look at the words and definitions next to the reading. Then read without stopping. If you see a new word, try to understand the sentence without it. You will learn the word later.

Behavioral Economics

1. An economist set up a table in a public place. Then he offered people walking by a choice of two chocolates. One was a gourmet[1] chocolate that he had priced at 15 cents, while the other was a smaller, more **ordinary** chocolate priced at just a penny.[2] More than 70 percent of the people who stopped at the table preferred the higher-quality chocolate. **Even though** it cost 14 cents more, they were willing to pay the extra money for it. Then the economist dropped both prices by a penny, so the gourmet chocolate cost 14 cents, and the other one was free. All of a sudden, the numbers were reversed:[3] Only 31 percent of the people who stopped would pay the 14 cents for the better-quality chocolate. The other 69 percent went for the smaller, more ordinary one—the free one.

2. Question: Why does the **thought** of getting something for free have such a strong effect on people's choices?

3. The same economist secretly visited some dormitories[4] at the U.S. university where he teaches, leaving a six-pack of soda in each of several shared refrigerators. In most cases, the sodas were gone within three days. The students had **helped themselves**. Then the economist returned, but this time, instead of a six-pack of sodas, he left a plate with six one-dollar bills. Three days later, all the money was still there.

4. Question: What made students decide it was fine to take a one-dollar soda but not a one-dollar bill?

5. The economist and a team of researchers carried out a test that involved giving volunteers electric shocks. After one set of shocks, the volunteers got a pill that was supposed to make them feel less pain. They also got one of two brochures[5] about the pill. Some of the volunteers read in their brochure that the pill they got was expensive, while others read that their pill had been marked down[6] to only 10 cents. There was no actual pain reliever[7] in any of the pills. **Nevertheless**, after taking the pills, when the volunteers **went through** another set of shocks, most of them reported feeling less pain. Of the people who got the "high-priced medicine," almost everyone said that it helped. Of the people who got the "cheap medicine," only half said that it did.

[1] *gourmet* = relating to very high-quality food and drink

[2] *a penny* = a U.S. coin worth $.01 or 1¢ (one cent)

[3] *reversed* = changed to the opposite of what they were

[4] *a dormitory* = a university building where students live (also *dorm*)

[5] *a brochure* = a thin book with information or advertising

[6] *marked down* = with the price lowered

[7] *a pain reliever* = medicine that makes you feel less pain

6   Question: Why do people believe that a higher-priced pain reliever works better?

7   For answers to these questions, read the work of Dan Ariely, the economist who **handed out** the chocolates and **fake** pills and made the secret visits to those college dorms. Ariely is a professor of behavioral economics, a fairly new area of economics that has to do with economic decisions. He studies the behavior of consumers, **borrowers**, and investors.

8   According to the teachings of traditional economics, when people make economic decisions, they act in their own best interests. That is, most economists assume that people are **sensible** and will make the choices that do them the most good. What behavioral economists are finding, however, is that this is **frequently** not true: People often make poor economic choices. Emotions **get in the way of** calculations,[8] and people often repeat the same mistakes. Ariely calls people "predictably irrational" because their decisions often don't make sense and because he can predict the mistakes they will make.

[8] *calculations* = work done with numbers to figure out amounts or costs

9   One thing that influences people's decision making is the way that a choice is presented to them. According to Ariely, "Most people don't know what they want until they see it in context." People need the context to make comparisons. Ariely uses an illustration like the one on the right to show that those comparisons cannot always be trusted.

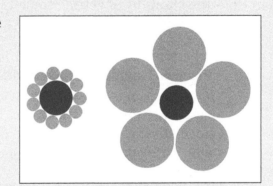

10 The two purple circles in the middle are the same size, but they don't seem to be, do they? The one on the right seems smaller because of the larger circles that **surround** it. Ariely says that this is exactly how the human mind works. People see things not as they are but **in relation to** other things. The same is true of how people view experiences, emotions, and other people. When faced with certain choices, presented in certain ways (for example, by smart salespeople), people don't see the choices as they really are, and they're likely to make poor decisions.

11 Ariely hopes that as people learn more about when, where, and why they make poor decisions, they will understand themselves better. Maybe consumers will learn to think differently and make better choices when shopping. Nevertheless, he **admits** to buying a thirty-thousand-dollar car (which was not the kind of car he truly needed)

after learning that it came with three years of free oil changes, even though compared to the cost of a new car, the cost of an oil change, or even three years of them, is insignificant.

12   Question: Is Professor Ariely as predictably irrational as the rest of us?

Quick Comprehension Check

A. Read these statements **about the reading**. Circle T (true) or F (false). On the line, write the number of the paragraph with the answer.

1.	Behavioral economists study economic decision making.	T	F	____
2.	Traditional economists expect people to know what's good for them.	T	F	____
3.	Dan Ariely is a traditional economist.	T	F	____
4.	In one of Ariely's studies, college students took someone else's money.	T	F	____
5.	Ariely says people often make the same kinds of mistakes.	T	F	____
6.	Ariely has learned not to make poor choices as a consumer.	T	F	____

B. Work with your class. Share your answers from part A. Go back to the reading to find the reason why a statement is true or false. Correct the false statements.

EXPLORING VOCABULARY

Thinking about the Target Vocabulary

A. Look at the chart with the target vocabulary from "Behavioral Economics." Two nouns, four verbs, and three adjectives are missing. Scan the reading to find them, and add them to the correct places in the chart. Use the singular form of any plural noun. Use the base form of each verb.

¶	Nouns	Verbs	Adjectives	Other
1				
				even though
2				
3				help yourself

¶	Nouns	Verbs	Adjectives	Other
5				nevertheless
7				
8				
				frequently
				get in the way of
10				
				in relation to
11				

B. Which words and phrases are new to you? Circle them in the chart. Then find them in the reading. Look at the context. Can you guess the meaning?

Understanding the Target Vocabulary

A. These sentences are **about the reading**. Complete them with the target words and phrases in the box.

admits	get in the way of	in relation to	thought
borrower	helped themselves	surround	went through
even though			

1. At first, people preferred the gourmet chocolates in spite of their higher

   price. _____ the price was higher, most people bought those.

2. People changed their minds when the one-cent chocolates became free.

   The idea, or the _____, of getting something for nothing was

   very powerful.

3. The students did not wait for anyone to offer them a soda. They went

   ahead and took what they wanted. They _____.

4. The volunteers in one study all experienced electric shocks. They

_____ two sets of shocks, and in between, they took a pill.

5. Sometimes a person gets money as a loan from family, friends, or a

bank. The person who gets the loan is a _____.

6. Our feelings can keep us from thinking clearly and making good

economic choices. Our emotions _____ our decision-

making skills.

7. In the picture on page 240, you see two purple circles with orange

circles all around them. The orange circles _____ the

purple ones.

8. Ariely says that we do not look at things all by themselves. We compare

them to other, similar things. We judge them _____ these

other things.

9. Sometimes a person agrees that something is true and says that it is, but

he or she says it unwillingly. For example, Ariely _____ that

he made a bad decision buying a car.

B. Read each definition and look at the paragraph number. Look back at the reading on pages 239–241 to find the **boldfaced** word to match the definition. Write it in the chart.

Definition	Paragraph	Target Word
1. average or usual, not special or different	1	
2. however	5	
3. give to each person in a group	7	
4. not real	7	
5. showing good thinking or judgment	8	
6. often	8	

EXPANDING VOCABULARY

Building on the Vocabulary

> ### Word Grammar: *Even Though* and *Nevertheless*
>
> *Even though* and *nevertheless* are both used to show a contrast between two facts, events, or situations. Notice how these words are used differently in the example sentences below.
>
> - *Even though* is used to stress that something surprising is true. It exists or happens in spite of the fact that something else has happened or is also true.
>
>   **Even though** she's almost 30, she still looks like a teenager.
>
>   He went to work **even though** he was sick.
>
> - *Nevertheless* is used to introduce information that is surprising because of what has just been said. It sometimes follows *but*.
>
>   She's almost 30 now. **Nevertheless,** she still looks like a teenager.
>
>   He was sick, but he went to work **nevertheless**.

Circle the correct word to complete the sentence.

1. (Even though / Nevertheless) the volunteers received no real medicine, they reported feeling better.
2. I knew I couldn't afford it, but I bought it (even though / nevertheless).
3. (Even though / Nevertheless) high-heeled shoes hurt Ann's feet, she still wore them.
4. It's true that he was to blame. (Even though / Nevertheless), it wasn't nice of you to tell him so.
5. In the park, you feel as if you're in the country (even though / nevertheless) you're in the middle of the city.
6. We don't agree with him, but we must (even though / nevertheless) respect his right to voice his opinion.

Using the Target Vocabulary in New Contexts

A. These sentences use the target words and phrases **in new contexts**. What is the meaning of each **boldfaced** word or phrase? Circle a, b, or c.

1. **Help yourself to** the cookies. Saying *Help yourself to (something)* means
   - a. help me do (something).
   - b. don't expect my help.
   - c. take whatever you want.

2. I hate the **thought** of paying for credit card debt month after month. In this sentence, *thought* means
   - a. a memory.
   - b. an idea.
   - c. a threat.

3. When the police arrested the man, he was carrying several **fake** ID cards. Something that is fake is meant to

   a. trick people.　　　b. benefit people.　　　c. educate people.

4. In soccer, the attacking players try to put the ball in the goal, and the defenders try to **get in their way.** When you get in the way of something, you

   a. consume it.　　　b. block it.　　　c. attach it.

5. Poor Beth! She is **going through** a lot these days. In this sentence, *go through* means

   a. experience something upsetting.　　　b. spend a lot of money.　　　c. get rid of something.

> **Vocabulary Tip:**
> Use *go through* + an experience that is difficult or painful: *They're going through a divorce.*

6. The apartment has six rooms, but it's small **in relation to** the size of their family because they have seven children. *In relation to* means

   a. in spite of.　　　b. in terms of.　　　c. in charge of.

B. Complete the sentences with the target words in the box. There is one extra word.

admit	frequently	ordinary	surround
borrower	nevertheless	sensible	thought

1. The bank charges different rates of interest depending on what the

   _____ will be using the money for: Is it to pay for college or

   to buy a house or a car?

2. The medicine isn't *always* effective but it _____ is.

3. Engineers designing appropriate technologies in developing countries

   are doing good work. They're taking a _____ approach to the

   problems in those countries.

4. When I spoke with my grandmother, I was sorry to bring up the subject

   of moving because I knew the _____ of it would upset her.

5. What started out as just another _____ day turned into

   the most exciting day of my life.

6. The man wouldn't _____ to being in the store until the

   police announced he had been caught on the security video.

7. Presidents who _____ themselves with "yes-men" are

   not open to considering new ideas or facing hard questions.

DEVELOPING YOUR READING SKILLS

Reading for Details

A. Reread "Behavioral Economics." Are these statements about the reading true or false? If the reading doesn't give the information, check (✓) *It doesn't say.*

	True	False	It doesn't say.
1. Dan Ariely studies people's behavior in relation to economic decision making.	☐	☐	☐
2. All the people he studies know that they are part of his research.	☐	☐	☐
3. He uses volunteers for some of his research.	☐	☐	☐
4. He teaches traditional economics as well as behavioral economics.	☐	☐	☐
5. He sometimes studies the behavior of college students.	☐	☐	☐
6. He says consumers' emotions help them make sensible choices.	☐	☐	☐
7. He says making comparisons will keep consumers from making mistakes.	☐	☐	☐
8. For most people, getting something for free is a very attractive idea.	☐	☐	☐

B. Reread paragraph 5. Then number the steps in order from 1 to 6.

_____ a. The volunteers went through another set of shocks.

_____ b. Each volunteer read a brochure with information about their pill.

_____ c. The volunteers went through their first set of shocks.

_____ d. Each volunteer got a pill that he or she believed was a pain reliever.

_____ e. Volunteers agreed to take part in a test involving electric shocks.

_____ f. Many volunteers reported feeling less pain, including almost all of those who believed their pill was expensive.

Understanding the Writer's Purpose

Circle a or b to complete the sentence with the writer's purpose.

1. The purpose of the reading is to
   a. explain to the reader what one area of economics is all about.
   b. help the reader understand how to make better decisions.

2. The purpose of paragraph 5 is to show that
   a. some pain relievers work better than others.
   b. the price of something influences our opinion of how much it's worth.

3. The purpose of paragraph 8 is to show that
   a. more people should study economics.
   b. a basic idea held by most economists might be wrong.

4. The purpose of paragraph 11 is to show
   a. how easy it is to go wrong when making economic decisions.
   b. that economists don't know much about cars.

Summarizing

A. Complete the summary of "Behavioral Economics." Include answers to the following questions:

- Who is Dan Ariely?
- What is behavioral economics?
- What is one difference between Ariely's views and the teachings of traditional economics?
- According to Ariely, why should we learn more about our decision making?

> The reading "Behavioral Economics" introduces Dan Ariely, who is a ...

B. Compare your summary with a partner's. Do you agree on how Ariely's views differ from the teachings of traditional economics?

CRITICAL THINKING

Discussion

Talk about these questions in a small group.

Complete the chart with information from paragraph 1.

	Situation 1		Situation 2	
	Price	Percent of Buyers Who Chose It	Price	Percent of Buyers Who Chose It
Gourmet chocolate	15¢			
Ordinary chocolate	1¢			

1. What happened when Ariely offered people the choice of chocolates? What reason for their behavior in "Situation 2" does the reading give? Was this an example of people making a sensible economic choice or not? Explain.

2. What did Ariely do the first time he secretly visited some college dorms, and what was the result? What about the second time? Does the reading explain the students' behavior? Why do you think the students behaved differently in the two cases?

3. Reread the last sentence of paragraph 10. What does the writer mean about "smart salespeople"? In this context, does *smart* have a positive or a negative meaning?

4. What influenced Ariely to choose the car he bought? Does he think he made a good choice? How do you know? What information can you find earlier in the reading that helps explain his decision-making in this case? How would you answer the final question in the reading?

5. What effect, if any, is this reading likely to have on your economic decision making? Why?

> **Critical Thinking Tip:** Being able to bring together information from different parts of a text is an important skill.

WRITING

A. Use the Target Vocabulary: Choose five of the target words or phrases from the chart on pages 241–242. On a piece of paper, use each word or phrase in a sentence and underline it. Find a partner and read each other's sentences.

B. Practice Writing: Choose one of these topics and write a paragraph about it. Then find a partner and read each other's paragraphs.

1. Write about question 5 from **Discussion**: What effect, if any, is this reading likely to have on your economic decision making? Why?

2. Think of a time when you had to make an economic decision, such as whether or not to buy something, or which of two things to buy. Describe the choice you faced and how you made your decision.

> **Writing Tip:**
> *Even though* and *nevertheless* are examples of transition words. Using transition words when you write can help make clear the relationships between ideas.

CHAPTER 20

The Economics of Happiness

The 10 Happiest Countries	Countries ranked among the 25 richest
1. Denmark	Denmark
2. Switzerland	Switzerland
3. Iceland	Iceland
4. Norway	Norway
5. Finland	
6. Canada	Canada
7. Netherlands	Netherlands
8. New Zealand	
9. Australia	Australia
10. Sweden	Sweden

The 10 Unhappiest Countries	Countries ranked among the 25 poorest
148. Madagascar	Madagascar
149. Tanzania	
150. Liberia	Liberia
151. Guinea	Guinea
152. Rwanda	Rwanda
153. Benin	Benin
154. Afghanistan	Afghanistan
155. Togo	Togo
156. Syria	
157. Burundi	Burundi

Data from The World Happiness Report 2016.

Data from 2016 rankings by Global Finance Magazine.

LEARNING OUTCOME

❯ Learn about how economics affects happiness

GETTING READY TO READ

Talk about these questions with your class.

1. Look at the chart above. How many of the 10 happiest countries are also among the richest? How many of the 10 unhappiest countries are also among the poorest? What is this chart saying about happiness and a country's economy?

2. Look at the graph on page 252. The happier countries (based on how people rated themselves) are higher up. The richer countries are further to the right. Look at the countries at the top and bottom on the graph and on the left and right. Do they surprise you in any way?

3. Find five countries on the graph that all averaged about 5 on the scale of life satisfaction. What does the graph tell you about their incomes? Do these countries surprise you in any way?

READING

Look at the words and definitions next to the reading. Then read without stopping. If you see a new word, try to understand the sentence without it. You will learn the word later.

The Economics of Happiness

1   People often think of economists as focusing on money, production, and the cold, hard facts of what happens in the marketplace. It may **therefore** come as a surprise to think of an economist asking, "How happy are you?" However, some economists very much want to know.

2   Richard Easterlin is an economist who has studied national happiness for years. In 1974, he presented a new theory.[1] He said that a nation's economic **growth** doesn't always lead to its people becoming happier. Poor people *do* become happier when they get enough money for basic needs, but beyond that, he said, more money does not mean more happiness.

[1] *a theory =* an idea that explains why something happens

3   Easterlin pointed to Japan as an example. In the years following World War II, Japan experienced an economic boom,[2] one of the biggest in the history of the world. Between 1950 and 1970, its economic production grew by more than 600 percent. Japan grew from a country **torn apart** by war into one of the richest nations in the world. Surprisingly, however, the people of Japan didn't seem to grow any happier. According to one **poll**, they actually felt less **satisfied** with their lives in the early 1970s than they had fifteen years before. They were richer, yes, but happier, no.

[2] *a boom =* a sudden increase in business activity

4   For years, economists accepted Easterlin's theory. The public[3] accepted it, too. It fit in with the popular idea that money can't buy happiness. Perhaps we want to believe in this idea because we all hope that happiness is within our reach even when **wealth** is not.

[3] *the public =* people in general

5   Easterlin's theory has been back in the news in recent years. The discussion began when two young economists, Betsey Stevenson and Justin Wolfers, **argued** against it in a 2008 paper that other economists found very interesting. Their **position** was that money is, in fact, likely to bring happiness. They based their argument on information that further polls had **revealed** over the 34 years since Easterlin's paper. They said, "Our key finding[4] is that income appears to be closely related to happiness. . . . Most countries get happier as they get wealthier, and wealthy countries have **citizens** with greater happiness than poor countries."

[4] *a finding =* a piece of information learned through research

6   Some of their information came from the Gallup Organization, a well-known and respected polling organization, which found that people in the richest countries are happiest with their lives. At least one-third of the people in those countries give themselves a score of 8, 9, or 10 on a happiness **scale** of 1 to 10 (with 10 being the highest possible level of "life satisfaction"). The very rich and happy nation at the top of the list is Denmark. Denmark also sits at the top of lists created by other economists who do similar research. Who is at the bottom? Poor African nations, among them Tanzania, Togo, and Benin.

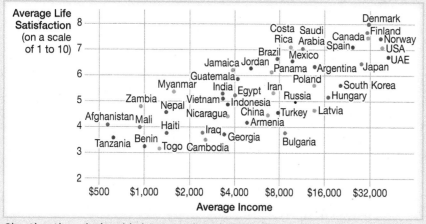

Charting the relationship between happiness and income.
(Source: Betsey Stevenson and Justin Wolfers, Wharton School at the University of Pennsylvania, USA.)

7   **As for** the case of post-war Japan:[5] Stevenson and Wolfers also looked back at the research done there. It turns out that the question in the poll changed over time. If you look only at the years in which the question stayed the same, then the **percentage** of people who **rated** themselves as "satisfied" or "completely satisfied" actually did rise.

8   The **central** idea, then, is that the economic growth of a nation does generally lead to more happiness for its citizens. In poor countries, it can lead to better food and housing and more choices in life. In rich countries, it can pay for research and medical care that help people enjoy longer, healthier lives. Easterlin, however, remains unconvinced.[6] He notes that China and the United States both grew richer in recent years without growing any happier.

9   Easterlin, Stevenson, and Wolfers would all agree on at least one thing: Money isn't the only factor[7] that influences happiness. Stevenson and Wolfers report that Latin American countries are happier than income alone would predict, and East European countries are less happy.

10 When Stevenson and Wolfers speak about income and its influence, they're saying that what matters is *absolute income*—how much you make (in dollars, pesos, euros, yen, etc.). Easterlin, on the other hand,

[5] *post-war Japan* = Japan in the years after World War II

[6] *unconvinced* = not made to believe in someone's argument

[7] *a factor* = one of several things that cause or influence a situation

believes that *relative income* matters more—how much you make in comparison with other people. After your basic needs are met, you compare yourself with the people around you. How happy you are depends not on how much you have but on how you think you compare with those others and on how much more you want.

11 Such comparisons may be human nature—or are they? Psychology[8] professor Sonja Lyubomirsky doesn't believe that happy people think this way. In her research, she has asked people who they compared themselves with. Less happy people, she reports, "went on and on." How did happier people respond? She says, "The happy people didn't know what we were talking about."

[8] *psychology* = the study of the mind and how it works

Quick Comprehension Check

A. Read these statements **about the reading**. Circle T (true) or F (false). On the line, write the number of the paragraph with the answer.

1. Some economists study national happiness.   T   F   _____

2. Postwar Japan affected economists' thinking about happiness.   T   F   _____

3. New information has come out about happiness in postwar Japan.   T   F   _____

4. The richest countries are among the unhappiest countries.   T   F   _____

5. Economists all agree on the role of income in happiness.   T   F   _____

6. People feel happiest when they compare themselves to others.   T   F   _____

B. Work with your class. Share your answers from part A. Go back to the reading to find the reason why a statement is true or false. Correct the false statements.

EXPLORING VOCABULARY

Thinking about the Target Vocabulary

A. Look at the chart with the target vocabulary from "The Economics of Happiness." Five nouns, three verbs, and two adjectives are missing. Scan the reading to find them, and add them to the correct places in the chart. Use the singular form of any plural noun. Use the base form of each verb.

¶	Nouns	Verbs	Adjectives	Other
1				therefore
2	growth			
3				tear apart
4	wealth			
5				
6				
7				as for
8				

B. Which words and phrases are new to you? Circle them in the chart. Then find them in the reading. Look at the context. Can you guess the meaning?

Understanding the Target Vocabulary

A. Complete these sentences **about the reading**. Use the words and phrases in the box.

argue	central	percentages	rated	scale
as for	growth	poll	revealed	torn apart

1. In 1974, economist Richard Easterlin said that a growing national economy did make citizens happier. He said economic _____ did not always lead to greater national happiness.

2. When a country has been "_____ by war," as Japan was, it has been badly hurt and has many problems.

3. To find out what people in general think about something, you can take a _____. That means talking to many people and asking them all the same question or set of questions.

4. In their report, the economists Stevenson and Wolfers explain what they believe and why. They _____ that national income is closely tied to national happiness.

> **Vocabulary Tip:** *Argue*, as used in the text, means "say something is true, giving clear reasons." *Argue* can also mean "fight with words, often in an angry way."

5. We know more about economic growth and national happiness now than we did in the past. Polls taken around the world have _____ information that no one knew before.

6. Gallup pollsters wanted to know how happy people were, so they asked people to give themselves a number on a _____ of 1 to 10. Each number was a measure of happiness.

7. The writer returns to the subject of Japan by saying, "_____ the case of post-war Japan, . . ." In this way, the writer introduces a paragraph on a new but related topic.

8. After someone takes a poll, they usually report the results like this: "Of the people who responded, 45% agreed, 35% disagreed, and the rest were undecided." They report the results in _____, as parts of a whole equal to 100.

9. When the people answered the question for the Gallup poll, they gave an opinion of themselves by giving themselves a number with a certain value. They _____ themselves.

10. When Stevenson and Wolfers speak about their "key finding," they are talking about the _____ idea from their research.

B. These sentences are also **about the reading**. What is the meaning of each **boldfaced** word? Circle a, b, or c.

1. People often think of economists paying attention only to buying and selling, spending and saving, etc. **Therefore**, you might be surprised that they study happiness, too. *Therefore* means

   a. after all.　　　b. to sum up.　　　c. for that reason.

Vocabulary Tip:
Therefore is usually used in formal English. In informal English, use *so*.

2. According to the Gallup poll, many people in rich countries say they are **satisfied** with their lives. *Satisfied* means

   a. happy.　　　b. confused.　　　c. stressed.

3. People often say that happiness does not depend on **wealth**. *Wealth* means

   a. your health and well-being.
   b. your personal development.
   c. how much money you have.

4. The economists mentioned in the reading have certain **positions** on the role of the economy in national happiness. In this context, *positions* means

   a. resources.　　　b. opinions.　　　c. treatments.

5. Economists disagree about whether a nation's economic growth makes its **citizens** happier. Citizens are people who

   a. have the right to live in a country.
   b. are political leaders in a country.
   c. study the economy of a country.

EXPANDING VOCABULARY

Building on the Vocabulary

> ### Studying Collocations: Prepositions
> Certain prepositions often follow certain nouns, verbs, and adjectives.
>
> Is he **arguing** for or against the plan?
>
> Your work has been **central** to the company's success.
>
> Anyone running for election must take **positions** on many issues.
>
> Stores want customers to be **satisfied** with the service they receive.
>
> Amina, Abdi, and their children just became **citizens** of Canada.

Complete each sentence with the correct preposition.

1. These values are central _____ the organization and its goals.

2. We weren't satisfied _____ the food or the service, so we rated
   the restaurant poorly.

3. What is the president's position _____ the trade agreement?

4. The phrase "a citizen _____ the world" describes someone who
   believes in being part of a global community.

5. I believe we aren't spending enough on public education, so I'm arguing
   _____ an increase in spending.

Using the Target Vocabulary in New Contexts

Complete the sentences with the target words and phrases in the box. There
are two extra words or phrases.

as for	percentage	rated	scale	torn apart
growth	polls	revealed	therefore	wealth

> **Vocabulary Tip:**
> Use *reveal* when
> something that
> used to be
> hidden or secret
> is made known:
> *The look on her
> face revealed
> her feelings.*

1. The X-ray _____ a break in the bone.

2. It's one of the richest countries, with oil as the major source of its
   _____.

3. I liked the movie, so when I _____ it, I gave it three stars.

4. The company has had a drop in sales in their stores but strong
   _____ in online sales.

5. On a _____ of 1 to 10, with 10 the worst pain you can imagine, how much pain are you currently feeling?

6. A large _____ of U.S. high school students have part-time jobs.

7. The plan presents too many risks. _____, we must argue against it.

8. Bob has had a very successful career. _____ his personal life, that's a different story.

9. Many voters have not yet made up their minds, according to the latest _____.

10. The country has been _____ by war for so long that thousands of children have grown up without ever attending school.

DEVELOPING YOUR READING SKILLS

The Main Idea

Reread "The Economics of Happiness." Which statement gives the main idea of the reading? Check (✓) your answer.

☐ 1. Economists disagree about the relationship between a country's economy and its citizens' happiness.

☐ 2. Economists have finally agreed that national wealth is based on national happiness.

☐ 3. Economists report that individual happiness depends on not comparing yourself with other people.

Text Organization

Reread paragraphs 2–5. Number these events in chronological order from 1 (the first to happen) to 6 (the most recent).

_____ a. Easterlin presented his theory.

_____ b. Easterlin studied information from polls done in postwar Japan.

_____ c. Stevenson and Wolfers presented their theory.

_____ d. Stevenson and Wolfers studied 34 years' worth of polls.

_____ e. Economists accepted the idea that economic growth did not always mean greater happiness.

_____ f. Japan experienced an economic boom.

> **Reading Tip:** You can scan a text for dates to find when events took place, but sometimes no dates are given and you must infer the timing or order of events.

Understanding Major Points

According to the reading, which researcher or researchers believe in each of the ideas below? In each column of the chart, write *yes* or *no* next to each statement or put a question mark if the reading does not say.

	Easterlin	Stevenson and Wolfers	Lyubomirsky
1. Getting the money to meet basic needs makes poor people happier.			
2. When a country's economy grows, it does not mean that its citizens get happier.			
3. Most nations become happier as they get richer.			
4. Money is not the only thing that affects national happiness.			
5. A person's happiness depends on how much he has compared to others.			
6. Happy people don't usually compare themselves with others.			

CRITICAL THINKING

Discussion

Talk about these questions in a small group.

1. In paragraph 4, the writer refers to a commonly held idea. What idea is that? How does this idea compare with Easterlin's thinking? The writer suggests a reason why this idea is so popular. What does the phrase "within our reach" mean? Do you agree with the writer's suggestion? Explain.

2. Where in the reading is each of these ideas discussed?
   a. If a poor country grows rich enough to meet people's basic needs, it's going to be happier.
   b. The richer a country grows, the happier it is.
   c. There are things besides money that affect how happy a country is.

   Which of these ideas does Easterlin agree with? Which ones do Stevenson and Wolfers agree with? Cite evidence from the reading to support your answers. Do you agree with any of these ideas? Explain.

3. In paragraph 7, you read that Stevenson and Wolfers pointed out a problem with the polls taken in Japan over a period of years following World War II. What was the problem? Why would that be a problem for a poll?

4. What does the phrase *relative income* mean in paragraph 10? How is that different from absolute income? Which one does Easterlin think is usually more important to someone's happiness? Why? Do you agree with Easterlin about what people's happiness depends on? Explain.

5. What did Lyubomirsky mean when she said that the less happy people in her research "went on and on"? What were the people talking about? What did Lyubomirsky mean when she said that the happy people "didn't know what we were talking about"? Does Lyubomirsky agree with Easterlin about what a person's happiness depends on? Explain. Can you infer from the text if the writer agrees with him?

Critical Thinking Tip: You may find a clue to a writer's opinion in the structure of the text. The writer might end the text with the argument that he or she thinks is stronger.

6. Much of the research described in "The Economics of Happiness" uses information from polls. Think about how you would answer the question "How satisfied are you with your life?" if the person asking the question were

   a. a pollster on the street

   b. a pollster on the phone

   c. a family member

   d. your best friend

   Would your answers be different? Explain. How could asking the same question in different situations lead to different results in a poll?

WRITING

A. Use the Target Vocabulary: Choose five of the target words or phrases from the chart on page 254. On a piece of paper, use each word or phrase in a sentence and underline it. Find a partner and read each other's sentences.

B. Practice Writing: Choose one of these topics and write a paragraph about it. Then find a partner and read each other's paragraphs.

Writing Tip: To develop your skills as a writer, do as much reading and writing as possible.

   1. Write about your country's wealth, in relation to other countries, and its happiness. What would make the citizens of your country happier?

   2. Do you believe it is human nature to compare ourselves with others? How do you think that would affect a person's happiness?

UNIT 5

Checkpoint

LEARNING OUTCOME

❯ Review and expand on the content of Unit 5

LOOK BACK

A. Think About This

Look back at your answers to the *Think About This* question on page 215:

When you hear the words the economy—*for example, from a TV news reporter—what topics do you think the reporter might talk about?*

Do you want to change any of your answers? Do you want to add anything new?

B. Remember the Readings

What do you want to remember most from the readings in Unit 5? For each chapter, write one sentence about the reading.

Chapter 17: Economics—What's It All About?

_____

Chapter 18: Supply and Demand

_____

Chapter 19: Behavioral Economics

_____

Chapter 20: The Economics of Happiness

_____

REVIEWING VOCABULARY

A. Match words with similar meanings. Write the letters.

1. _____ assume   a. chance
2. _____ exchange   b. personal
3. _____ frequently   c. needed
4. _____ growth   d. believe
5. _____ individual   e. work
6. _____ labor   f. often
7. _____ necessary   g. trade
8. _____ opportunity   h. development

B. Match words with similar meanings. Write the letters.

1. _____ ordinary   a. wise
2. _____ reveal   b. riches
3. _____ sensible   c. word
4. _____ since   d. so
5. _____ term   e. idea
6. _____ therefore   f. because
7. _____ thought   g. show
8. _____ wealth   h. average

C. Complete each sentence with a phrase from the box. There are two extra phrases.

after all	brings in	get in the way	in relation to
as for	drive up	handed out	other than
bring it up	even though	help themselves	ran out

1. I don't see them often _____ we live in the same building.

2. He's lucky—the cost of living there is low _____ his income.

3. Be patient with him. _____, he's only a child.

4. We don't always agree, but we don't let our differences

   _____ of our friendship.

5. Jack put the pizza on the table for his brothers and told them to

   _____.

6. The company is doing well. It now _____ over a million

   dollars a year.

7. The tomatoes in the garden are doing well, but _____ the spinach, that's been less successful.

8. The latest poll brought bad news, and the president didn't want to talk about it, so his advisors didn't _____ at the meeting.

9. One student _____ the papers to everyone in the class.

10. A tree came down in the storm, but _____ that, there was no damage.

EXPANDING VOCABULARY

Word Families

Use words from the six word families to complete the sentences below. Use your dictionary if you have questions about word meanings.

	Nouns	Verbs	Adjectives	Adverbs
1	attraction	attract	attractive	
2	economics economy	economize	economic economical	economically
3	fake	fake	fake	
4	satisfaction	satisfy	satisfying satisfied	
5	surroundings	surround	surrounding	

1. a. These flowers _____ a lot of bees.

   b. The beach is the island's top tourist _____.

   c. If something is scarce, that makes it more _____ to many people.

2. a. Pat decided to _____ by going out to eat less often.

   b. The region needs _____ development.

   c. It's more _____ to buy certain household products in large quantities.

3. a. Is that watch a real Rolex, or is it a _____?

   b. Sometimes players really get hurt in a game, but sometimes they just

      _____ it.

4. a. We enjoyed a _____ meal.

   b. He became a very wealthy man but nevertheless that didn't

      _____ him.

5. a. "Your _____" is another way to say your immediate

      environment.

   b. The fire was so huge that police blocked off the _____

      streets.

A PUZZLE

Complete the sentences with words you studied in Chapters 17–20. Write the words in the puzzle.

Across

1. One economist _____ that the crisis could have been avoided, but most disagreed.
6. I'm going to have to move, _____ the rent on my apartment is going up.
7. I needed a loan, so I _____ some money from my brother.
9. A large _____ of the bees died during the winter.
11. There's been only a little growth in the economy, nothing truly _____.
12. My sister advises me on taxes and other _____ matters.
13. Albert Einstein became a U.S. _____ in 1940.

Down

1. They're open to a new _____ to solving the problem.
2. Sellers want to find a _____ between supply and demand.
3. Gas is getting expensive. Fuel costs _____ for the third month in a row.
4. Some lawmakers support the plan, some are opposed, and some have not yet taken a _____.
5. He didn't want to _____ that he was to blame.
8. I spent years repaying my loans until finally I was out of _____.
10. This medicine works well for many patients, but it's not _____ for everyone.

BUILDING DICTIONARY SKILLS

Phrasal Verbs with Multiple Meanings

Look at the dictionary entry for each phrasal verb. Then read each sentence and write the number of the meaning.

> **go through** *phr v*
> **1 go through** sth to have a very upsetting or difficult experience: *She's just gone through a divorce.*
> **2 go through** sth to use all of something: *Jeremy goes through at least a quart of milk every day!*
> **3** if a deal, agreement or law **goes through**, it is officially accepted: *My car loan has finally gone through.*
> **4 go through** sth to look at, read, or explain something carefully: *She had to go through all her uncle's papers after he died.*
>
> **go through with** sth *phr v* to do something you had planned or promised to do: *I'm not sure if I can go through with the wedding.*

1. _____ a. Runners go through shoes quickly.

   _____ b. Pam has been going through a lot since she lost her job.

   _____ c. We finally have a sales agreement—the deal went through yesterday.

   _____ d. Get a lawyer to go through the details with you.

> **tear apart** *phr v* **1 tear sth ⇔ apart** to make a group, organization, etc. start having problems: *Scandal is tearing the government apart.* **2 tear** sb **apart** to make someone feel extremely unhappy or upset: *It tore me apart to see her leave.*

2. _____ a. It tears me apart to see you so unhappy.

   _____ b. Their competition for power is tearing the organization apart.

> **run out** *phr v* **1** to come to an end: *The rental agreement runs out in June.* **2** (+ *of*) to use all of something and not have any left: *I can lend you some money if you run out.* | *The car ran out of gas.* **3** to be all used up so nothing is left: *While I was in the shower, the hot water ran out.*

3. _____ a. I've run out of juice, eggs, and bread, so I need to get to the store.

   _____ b. I have a free 30-day membership, but it runs out on Friday.

Vocabulary Self-Test 3

Circle the letter of the word or phrase that best completes each sentence.

1. Only _____ can vote in a national election.

   a. clients   b. experts   c. citizens   d. consumers

2. Several economists _____ that the cost-benefit analyses were incomplete.

   a. argued   b. occurred   c. rated   d. attached

3. They looked like _____ dollar bills but were actually fake.

   a. individual   b. renewable   c. portable   d. ordinary

4. Mike _____ his mistake and said that he was sorry.

   a. rose   b. attended   c. tricked   d. admitted

5. They have little hope of success. _____, they will keep trying to reach their goal.

   a. Nevertheless   b. Besides   c. Beyond   d. In return

6. I didn't bring up the meeting because I _____ that you already knew about it.

   a. rose   b. assumed   c. forced   d. solved

7. The actor wouldn't take the role _____ they offered him a million dollars.

   a. other than   b. at least   c. even though   d. as for

8. The toy was so popular that stores _____ it.

   a. ran out of   b. drove up   c. called on   d. got rid of

9. A _____ increase in pay made a big difference in his life.

   a. grateful   b. significant   c. willing   d. physical

10. We decided to go home, _____ it was getting late.

    a. therefore   b. in charge of   c. as   d. in spite of

11. Let's try a new _____ to solving the problem.

   a. property   b. approach   c. vehicle   d. border

12. We buy fresh vegetables in small _____ to use immediately.

   a. terms   b. diameters   c. methods   d. quantities

13. My doctor says exercise is an _____ way to reduce stress.

   a. economic   b. environmental   c. effective   d. emotional

14. The house is _____ by trees so it gets plenty of shade.

   a. crossed   b. surrounded   c. hunted   d. replaced

15. When you're _____ a crisis, it often helps to talk to someone.

   a. setting out   b. carrying out   c. going through   d. setting up

16. Before we start the meeting, _____ coffee or tea if you'd like.

   a. tear apart   b. look into   c. take off   d. help yourself to

17. The company wanted very much to hire her, so they made her an

   _____ offer.

   a. uncertain   b. attractive   c. advanced   d. unscientific

18. He can't borrow any more money. He's too deep in _____.

   a. soil   b. fuel   c. wealth   d. debt

19. When resources are _____, then there's likely to be strong
   competition for them.

   a. scarce   b. rural   c. satisfied   d. recent

20. The use of pesticides can upset the _____ of Nature.

   a. loss   b. balance   c. harm   d. risk

21. The phrase *international* _____ refers to buying and selling
   between countries.

   a. opportunity   b. service   c. treatment   d. trade

22. The manager was pleased at the _____ of getting some free
   advertising.

   a. scale   b. right   c. thought   d. limit

23. A high _____ of voters voted in favor of changing the law.

   a. percentage   b. profit   c. growth   d. load

24. The two economists do not agree. Their _____ are very different.

   a. liquids   b. proteins   c. volunteers   d. positions

25. If your emotions get in the way, I'm afraid you might not make

   _____ economic decisions.

   a. sensible   b. confused   c. political   d. high-tech

26. The bill for the repairing the washing machine had separate charges for

   parts and _____.

   a. culture   b. labor   c. grain   d. oxygen

27. I _____ to call her, but I forgot.

   a. pressed   b. meant   c. blocked   d. designed

28. It will take a lot of work to reach my goal, but I think I'll _____.

   a. make it   b. hand it out   c. make it up   d. come up with it

29. It seemed a good idea at first, but then they _____ that there would be few actual benefits.

   a. consumed   b. destroyed   c. realized   d. flowed

30. The committee announced its decision but did not _____ the reasons for it.

   a. blow   b. earn   c. appear   d. reveal

31. The population of Alaska is small _____ the size of the state.

   a. after all   b. in relation to   c. since   d. as well as

32. A car won't last long if you don't _____ it.

   a. maintain   b. avoid   c. invest   d. set

33. It would not be _____ to wear a bathing suit to class.

   a. accurate   b. financial   c. appropriate   d. equal

34. The Galápagos Islands _____ 600 miles west of Ecuador.

   a. gain   b. differ   c. improve   d. lie

35. We plan to go to the beach on Saturday _____ it rains.

   a. meanwhile   b. immediately   c. within   d. unless

36. Separating the light clothes from the dark ones is the first step in the

    _____ of doing the laundry.

    a. process   b. income   c. decrease   d. society

37. The reporter asked the president for his _____ on recent events.

    a. styles   b. crops   c. views   d. goods

38. The hospital _____ was not prepared to deal with such a large number of patients all at once.

    a. material   b. staff   c. imagination   d. surface

39. Barbara would not take such a big risk—it's not in her _____ to do a thing like that.

    a. adventure   b. blame   c. rate   d. nature

40. Has any other sport _____ around the world like soccer has?

    a. signed up   b. spread   c. responded   d. provided

41. The _____ economic conditions, uncertain as they are, are making investors nervous.

    a. independent   b. current   c. huge   d. fair

42. He said, "Don't blame me for the decision—I _____ it."

    a. kept up with   b. made a   c. had nothing   d. turned
                           living at   to do with   something into

43. If you get a loan from a bank, you'll have to pay _____.

    a. development   b. condition   c. influence   d. interest

44. I enjoyed listening to all his stories, but the last one _____.

    a. fairly   b. further   c. on the other   d. in particular
                                              hand

45. Did the researchers find any differences _____ how much the children learned?

    a. in terms of   b. throughout   c. as long as   d. at least

See the Vocabulary Self-Test Answer Key on page 272.

Vocabulary Self-Tests Answer Key

Below are the answers to the Vocabulary Self-Tests. Check your answers, and then review any words you did not remember. You can look up the word in the Index to Target Vocabulary on pages 273–274. Then go back to the reading and exercises to find the word. Use your dictionary as needed.

Vocabulary Self-Test 1, Units 1–2 (pages 107–108)

1. b. goods
2. d. drove
3. a. as long as
4. c. mean
5. b. had something to do with
6. a. break the habit
7. d. actually
8. b. right
9. c. willing
10. a. make it
11. c. process
12. c. response
13. b. avoid
14. a. particular
15. d. simply
16. d. view
17. c. spread
18. b. provides
19. a. likely
20. a. react
21. d. developments
22. a. blocking
23. b. besides
24. a. improving
25. d. rate

Vocabulary Self-Test 2, Units 3–4 (pages 211–213)

1. b. sources
2. b. occurred
3. d. exact
4. c. ink
5. a. attend
6. c. demand
7. a. in spite of
8. d. practice
9. c. realize
10. d. section
11. c. appropriate
12. b. descriptions
13. b. involved
14. b. estimating
15. c. imagination
16. d. society
17. b. accurate
18. a. carry it out
19. b. resource
20. d. set out
21. a. yet
22. b. at least
23. b. scientific
24. d. models
25. d. requires
26. c. production
27. b. environmental
28. a. be better off
29. c. engine

Vocabulary Self-Test 3, Units 1-5 (pages 267–270)

1. c. citizens
2. a. argued
3. d. ordinary
4. d. admitted
5. a. Nevertheless
6. b. assumed
7. c. even though
8. a. ran out of
9. b. significant
10. c. as
11. b. approach
12. d. quantities
13. c. effective
14. b. surrounded
15. c. going through
16. d. help yourself to
17. b. attractive
18. d. debt
19. a. scarce
20. b. balance
21. d. trade
22. c. thought
23. a. percentage
24. d. positions
25. a. sensible
26. b. labor
27. b. meant
28. a. make it
29. c. realized
30. d. reveal
31. b. in relation to
32. a. maintain
33. c. appropriate
34. d. lie
35. d. unless
36. a. process
37. c. views
38. b. staff
39. d. nature
40. b. spread
41. b. current
42. c. had nothing to do with
43. d. interest
44. d. in particular
45. a. in terms of

Index to Target Vocabulary

accurate, 111
actually, 57
ad, 3
admit, 240
advanced, 11
adventure, 145
advertising, 15
affect, 69
after all, 217
agriculture, 197
announce, 15
appear, 15
approach, 217
appropriate, 134
argue, 251
as for, 252
as long as, 15
as well, 57
as, 228
assume, 229
at least, 122, 197
attach, 135
attend, 111
attractive, 229
avoid, 15
balance, 228
be better off, 135
be in favor of, 186
be open to, 186
behavior, 123
believe in, 38
benefit, 91
besides, 37
beyond, 57
blame, 163
block, 69
blow, 80
border, 164
borrower, 240
break a habit, 68
bring in, 228
bring up, 229
call on, 196
carbon dioxide, 174
carry out, 122
central, 252
century, 146
chemical, 81
chemistry, 69
citizen, 251

client, 4
come up with, 3
committee, 38
community, 38
competition, 164
condition, 38, 92
confused, 145
consume, 175
consumer, 15
crisis, 197
crop, 196
cross, 228
culture, 92
current, 185
deal with, 26
debt, 217
decrease, 163
demand, 112
description, 145
deserve, 123
design, 3
destroy, 185
developing, 15
development, 91
diameter, 175
differ, 80
difference, make a, 57
drive up, 229
drive, 3
drop, 92
earn, 3
economic, 27
economics, 217
educate, 185
effective, 229
electronic, 122
emotional, 80
employee, 27
engine, 163
engineering, 134
environment, 136
environmental, 185
equal, 111
essential, 196
estimate, 163
even though, 239
exact, 112
exchange, 218
exist, 145
expert, 186

explanation, 69
fair, 3
fairly, 111
fake, 240
financial, 27
flow, 80
force, 185
forever, 57
frequently, 240
fuel, 164
further, 69
gain, 26
generally, 57
get in the way, 240
get rid of, 15
go ahead, 81
go through, 239
goods, 15
grain, 135
grateful, 175
growth, 251
habit, 68
hand out, 240
hand, on the other, 122
harm, 163
have something to do with, 69
help oneself, 239
high-tech, 112
hire, 3
hug, 91
huge, 26
hunt, 196
imagination, 145
immediately, 197
improve, 92
in charge of, 37
in favor of, 186
in particular, 122
in relation to, 240
in return, 16
in spite of, 146
in terms of, 186
income, 164
increase, 57
independent, 91
individual, 217
influence, 26
ink, 175
interest, 163
invest, 27

involve, 175
keep up with, 174
key, 91
labor, 218
least, at, 122, 197
lie, 197
lifestyle, 57
likely, 57
limit, 57
liquid, 80
living, make a, 4
load, 135
loan, 163
look into, 174
loss, 217
maintain, 163
major, 16
make a difference, 57
make a living, 3
make it, 57
make up, 145
market, 27
material, 80
mean, 3
meanwhile, 164
measure, 111
mental, 81
method, 134
model, 134
modern, 112
motor, 197
nature, 26
necessary, 218
neither . . . nor, 145
nevertheless, 239
normal, 81
notice, 80
occur, 196
on the other hand, 122
open to, 186
opportunity, 217
ordinary, 239
organize, 37
other than, 229
oxygen, 174
particular, 26, 122
passenger, 164
percentage, 252
pesticide, 197
physical, 91
plenty, 134
political, 27
poll, 251
pollution, 135
population, 174
portable, 111
position, 251

possibly, 57
practice, 123
predict, 145
press, 91
process, 57
production, 135
productive, 197
profit, 37
property, 218
protein, 186
prove, 69
provide, 37
quality, 26, 37
quantity, 228
quite, 26
raise, 91
rate, 80, 111
react, 37
realize, 134
recent, 69
reduce, 92
renewable, 175
replace, 122
require, 186
resource, 122
respond, 122
response, 68
reveal, 251
right, 37
rise, 217
risk, 4
role, 68
rubber, 175
run out (of, 229)
rural, 135
satisfied, 251
scale, 252
scarce, 217
scientific, 145
section, 122
security, 38
sensible, 240
seriously, 123
service, 4
set out, 185
set up, 3
set, 92, 111, 145
shade, 174
shadow, 111
sign up, 16
significant, 229
similar, 57
simply, 68
since, 217
so far, 122
society, 145
soil, 174

solve, 134
source, 186
speak out, 186
spread, 26
staff, 69
stress, 92
style, 145
such, 38
surface, 80
surround, 240
take (something) seriously, 123
take off, 146
tear apart, 251
technology, 111
term, 186, 229
the environment, 136
therefore, 251
though, 239
thought, 239
threat, 196
throughout, 80
to sum up, 229
trade, 218
transportation, 112
treat, 57
treatment, 68
trick, 68
turn (something) into, 3
uncertain, 37
unless, 185
valuable, 174
vehicle, 163
view, 81
volunteer, 16
wealth, 251
while, 16
willing, 4
within, 16
yet, 197